Aaron Spelling

A Prime-Time Life

ALSO BY JEFFERSON GRAHAM

The Salesman of the Century with Ron Popeil
(Delacorte Press, 1995)

Life is a Contact Sport: The Ten Point Strategy to Turbo-Charge Your Career
with Ken Kragen
(Morrow, 1994)

Vegas: Live and In Person
(Abbeville Press, 1990)

Come On Down: The TV Game Show Book
(Abbeville Press, 1989)

Aaron Spelling

A Prime-Time Life

AARON SPELLING
WITH JEFFERSON GRAHAM

ST. MARTIN'S PRESS NEW YORK

Grateful acknowledgment is made of New World/Genesis Distribution, a New World Entertainment company, for permission to reprint "Unrelenting Sky" and "Silent Sentry Memoirs" from *Zane Grey Theater*.

Design by Ellen R. Sasahara

Library of Congress Cataloging-in-Publication Data

Spelling, Aaron.
Aaron Spelling : a prime-time life / by Aaron Spelling with Jefferson Graham.—1st ed.
p. cm.
ISBN 0-312-14268-4
1. Spelling, Aaron. 2. Television producers and directors—United States—Biography. I. Graham, Jefferson. II. Title.
PN1992.4.S64A3 1996
791.45'0232'092—dc20
[B] 96-5225
CIP

First Edition: August 1996

10 9 8 7 6 5 4 3 2 1

For Candy, Tori and Randy

Without you, my life would be nothing

Acknowledgments

THIS BOOK is something I've wanted to do for many years, to let young people know that if they follow their dreams, anything can come true. I'd like to thank Jefferson Graham for working so hard with me on this book, Ron Castell for bringing the book to St. Martin's, and our editor, Jennifer Weis, who was a tremendous help. Additionally, my wife, Candy, was an incredible resource for us. She's been saving all the articles that have been written about me over the years. Doing this book finally gave us a reason to pull all the scrapbooks out of the closet.

There wouldn't be a book in your hands right now had we not been lucky enough to produce over 3,000 hours of television, and the opportunity to work with some of the most talented people in our business. I'd like to thank Dick Powell for giving me my first big break, Leonard Goldenson and the late Elton Rule for putting me in business at the then-young ABC network, and Barry Diller and all of his associates for making it happen all over again on the Fox network with *Beverly Hills 90210* and *Melrose Place*.

Foreword

WE HAVE this little house that my wife, Candy, built. You may have heard about it. I'm still trying to find our bedroom.

Anyway, every day the tour buses come around, and I often go out and talk to the tourists and welcome them to Hollywood. I'm asked this question all the time, "Why do you go out there and talk to them?" Simple answer. They built our house; they made our lives. I also like to discuss television with them.

"Forget about our shows," I always say to the viewers. "What do you like? What do you watch?"

You can't get a gauge on what the American public likes by listening to the Beverly Hills and Bel-Air crowd. They won't admit to watching *Dynasty* or *Melrose Place*. Instead, it's always *60 Minutes*, news, and sports. And if you believe that, there's a bridge I'd like to sell you in Brooklyn.

You can find out so much from these tourists. They tell me they want more fantasy in their lives. Times are tough. They'd like to go home and enjoy television. They want to relax and have some laughs, but they also want something uplifting. I can't tell you how many good ideas I've stolen from those tour buses.

I'm asked all the time to sum up the secret ingredients of our shows, but the truth is, every show is different. If you look at our library, you'll see Westerns, sitcoms, soaps, cop shows, teen and young adult drama, and anthologies. That's the thrill. Entertaining people no matter what kind of show you do. Do you know how lucky I am to be able to entertain? There's no greater gig in the world.

My fantasy when I was poor in Texas was to live a glamorous

lifestyle, and I think everybody wants that. That was my dream. We had some glamour on *Burke's Law*, but I didn't fully realize it all the way until *Dynasty* and *The Colbys*. I can list three trademarks of our most popular shows. Beautiful people in beautiful clothes in front of beautiful sets. If you lived in a little house with wall-to-wall people on a road that was never paved, you dream about beautiful people, beautiful clothes, and beautiful styles of living. That was my dream and I've realized it many times over.

I've had a career that I continue to find hard to believe—I've produced over 50 TV series, ten theatrical films, nearly 150 made-for-TV movies, written over 100 scripts, been awarded two Emmys, lifetime achievement awards from the People's Choice and National Association of Television Program Executives, five NAACP awards, 37 other awards, and I'm known around the world as Tori's dad! Just kidding. I'm very proud when some people refer to me that way.

This book is the story of that little kid from Texas and what could eventually happen if you follow your dreams. I started with truly nothing, and look at what's happened. It's like I boarded *The Love Boat* and landed on *Fantasy Island*. I've achieved every career dream, and it happened because I followed my dreams, stuck with them, worked hard at it, and got very, very lucky. Thanks, Mr. Roarke, for making my dream come true.

Here's how it all began.

Aaron Spelling

A Prime-Time Life

One

I WAS BORN in Dallas, Texas, literally on the wrong side of the tracks, on Browder Street, a dusty, dirty, unpaved street. The well-to-do people lived on one side of the tracks, and we were on the side that was considered Dallas' worst slum.

My parents were immigrants. My mother was from Russia and my father from Poland. They spoke mainly Yiddish and a little English, although not much. Their English had such a heavy accent that they sounded like foreigners. My dad was a tailor who never made more than $45 a week, and my mom tended to the kids. My three older brothers, my sister, her husband, and my parents were all crammed into a small $6,000 house. It had one bathroom and wall-to-wall people.

Browder Street was six blocks long. At one end were the railroad tracks. At the other was the cotton mill. It was a noisy, dirty, and dangerous street.

Our house was a small, white frame building with a porch, three bedrooms, a living room, kitchen, and a garage that never had a car in it. For my parents, a car was something other people owned. We kids used to sleep three in a bed, head to toe. I didn't know at the time that this was the economical approach. Mom told us it was fun sleeping that way, and I thought everyone did it.

My mother, Pearl Wald, was a tiny, energetic woman from a prominent and respected Russian-Jewish family. As a young woman she had fallen in love with a handsome Polish man, but her grandfather, the patriarch of the clan, had objected to the man and had forbidden her to marry him. Then when the pogroms began, the family reluctantly decided to emigrate. Like so many others, they stood in line at Ellis Island and didn't know where to go from there. My grandfather knew two words of English—"New York" and "cowboy." That last word sent the family to Texas. The immigration officials were trying to ensure that not all Jews would reside in New York, so when they heard "cowboy," they shuffled my family off to Texas. Makes sense to me.

My mother was in her late teens when her family arrived in Dallas, and she soon married a professional wrestler with the hope of getting out of poverty. She was married long enough to produce two children: my sister Becky and my brother Max. But she lost her husband when he got into a fight with a vulgar neighbor and was stabbed to death.

She was then a penniless widow with two children to support. Her family did everything they could to help, and they wrote a letter to the man in Poland who my mother had always loved. He arrived in Dallas a few months later, immediately married Mom, and raised her two kids as his own. His name was David Spurling, and when he arrived at Ellis Island, the officials didn't understand it, so they renamed him Spelling.

Mom and Dad had two more children, Sam and Danny, and then little Aaron, the fifth and final child, the smallest and sickliest. People were always expecting me to waste away and die—that's how small I was. One of my chores as a kid was to buy groceries at a bakery where sacks of day-old bread and cakes were put on sale. The family chose me, the puny kid, to stand in line. The man behind the counter, seeing this pitiful sight, would stuff in a few more pastries because he felt sorry for us. Growing up, we ate little bread and no meat but lots of stale cookies, cream puffs, and cake. Perhaps that's why to this day I can't eat dessert.

We were so poor that everything which seems like a given today was a struggle. Clothes and school supplies were hard to come by. We didn't have a car. We never went anywhere. We rarely left our neighborhood, and ordinary things such as picnics or trips to the amusement park were out of the question. To the day Dad died, I don't remember him ever making more than $45 a week. One of my saddest memories is when my mother called me outside to have my picture taken on a rocking horse. I was so thrilled. I had never had a rocking horse, but I had seen pictures of them. They put me atop the rocking horse, and I just beamed. I don't think I had ever been happier. But then, after the picture was snapped, they pulled me off the horse, crying. It turned out they had paid a nickel to get my picture taken and paid another nickel to rent the rocking horse from the photographer for the picture. I thought the horse was mine, a wonderful present. Mom said that I cried the entire day. When Tori was born, the first present I bought her was a rocking horse. She was two days old.

Dad was a good tailor. He worked all day in his shop, and then after dinner, he would go to the garage and work some more. He was stern and unaffectionate, yet he somehow communicated his love to us by his devotion to Mom. He made all of our clothes on the weekends. His whole aim in life was to keep us all fed and clothed.

One of my favorite stories about my dad concerns my first lesson in racial tolerance. He met and befriended a black man, a person in the same economic boat as himself. He brought his friend over for a Friday dinner, and thereafter brought him around to join us on holidays. Whites and blacks didn't spend time with one another back then in Texas, but that never meant anything to my dad.

I grew up thinking "Jew boy" was one word. You never saw so many rednecks in your life. Whenever my parents would come to the school playground, the other kids would turn on me. Suddenly I was different because my parents spoke another language. I would beg my folks to speak English, and I later hated myself 15 million times for having done that to them.

My brother Danny, the next to youngest, and I both went to Lamar School, a small neighborhood school, where most of the kids were poor and tough. We were the only Jews in the school, which made it even rougher for us. Every day I was chased home from school and got my butt kicked. There were fights every day, and at least once a week Danny would have to rescue me from another beating. My mom finally went to the school principal to ask him to do something about the fighting, but, with her thick accent and the school administrator's attitude about Jews, she got nowhere.

As a child, I was always sick. I think I often made myself ill so I wouldn't have to walk to school because I knew that I would get beaten up along the way, by the bigoted sons of the tough cotton mill workers. Most of it had to do with being Jewish. There weren't a lot of Jews in Dallas at the time, and racism was rampant in the area. Those kids weren't born hating; they were taught to hate by their parents.

Danny was my protector, and I loved him. I did well academically at school as long as he was there with me. But then he got transferred to another school, and I was on my own. From then on, I got chased every day of my life. There wasn't a day when I didn't get beaten up. I didn't want to go to school, so my mother had to accompany me, which made me look even more like a nerd. They would curse her, and at home she would curse them.

And then one day I totally lost it. I went to bed thoroughly depressed, and couldn't find the energy to get up. In fact, for several months I couldn't even walk. I didn't go back to school for a year. I later called this my nervous breakdown, but back then we knew of no such terms. The kids at school called it "chicken." I think they were right.

A doctor came to examine me and he found nothing wrong. Then the rabbi came to visit, and he was still mad that I had come to Hebrew school barefoot one day. (That was because my one pair of shoes were being repaired, and I had nothing else to wear.) He accused me of disrespect and told me that everything was a matter of life and death, and if I continued to stay in bed, I would die. "There's life, religion, God, and death," he said.

So after he left, I made a decision—I was going to lie in my bed until I died.

And then my teacher, Miss Emma Jones, came to see me.

I really liked her. She had been very nice to me, and she made me a wonderful offer. She told me that I had been a good student and that she had been impressed by the stories I told in class. They were mostly ghost stories I invented on Halloween. She handed me six books and said, "If you turn in six book reports during the semester, I'll allow you to go on to the next grade when you return to school."

Miss Jones did more for me in her brief visit than all of the others combined. When she returned a week later to see me, I handed her all six books and six book reports. By the end of the year my six book reports had become 64 book reports. I discovered the wonders of reading, and fell in love with the stories of O. Henry, Mark Twain, and others. I loved O. Henry's twists and Twain's humor and adventures. Every book was an escape from my world and a chance to visit wonderful, imaginary places. In my mind, I had forgotten, momentarily, that I was little sickly Aaron Spelling.

I was not only able to lose myself in books, but at the movies as well. As I said, Dad was a tailor who for some reason had gotten a reputation for making great men's suits. Occasionally, he made clothes for visiting entertainers. I remember Eddie Cantor coming to the house once to get fitted for a suit. Some of the entertainers gave the family passes to see their vaudeville shows in Dallas. I guess that was my first inkling that there was this other world out there. I don't think I was ever happier as a child than when I was at those shows.

My favorite film was *Tales of Manhattan*, a story about the effect one tuxedo had on various owners. Edward G. Robinson, Ginger Rogers, Charles Boyer, and Henry Fonda starred. One guy was very rich, and he bought the tuxedo and wore it to a lavish party. Then he hocked it, and it went to a rental shop where any guy who was too poor to own one could, for very little money, wear it for one night. And this tux transformed everyone who wore it.

The movie had a great effect on me. It had glamour and multiple story lines, all the elements that would one day be two of my television trademarks.

Reading became the primary activity of my life, with movies running a close second. In third place was listening to the radio. *The Lux Radio Theatre*, hosted by Cecil B. DeMille, gave me my first taste of drama, and because of the way it promoted its stars, my first fascination with the glamour of stardom.

When my mother began to understand what was happening to me, she started taking me to movies on Saturdays. The movies were usually serials and westerns, and on the way there we'd talk about the previous week's episode and build up our excitement for the newest installment. I loved the serials for the adventure and my mother enjoyed the Westerns because the English spoken was brief, and even when she couldn't understand what the actors were saying, she could still understand the plot.

Once my parents had determined my interests, and had observed the changes in my life, they also exposed me to theater. They took me to Yiddish plays, even though I barely understood what I was hearing. But I got the idea.

I eventually went back to school and had a new weapon to use to combat the bullies: storytelling. Whenever they would try to pick a fight, I would just tell them a story and not finish it. I told them I would finish it the next day, and they let me go home. I'd run like hell before they changed their minds, and so I could change my shorts!

I joined the Air Force in 1943 on my eighteenth birthday and went into basic training in Massachusetts. A few weeks later I was back in Texas, at the Fort Worth Army Airfield, where I started submitting sketches to the camp revues. The first offerings were rejected, but I kept at it and finally scored with something called "Wacky-Khaki," your basic barracks-room humor. I knew immediately after hearing the applause that this was what I wanted in life—to entertain an audience.

In the service, I became famous on mail day, because I started receiving cards from the likes of Fred Astaire, Elizabeth Taylor, Ava Gardner, and Mickey Rooney. Not that they really knew me. It was because I was such a big movie fan that I wrote to all the stars to wish them a Merry Christmas, and so I got a lot of return thank yous, and the soldiers therefore thought I had big connections in Hollywood. And I didn't do anything to try to persuade them that I didn't. That's how I got into the Special Service, entertaining the troops.

I later started submitting material to the *Stars and Stripes* armed forces newspaper, where I did well enough to warrant a trip to France to write about the invasion. My job was to function as a field correspondent in France and later in Germany. Don't get me wrong—I just interviewed our soldiers and sent their stories to their hometown newspapers so that their wives and parents would know how they were doing.

It was in Bavaria that I received a Purple Heart. My unit was in a war zone. I was working with a cameraman, and we were going to do a story about the "Battered Bastards of Bostogne." We were driving a command car, and a sniper shot at us. The car overturned and killed our driver and hurt our photographer very badly. We stopped rolling over in an apple field. I was shot in my left hand and knee by a sniper. In the hospital they wanted to amputate my two fingers, but I talked them out of it by telling them I was a pianist, so they sewed them up and to this day I still can't straighten them out completely. But what the hell, I still have them! And even now I think it's the best story I've ever concocted.

While in the armed forces I developed my phobia about flying on airplanes. I had been in the service for six months and we were scheduled to fly to Ohio to do "Wacky-Khaki" at an air base there. I had the flu that morning, and the flight surgeon wouldn't allow me to fly. I got yanked from the flight two minutes before it took off. That medic saved my life because the plane crashed and everybody aboard was killed. The authorities didn't know that I was alive and was driving home to Dallas from Fort Worth to see my folks. They telephoned and told my mother I was dead. When I arrived home later that day, there were all these cars in front of the house. That seemed strange since my parents didn't own a car. When I walked through the door, my mother fainted. When she came to, she looked at me as if I were a ghost. She made me promise never to fly again, and I've remained true to my word. If we travel, it's by boat, train, or car.

After the Army, I came home to Texas to attend Southern Methodist University on the G.I. Bill. At SMU I had a ball. I was elected head cheerleader and became the first student to direct a senior class production. Before that, I auditioned for a small part in the play *The Hasty Heart* and, to my surprise, I got the lead. In 1947 I won the Eugene O'Neill award for writing the year's best original one-act play. It was called *Is Everything Always Black and White?* and dealt with a cat and a dog who fell in love, to the horror of their owners. Then a South Dallas street cleaner, their God, magically changed them into human beings, so they could love one another. But the cat was a black woman and the dog a white man, so they faced the same prejudices again.

I formed a comedy team with a friend named Bill Slack (Slack and Spelling) and we did Laurel and Hardy and Abbott and Costello rip-offs at frat parties and pep rallies. I lived at my sister Becky's house and got hired by two friends, Leon and Idelle Rabin, to direct plays for their Jewish community theater group and other theater groups.

I didn't spend much time on my studies at SMU, but it was very hard for my instructors to grade me harshly when I was directing them in off-campus productions at night.

Oh, a funny story about how I got elected head cheerleader at SMU. At that time, SMU was known as the Country Club on the Hill, and I soon found out why. There was no limit to the money that could be spent by those running for election for head cheerleader. The other nominees hired bands, threw big parties, passed out T-shirts, etc. I was desperate. I didn't have any money to spend, but Bill Slack and I had a funny idea. Every day before school and between classes I would sit on a hundred-pound block of ice with a card around my neck that said "Elect This!"

Would you believe I won by a landslide? It was my first dream to come true and it cost about six dollars.

I moved straight from SMU to directing full-time at the Edward Rubin Playhouse. We churned out 36 plays in three years, and won several critics awards. One directing experience I'll never forget: For one of our plays, we brought in a group of drama students from a local black high school to see the play, and they asked me if I would help them put on their own production of Richard Wright's *Native Son*, one of the pioneering pieces of black theater literature. Of course I agreed.

The day the reviews came out, my father was suspended from his job as a tailor for Sears, Roebuck & Co. He wasn't given an explanation, but the answer was obvious to all of us. They weren't happy about his son's work on *Native Son*. Equal opportunity had a long way to go in Dallas.

Fortunately, a member of the SMU theater arts department went to speak to the Sears officials and my dad got his job back. Still, after watching what had happened to him, I knew I couldn't stick around Dallas anymore.

Two

I DROVE FROM Dallas to New York in my little Plymouth, but soon discovered that the Big Apple wasn't for me. All my awards and achievements didn't mean anything there. I was five steps below an apprentice actor and was never so lonely in my life, so I left three months later and drove across the country to Los Angeles, where I rented a room at the Franklin Hotel and looked for any kind of theatrical work I could find.

My son, Randy, once asked me what was the lowest I'd even been, and it's hard to top this time of my life. One day I was so broke that I woke up early on a Sunday morning at six A.M. and scooped up copies of the *Los Angeles Times* from people's driveways and sold them back to a newsstand to make money—all so I could afford a little breakfast.

Not that I needed much to satisfy my hunger. I only weighed 118 pounds and had lived on peanut butter for so long that it didn't take much to fill me up. But I did like to go for breakfast at a local coffee shop, for the social interaction, and I became friendly with another actor who used to come in every morning with the Hollywood trade papers, *Daily Variety* and *The Hollywood Reporter*. He was kind enough to share them with me. He was from the southwest, like me, from Oklahoma, and he wanted to be an actor. His name was James Garner. I wonder what ever happened to him?

Luckily, I never had to do my sidewalk swipe of newspapers again. Within a month I finally had a legitimate job. I answered an ad in the paper for a reservations clerk at the Western Airlines office on Hollywood Boulevard. My pay was $50 a week, good money, but I wasn't happy. I didn't come to Los Angeles to sell airline tickets.

Each night I would go home and bang out spec scripts for TV shows. Westerns and anthologies were hot at the time, and since I had written several one-act plays at SMU that had won awards, I figured writing TV shows would be a snap. I went to Larry Edmund's bookshop on Hollywood Boulevard and bought a used script to learn the proper form, and went to work on my battered Royal.

I'd write scripts and sent them out, and I received a lot of rejection letters.

Then one day a man named George McCall came into the Western office. He was the manager and booker for his wife's all-female band. Her name was Ada Leonard, and she was a popular local TV attraction in L.A. at the time. Ada had a show on KTTV, a local TV station that's now the Fox affiliate, an amateur hour with all-female contestants. George was a writer who once coined the famous headline for *Variety*—"Hicks Nix Stix Pix."

One day he came into the office to pick up some tickets, and said, "You know, I've been looking for a band boy to work with me and the girls. Would you be interested?" He offered me $40 a week, $10 less than I was making, but it was show business. There was no way I could say no.

But I soon found out that being a band boy was not a glamorous occupation. I spent most of my time at an old theater on La Cienega Boulevard, where the show was televised, setting up the bandstands, going for coffee, and doing whatever needed doing. When the show was done, I'd pack everything up, help load it on a truck, and then hop on the bus to travel wherever our next performance was—Bakersfield, Azusa, Pomona, Twenty-nine Palms, etc.—carrying cellos and drums and all those other instruments. It was horrendous, back-breaking work. This was easily the worst time of my work life, and I almost packed up and went home.

There were many nights of crying myself to sleep because I was so lonely. It was tough and I could have gone home, but you know what—I thought my parents would have been so disappointed that I hadn't made it. I couldn't give up.

One of the gimmicks for the Ada Leonard TV show was a competition among the female performers. On each show there were five contestants, and the winner would come back to compete the following week. After a number of weeks, a winner would be declared. It became painfully obvious that I was in no shape to be a band boy. But they took a liking to me anyway and promoted me. I was given the job of finding the contestants. I didn't get a raise, but at least I didn't have to carry instruments anymore. So I went to every music school and tap-dancing class, checked out the baton twirlers and vocalists and came up with performers for the show.

One young performer caught my attention. She was small, blond, pretty, and had a big voice. But that wasn't what caught my eye. What intrigued me was that she had a manager. I had to assume they were dating, since all any of the contestants got for winning was a gown.

The manager's name was George Schlatter, and he told me that each week he and the singer would sell the gown immediately and split the money. George eventually shifted his focus from singers to comedians and went on to become, among other things, a prolific producer of network TV specials and the executive producer of NBC's old *Rowan & Martin's Laugh-In* series. We're still close friends today.

When we weren't at the theater, we were at the show's office, which was in the old KTTV-TV studio on Sunset Boulevard. I got to know a lot of the people there, especially the mailroom boys. In this town, everybody is an actor, and most of the KTTV mailroom boys were budding thespians. They had heard that I was a director back in Dallas and asked if I would direct them in a one-act-play contest in Long Beach. Of course I would, I said, but first I'd need to find the right play. The next day, in my best Orson Wellesish tone, I said, "I can't find a one-act play for all of you, so I'll write one instead."

My play, *Thorns in the Road*, was about a group of GIs who dreamt of going home, but who were, in fact, stuck in a small barracks in occupied Germany during World War II. Next to the barracks was a road leading off into the horizon. The soldiers had been told to remain where they were, that it was dangerous to leave and they were to stay off the road. With that warning, the road became the object of their dreams, their ticket home to wives, sweethearts, mothers, a new life. And eventually the tension became too much to bear and one of the soldiers set off down the road, only to find it was a dead end, leading nowhere, just like their lives.

It may sound corny now, but it won the competition. And writing it was a psychological turning point for me. I knew I had strayed from my original dreams yet somehow had found a way back.

The kids in the mailroom enjoyed working in the show, and realized that if we could mount one play we could do more, so they came to me with a proposal. If we all pooled our money—and kept our day jobs—we could rent a theater in Hollywood and do a full three-act play.

I had the perfect production for them, Garson Kanin's *Live Wire*, a play I had directed in Dallas about a group of young actors living in a Quonset hut in New York. The play, as written, had 12 speaking parts, and our troupe had eight members, so I combined roles to fit our mailroom gang. I called the art director in Dallas who had done our play and asked him about the old sets. He had them, and he also had a burning desire to come to Hollywood. So he loaded up a truck, drove west, and we were in business. (It sounds like an old Mickey Rooney/Judy Garland "let's put on a show" musical, but it really happened.)

We rented—for almost nothing—the old Cahuenga Theater, which was over the bus depot right off Hollywood Boulevard. The fumes, during the busiest hours, were deadly, and the whole theater rattled every time a bus pulled into the depot, but we were in show biz, and we loved it.

We rehearsed at KTTV during our lunch hour, and headed directly for the theater as soon as we finished for the day. The theater had 34 seats, and I dreaded trying to fill them for opening night, let alone the three weekends we'd committed to. Ada Leonard, bless her heart, heard about our enterprise, and bought tickets for everyone in her band. And they all came for opening night. We were sold out!

One of the mailroom guys went downtown to the *Los Angeles Times* and met Edward Shallert, who at the time was the most powerful theater critic in town. He told Shallert how this crazy little group of mailroom boys and band luggage carriers had put together their own little theater company and convinced him to come and watch the play.

The next morning, I received what I still think is the best review of my life. "There's a new young director on the scene," Shallert wrote, "in a theater above the bus station where the buses shake the sets, but they didn't shake my faith in the future of this man."

His review was so powerful it reached one of Hollywood's greatest writer-directors, who decided to come to our little theater the next night to check out the show.

I'll never forget it. As a director, I had nothing to do before the show, so I helped take tickets. And that's where I found this dignified but bombastic man. In the lobby.

He was dressed in all black, topped with a billowing cape and a Borsalino hat. He had a deep, deep voice which seemed to shake the place more than the buses downstairs.

"I would like to see Aaron Spelling," he said.

"I am Aaron Spelling."

"I am going to see your show."

I reminded the man that he needed a ticket.

"I don't need a ticket," he said. "I am Preston Sturges. I will talk to you later."

And with that, he walked into the theater and sat down.

I couldn't believe that Preston Sturges had come to see our show. Growing up in Texas, I used to love seeing his great comedies—*Christmas in July* with Dick Powell, *The Palm Beach Story* with Rudy Vallee and Claudette Colbert, and *Miracle of Morgan Creek* with Eddie Bracken. There were only three writer-directors I could even name—John Ford, Frank Capra, and Preston Sturges.

"Are you all members of Equity?" he asked after the show.

Not one of us was, although we wanted to be. We just hadn't gotten to that point in our careers yet.

It didn't bother him. "I would like to open this show in my theater in two weeks. You will all have to join Equity. I will pay you minimum wages, and I will include you"—the cape billowed as he pointed at me—"as director."

At this time, Sturges was down on his luck in Hollywood. His directing career was over, and so he turned his sights toward theater. He built one of the first dinner theaters, located in a perfect spot along the Sunset Strip. The theater had revolving stages and the most complete and elaborate lighting system I had ever seen.

Sturges told me to be at the theater the next morning.

"What time?" I asked.

"It's a real theater, what time do you think you should be there?"

"Nine?"

"Be there at nine. I won't be there. But you will."

And with Sturges as our backer, we all quit our day jobs and immediately went to work uncondensing the parts in *Live Wire* since Sturges agreed we could add cast members.

Fast-forward to two days before opening, when our leading lady quit at the last minute. She said she had a date with a movie star and couldn't show up, and we were all understandably panicked. But the actress found a replacement for us, a wonderful young actress named Carolyn Jones, who was talented, beautiful, and very outspoken.

Carolyn read for us and was sensational. The following day she arrived at rehearsal. She already knew her lines and had learned all the blocking. I took an immediate liking to her.

Opening night was a black-tie event complete with klieg lights in front of the theater. I thought I knew what a director felt on opening night, but my previous experience was nothing compared to the pressure of this night. I wished the cast well, gave a few last-minute instructions, and sent them on to do their best.

I couldn't bear to watch the show with the audience, so I sat downstairs at the bar drinking a Coke. I lasted about six minutes, and then I heard a great roar of laughter from the theater upstairs. I was up, out of my seat, up the stairs, and in the back of the theater in seconds. Carolyn was signed to a contract by Warner Bros. that night.

We were a hit! By the time the evening ended, three members of our company had their first agents. One of those was our last-minute addition, Carolyn, who had quickly became popular with the whole company.

Within a week, Carolyn and I started dating, if you can call it that. Neither of us had any money to speak of, so our dates as often as not consisted of dinner after the show, usually leftovers from the theater kitchen. Sometimes we splurged and went out, but not to the sort of places that featured tablecloths.

Carolyn had a wicked sense of humor. Brunette, with a model's figure, she was a real knockout, and Hollywood took an immediate liking to her. Carolyn's agent got her a part in the film *House of Wax*, now famous as Hollywood's first 3-D production. Even though I was now a "big-time" theater director, working for the great Preston Sturges, I was still as broke as ever. I hocked my Plymouth, and Carolyn bought herself a Chevy convertible, insisting on driving us on our dates and quite often paying for them too.

My fortunes picked up soon after the night Jack Webb came to our show. Webb was at the height of his success with *Dragnet*, and in person sounded nothing like the monosyllabic Joe Friday from the TV show. He came backstage after the show and gave me the facts. He had seen *Live Wire* in New York and he loved our version of it. "I don't need any directors," he said, "but do you have any acting experience? I'd like to give you a job."

Without hesitation, I said, "I've been acting all my life." In a way, it wasn't really a total lie.

Mr. Webb said he'd have a script delivered the next day.

It arrived and he attached a note to the script asking for my agent to call him to set the deal. I didn't have an agent, but Carolyn did. So I had her man, Meyer Mishkin, make the deal, and he got me the sum total of $90 for a day's work.

"You'll be on the shoot with two other clients of mine," he said. One of the guys was another new person in town, a Charles Buchinski, who later shortened his name to the more manageable Charles Bronson. And the other client was a fellow named Lee Marvin. Try doing your first gig opposite those talented guys!

On *Dragnet*, I played a retarded young man. Wardrobe fitted me out in clothes that were far too big, with a couple of extra inches in the shirt collar and a tie that hung down to my knees and a hat that covered my ear lobes. Jack later told me that all he could really see of me was my eyes, and they were enormous. "That was the look I wanted," he said. In my scenes, I played a witness who sat on a slat chair in a bare police room.

"I know what you're going to do to me," I said very theatrically in the rehearsal. "You're going to arrest me. I'm never going to see my mother again, am I?"

Although I thought I was doing well, Mr. Webb had other ideas. He told me to forget that I had memorized my lines, pushed a TelePrompTer (a machine with the written dialogue in it) in front of me and said, "Don't act, Aaron. Just read. That's the kind of reality I want on the show." He called it "dramatic monotone."

He was the boss, so I did it his way. As I came to the end of my scene, I slid behind the chair and peered out from the slats as though they were prison bars. He loved my performance, and invited me back the next day for another scene. He also called my new agent, Meyer Mishkin, and told him how much he liked my work. When I called my folks to tell them the good news, my mother cried and my dad kept saying, "Ninety dollars for one day's work! Only in Hollywood!"

I did two more *Dragnet* episodes that year and eventually did four over a period of three years. I played every imaginable kind of pyromaniac, dipsomaniac, and sex maniac you can think of. I still weighed about 118 pounds at the time, always wore clothes that were too big, and had these giant eyes that bulged out of my tiny body.

Even so, Meyer was able to take the *Dragnet* experience and parlay it into other paying jobs. I began to pick up lots of one-day jobs on TV shows for which I continued to get $90. Meanwhile, Carolyn was thriving. Meyer got her a raise on her Warner Bros. contract to $250 a week, which to us then was an enormous amount of money. She was in their contract players division, and went from one quick job to another.

Whenever I trot out the film clips of my acting appearances, two highlights always get everyone's interest: my appearance with Lucille Ball and Tennessee Ernie Ford on *I Love Lucy*, and my 1955 date on *Gunsmoke*, in which I probably did my best acting ever. Actually, there are four acting highlights, and they begin in May 1954 with the most rerun show of all time—*I Love Lucy*.

Like any actor I went out on open calls. On this particular open call for *I Love Lucy*, I did well enough to warrant a callback, where I read a scene with Lucille Ball and Desi Arnaz, who, of course, were the stars and producers of the show. They liked me and I got the job.

Ford played a country cousin of the Ricardos from Bent Fork, Tennessee, who eventually got Lucy, Ricky, Fred, and Ethel to dress up as bumpkins and sing "Ya' All Come to Meet Us When You Can" on a New York talent show in order to win enough money to send him home. The next week they went to Tennessee to visit Ernie, and I played this very funny part of a gasoline attendant. They stop to get directions from him and I had this marvelous scene where I tell them every which way to get there but the right way. Meanwhile, the local sheriff stops them and demands that Ricky put his two obese daughters in the movies. Ricky refuses and then the sheriff throws them in jail. They come up with a plot to get out, and by the end of the show, we're all square dancing together at the town hall.

I hadn't done a lot of television acting by the time I got the part on *Lucy*, just the few *Dragnet* episodes. This was my first sitcom, and the atmosphere was totally different. On *Dragnet*, we read our lines from the TelePrompTer and had no rehearsal. On *Lucy*, we rehearsed for four days, starting off with a table reading of the script on a Monday, and filming in front of a live audience on Friday.

I walked in that Monday morning in total awe of Lucy and Desi. I was such a big fan of theirs. At the table, everyone was very serious. They read the script as if it was a drama, and the only time we laughed was when Lucy and Desi disagreed about something and they went into this planned disagreement act, which broke everyone up. By the time the actors got out of their seats and started doing the scenes a few times, it suddenly became hilarious. I've never seen a set where so many people clowned around. Lucy was as funny in rehearsals as she was on TV. *Dragnet* was a very controlled and calm set; on *Lucy* everyone talked at the top of their lungs and had outrageous fun with each other.

Lucy was a great experience. Despite their bitter breakup years later, when I was at the set in 1954, it was a ball. And because we hit it off, Lucy found a recurring role for me on a new Desilu series called *Willy*. The show premiered the following September and starred June Havoc as a small-town lawyer. I played the dogcatcher, and am still embarrassed to this day about what happened during the first episode. I was supposed to make an entrance, but I suddenly drew a total blank. I'd done play after play as an actor and had never gone blank, and I don't know what happened that night. Driving home that night, I couldn't help but think of that great story about the time the actors John and Lionel Barrymore were doing a scene on Broadway together and they both couldn't remember their lines. The prompter offstage kept whispering the line to them, but neither man responded. The prompter whispered the line again and again, and finally John Barrymore said, "We know the damn line . . . but who says it?"

I had better roles, but more people saw me on that *Lucy* episode than all of my other acting work combined. To this day I still get letters about it. People see me on the street and talk to me about it, and there's even an edition of *I Love Lucy* baseball cards with a picture of me square dancing on the back, and the trivia question is "Guess what TV producer is dancing with Lucy?"

Lucy was the most-viewed, but the best acting job of my career was on *Gunsmoke*. Like *Lucy*, it began with a reading. I remember catching a bus to audition at Paramount, where *Gunsmoke* was filmed on a soundstage. I read the scene, the producers were curt, excused me, and I went back outside to Melrose Avenue and took a seat on the bench to wait for the bus.

A man with grungy clothes and a scraggly beard walked over. "How ya' doin'?" he said.

"Fine, thank you."

You have to remember, I was from Texas, and I'd read all these wild stories about Hollywood. This man had these intense eyes and spoke in such a deadly tone that I didn't know whether I was going to be robbed or abused.

"I didn't ask you, 'How you doing?' " he said. "I asked, 'How *did* you do?' "

"How did I do what?"

"In your reading. How did your reading go?"

"I think they liked me, but I don't know."

"You're going to do it."

"How do you know?"

"Because I wrote it for you. My name's Sam Peckinpah, and I wrote it for you."

Peckinpah, who would go on to become one of Hollywood's greatest directors (best known for films like *The Wild Bunch* and the original *Getaway*) had seen me on *Lucy* and was looking for somebody to play a shell-shocked soldier. The way I looked back then, I was perfect for the part.

Gunsmoke, you'll recall, starred James Arness as Marshal Matt Dillon, who kept the peace in Dodge City, Kansas, in 1873. Doc Adams (Milburn Stone), the town physician, spent most of his spare time at the Longbranch Saloon, owned by Kitty Russell (Amanda Blake). Matt's deputy was Chester Goode (Dennis Weaver).

I played a retarded Civil War soldier who just sat there playing the guitar. His name was Weed Pindle, and he was going to be hung because he wasn't like the rest. I came out wearing a black hat, a long western jacket, and holding onto a guitar. Matt Dillon came out and took a look at me and said, "What's going on around here anyway?" A stranger says, "I'd like you to meet Weed. We've been showing him every saloon in Dodge."

"The minute they found out I was from Texas, Marshal, they just couldn't do enough for me."

By the end of the episode, there was a man hanging from the rope, and you expected it to be me, but instead it was the heavy. Chester and Doc had strung up the bad guy. It was the first time on *Gunsmoke* that something like that had happened. At that time, you were supposed to pay for a crime on TV. Good guys didn't get away with murder.

After *Gunsmoke*, I was asked to read for another Western, the film *Three Young Texans*, at 20th Century–Fox. The producer asked me if I could ride a horse. I was too frightened to lie by saying yes, and I knew if I said no I wouldn't get the role.

"Mr. Goldstein," I said, "I'm from Texas."

"OK, then," he said, "you're set."

So I started going to Griffith Park every day for two weeks to take riding lessons, and my butt was sore for months. But I kept the job and got to do a movie with Mitzi Gaynor, Jeffrey Hunter, and Keefe Brasselle.

My acting career came to an end in 1955. The great director Vincente Minnelli used to say, "I started Aaron Spelling," and he was right. I got a call one day to meet Mr. Minnelli to read for *Kismet* and I was thrilled sick. *Kismet* was the film version of the Broadway musical about Arabian nights with songs such as "Baubles, Bangles and Beads" and "Stranger in Paradise," and Minnelli was one of my idols. His wife, Judy Garland, dream-danced before my eyes. . . . Vincente directed all of those great musicals.

Anyway, I was to report onto Stage 17 at MGM. I was sent to wardrobe, and they fitted me in sack clothing and horrible sandals. I played a beggar with one line: "Alms for the love of Allah." I was so embarrassed about the way I looked, I wouldn't even go to the commissary. I brown-bagged my lunches. I worked three weeks, saying that miserable line over and over.

Carolyn visited the set one day, unbeknownst to me, and saw how miserable I was saying my one line over and over. She came over after a take and whispered, "Good-bye, acting; hello, typewriter." And that was the end of that.

That's why Vincente always said he was responsible for my career. "Had I not put you in *Kismet*, you'd still be an actor somewhere."

I can look back and laugh at my acting days now, but the truth is, I was dying on the inside. I went back to my typewriter and wrote more spec scripts for TV shows. I used to sit in the apartment and bang out the pages for a script in hours. When I left the apartment, I was so worried they might burn up while I was out that I would store them in the refrigerator. I had the coldest scripts in town.

Since I had an in at *Dragnet*, I wrote a spec script for the show and sent it to Jack Webb. He read it and was nice enough to call and invite me over to the studio. He couldn't have been more gracious or generous. "You've got the beginnings of good writing," he told me, "but you know nothing about film technique." Instead of discouraging me, he said I'd be welcome to hang around any time I wanted and watch him direct, and that I was free to read any script he had. Jack Webb was my first great mentor. I started going to the set every day to watch one of the great TV pioneers at work doing his craft and I learned an awful lot.

I didn't make a sale on a *Dragnet* script, but I certainly learned how the process worked, which helped me eventually break into the business.

Meanwhile, Carolyn and I had by now become very serious. Carolyn had been hinting at marriage, but I just couldn't see it. How do you propose to someone who is making ten times more than you? Someone who even owned a car! It's an impossible task, and she knew it. So one night, we went to dinner at a little Italian restaurant in the San Fernando Valley that we loved. As we sat down, the restaurant's accordion player came to our table and started to play and the waiter brought me a note. It was very simple.

"You'll never ask, so I guess it's up to me. Will you marry me?"

How can you say no in front of an accordion player? We were married five days later.

Three

WHENEVER I looked at pictures of writers in Hollywood, they were always smoking a pipe. So I started pipe smoking when I moved here. I figured it helped make you a better writer. I also learned that smoking a pipe is the greatest crutch a writer has in the world. The producer asks you a story question, and you take your time, load your pipe, and light it. By the time you're finished, you've thought of an answer for him.

Pipe smoking didn't help me break into script writing. That all came from contacts. The late, great Stan Kamen from the William Morris Agency got me an appointment to see Jane Wyman, who then had one of the first TV anthologies, *Fireside Theatre* (later called *The Jane Wyman Show* and in rerun as *Jane Wyman Presents the Fireside Theatre*). The anthologies, at the time, were like the TV movies of today. Great stars would appear in original works every week, with the only difference being that hosts like Jane Wyman, Robert Montgomery, or, later on, Rod Serling, Alfred Hitchcock, and Dick Powell, would introduce the story and help set it up.

Anyway, I came up with an idea for Jane Wyman, who also co-produced the series, to play on her show. Stan was lucky enough to know her and got me an appointment to see her. I typed up the story, which I called "Twenty Dollar Bride," and I brought it with me. When I walked into her office, she was there with her producers, but she didn't want to read my piece. "Just tell it to me," she said.

I knew she hadn't done a Western before, so I figured I'd give it a try. It was about a fellow who picked up a mail-order bride in the Old West, married her, and then bet her in a poker game. It was very touching and quite charming, and she loved it. She bought it on the spot.

I was thrilled. My first big sale. Then the bubble burst. When I got home, Stan called me. "The producers won't let you write the script because you don't have enough experience," he said, "but they will buy the story from you for $600." Well that just about decimated me, but I needed the $600, so I sold them the story.

Two weeks later Stan called again and told me to return to Miss Wyman's office. I figured they wanted to buy another story, so I thought of a new one on the way over there. When I walked in she literally attacked me. "What happened to your story?" she said. "Why did you change it? I loved what was there." I explained that I didn't write the script and she scowled at her producers, who I thought were going to crawl under the chairs.

"Oh, great guys," she said. "I finally find a story that had everything in it that I want, and you give this story to somebody else? Aaron, go home and write the script." This was a Thursday. I went home and handed in the script the following Monday. They never changed a line.

Now that I had a professional credit, Stan was able to send me out to meet with other producers. He got me an appointment to meet with Dick Powell at Four Star. Like Jane Wyman, Dick Powell was one of the first Hollywood actors to get into television, forming his Four Star studio with pals Charles Boyer, Ida Lupino, and David Niven in 1952. And Four Star was the first Hollywood independent TV house at a time when the major studios produced most of the shows. Besides the fact that I was thrilled at the prospect of a second sale, I was also a big fan. I loved the movies Dick Powell made with Ruby Keeler (*42nd Street*) and the great Preston Sturges comedy, *Christmas in July*.

At the time, he was just preparing to get his first production off the ground, *Dick Powell's Zane Grey Theater*. This was during the era when Westerns were one of the most popular forms of TV fare. Everyone remembers the middle 1950s as the time of *I Love Lucy* and *The George Burns and Gracie Allen Show*, but in 1955 there were also two shows that debuted and helped launch a new era of TV Western—*Gunsmoke* (then in 30-minute form) and *The Life and Legend of Wyatt Earp*. Eventually there would be as many as 40 Westerns in prime-time by the end of the decade, with such Four Star series as *The Rifleman* (created by occasional *Zane Grey* writer Sam Peckinpah) and *Wanted: Dead or Alive* (starring Steve McQueen.)

Zane Grey, which debuted in 1956, was originally developed to be adaptations of short stories and novels by the great Western author Zane Grey. But, as often happens, eventually the material ran out (the books were also way too long for a half-hour show) and original work was commissioned. Dick was the host and executive producer, and was set to also star in four episodes per year.

Some of the great stars who also eventually appeared on the show included the best of Hollywood: Jack Lemmon, James Garner, John Forsythe, Ronald Reagan, Joan Crawford, Ginger Rogers, Danny Thomas, Anne Bancroft, Walter Brennan, Lloyd Bridges, Sammy Davis, Jr., Dennis Hopper, Claudette Colbert, Hedy Lamarr, and Esther Williams. The pilot for *The Rifleman*, which starred Chuck Connors as Lucas McCain, the widowed rancher who moves to North Fork, New Mexico, to make a new life for himself in a land of bad guys, was first seen as an episode of *Zane Grey*. Besides me, other writers who got early breaks on *Zane Grey* include Sterling Silliphant (*Route 66*) and Christopher Knopf (*Equal Justice*) and directors like Richard Donner (*Lethal Weapon*), Arthur Hiller (*The Babe*), and Robert Ellis Miller (*Reuben, Reuben*) also started on *Zane Grey*.

Zane Grey stood out because it was the only Western anthology at the time. And because of that great format, it was a great magnet for stars to want to do the show. We always used one star per episode, and the stories were always great showcases for them.

Stan Kamen brought me to meet Hal Hudson, Dick Powell's producer, at the old Republic studio on Radford Avenue in Studio City, now the CBS Studios where *Seinfeld* and *Roseanne* are filmed. I told him a few stories and he was encouraging, but noncommittal. "Let me think about them," he said. "I'll get back to you."

I started walking off the lot, and I saw Dick Powell standing outside a projection room, arguing with Stan and Abe Lastfogel, the legendary head of the William Morris Agency. They handled Four Star and the sponsors of the show, Lorillard cigarettes.

"I'm not going to do that," I heard Dick say, as he went into a tirade about the hokey host spots for the show. "I'm not going to say, 'In tonight's story, Tom meets Jane, Jane turns out to be already married, and you'll find out how they resolve their problems on tonight's *Zane Grey Theater.*' I'm sick of that. I'm just not going to do it."

"But Dick," said Mr. Lastfogel, "you agreed to do the host spots for the show. It's called *Dick Powell's Zane Grey Theater.*"

"I don't care," said Dick. "I'm not going to do it." And he walked off in a huff.

While driving home from the studio, I came up with an idea. I waited a few hours, as I didn't want to sound incredibly opportunistic, and called Stan, telling him that I had a great idea for the host spots. "What are you talking about?" he said.

"Well, I was walking across the lot and I heard you all chatting—"

"One thing you'll learn in this business, kid," he said, in a condescending tone, "is when you walk across the lot or in front of someone's office, you forget what you hear. I don't want you to ever repeat a word of what you saw today or we'll drop you."

Well, that scared me to death. William Morris had only signed me because of Carolyn. It was a package deal and I knew that. I apologized profusely and sat at home for two days, afraid to have any contact with the human race. But then, out of the blue, Stan called, and this time he was interested in my idea for the host spots. Dick Powell was still refusing to do the show the old-fashioned way. "Meet me and Mr. Lastfogel in Mr. Powell's bungalow at 20th Century–Fox (where Powell was directing a movie) tomorrow at 2 P.M."

(Mr. Lastfogel was the most powerful agent in town, and when he called, people picked up the line. Everybody called him Mr. Lastfogel to his face, even studio chiefs, but behind his back, everyone referred to him as Uncle Abe.)

Dick Powell's office was typical of big-shot digs. Once you entered, his desk was so far away that by the time you started walking toward the chair opposite his desk, he grew to be 15 feet tall and I shrunk to 15 inches. It was that awesome.

I brought six copies of my host spots with me, and Mr. Lastfogel had me read one out loud to Mr. Powell. Instead of doing the traditional "Tonight we'll tell you the story of . . . ," I came up with a different concept. I made up little stories of Western lore to anchor the show. I had Dick come out, dressed in a Western outfit, talking in a graveyard.

"Some of the greatest messages, poetry, and feelings went onto these small little gravestones," I wrote. "Some were humorous, some were sad. Here's one that says, 'I died, but my love for you will never die,' and that was a father's tombstone to his daughter. And here's one that says, 'Stole a cow that wasn't his'n, was hung before he got to prison,'" and then the whole room broke up.

"I like this," said Dick. "We're going to shoot it. Be on the set Thursday at 9 A.M."

It sounded like a staff writer job to me. I later found out it was only to write three host spots for $125 a pop. I was disappointed, but it was another writing credit, and who knew what it would lead to? I ended up writing all 39 host spots that season, which, when it was all added up, was more money than I had ever seen in my life.

In 1959, Carolyn introduced me to the great actor Alan Ladd. They had worked on a movie together (*Man in the Net*) and they had a wrap party at Alan's house. "I hear you love Westerns," Alan said to me.

"Sure," I replied, "I'm from Texas."

I always used that line. I actually had never seen a horse in my life until I came to Hollywood.

"Here," he said, "read this script. I have a deal with Warner Bros. and I have to do the damn thing. I don't think it's any good, so I'm going to turn it down. Let me know what you think and give me some notes."

This was on a Friday night. I didn't know how to give notes to America's number-one box-office attraction. So I did the only thing that made sense to me. I went home and rewrote the script.

I showed up at Alan Ladd's house the following Monday at 10 A.M., as he asked, and he told me to sit down while he read it. Incredibly nervous, I went over to his window and looked out at his beautiful swimming pool and counted every blade of grass while he slowly read the script. When he was done—and I'll never forget this as long as I live—he picked up the phone.

"Jack Warner, please. . . . Is he in? Alan Ladd calling."

Mr. Warner came to the line.

"Jack, I've had a rewrite on the script and now I like it. I'm going to do it. I'm working with the script right now. And Jack, my producer's name is Aaron Spelling. That's S-P-E-L-L-I-N-G."

He then turned to me and said, "All right, kid, let's get to work."

The movie was called *The Guns of the Timberland.* Gilbert Roland, Frankie Avalon, and Jeanne Crain costarred in a tale of loggers versus the townspeople, and it was directed by Robert Webb. Here I was, with hardly any credits to my name in Hollywood, a guy writing $125 host spots for Dick Powell, and the next thing I knew I was on a train heading to the timberline country of Nevada to produce a movie for the great Alan Ladd.

However, I almost lost my job four days into the production. Sue Ladd, Alan's wife, came up to me and said, "Alan loves you, but he never should have made you producer. Aren't you even interested enough to come to dailies?"

"Am I allowed to?" I said.

That's how naive and young I was.

Four

I CONTINUED cranking out the host spots for Dick Powell. After I completed the twelfth one, he said, "Hey, Skinny, you know the show now. Why don't you write one?" That sounded great to me, except that Hal Hudson didn't seem so interested. Mr. Powell changed that when he called him and asked his producer to meet with me again.

Mr. Hudson remembered the stories I had pitched, selected one, "The Unrelenting Sky," and asked me to write it.

THE UNRELENTING SKY

by Aaron Spelling

OPENING:
EXT. WESTERN PLAINS—DAY

CAMERA PANS from SHOT of sky of blowing sand to a two-horse wagon, loaded with personal belongings—an old battered truck, a washtub, an iron bed, a wire coop with two chickens, and other furniture and paraphernalia, rolls into CAMERA. The wagon stops for a moment in front of a grave marked with a relatively new wooden headstone. A weary-looking woman drives the wagon and a young boy, of about ten, sits behind her. The woman looks for an anguished moment at the gravestone. The boy doesn't look at the grave. He is interested only in his mother's welfare now. The woman finally slaps the horse with the reins, and the wagon rolls on again. As they move out, the boy turns and darts a last look at the grave. The dust from their wagon almost obscures the mound from view. CAMERA DOLLIES through dust to CLOSE SHOT of the roughly marked tombstone.

NARRATOR
(reading epitaph)
Branch Williams
Took sick in the heat of '58
He fell
Before the rain

FADE OUT.

FADE IN:

EXT. RANGE DAY MED. SHOT CLINT HOWARD

walking slowly toward CAMERA, a rifle in his hands. The strong, hot sun beats down harshly. He is a strong, lean rancher in his early thirties, dressed in the typical rancher's garb of the period. Lacking a formal education, Clint has the intrinsic intelligence and moral strength necessary to exist in the unsettled wilderness of the West. Under easier and less demanding circumstances, he might have been considered an aesthetic man . . . yet he has now successfully adapted himself to the grueling hardships and adversities of a cattle rancher. His determination is motivated by a single dream—a dream of making a home in the barren vastness of Arizona. Others have failed and moved on . . . Clint Howard is no mover.

He walks into a CLOSE SHOT. Slowly, he raises the rifle to his shoulder, but stops halfway. He takes a deep breath . . . and in one motion, whips the gun up and fires to right of CAMERA.

CAMERA PULLS BACK as Clint moves to the scrawny, sick steer he has slain. He looks down at the animal and wipes the sweat off his face with a kerchief. He looks up at the sound of horses' hooves.

POV SHOT RIDER
ALEX ROZKY rides in and pulls his horse to a stop by Clint's side.

MED. SHOT ROZKY

A slight Polish man of about forty-seven, his face is shiny with sweat. He has the enduring stamp of a farmer trying to adapt to this rugged new life. Rozky is a mild, gentle man who speaks with a sight accent. A small, handmade crib or cradle is tied on the back of his saddle. He looks down at the dead steer for a moment, dismounts, and walks over to Clint. CAMERA PANS with him. Clint rises as his friend approaches. As he looks at his steer, Rozky says:

ROZKY
They are not pretty when
they get like that.

CLINT
Fourth one this week.

ROZKY
(sympathetically)
It is not easy . . . to kill this way.

CLINT
He was half-dead. Better to
shoot him than let him suffer.
That or the mountain lions will
get him.

ROZKY
They are getting worse. A cougar
attacked one of Mr. Beecher's
steers last night. It was not more
than fifty feet from his house.

CLINT
An animal crazy with thirst
will kill just for the blood.

ROZKY
(nods, pauses)
I passed the Williams wagon
on the way over. Mrs. Williams
and the boys have moved on.
They go to California.
(pauses, smiles wistfully)
They say it is green there all
year round.

He picks up a handful of hot sand and lets it drizzle between his fingers.

ROZKY
(continuing)
I do not believe it.

CLINT
(disturbed)
You're not thinkin' of leavin', too?

ROZKY
(smiles)
My family and me, we
have already come a
long way. No, God
willing, we will stay.

CLINT
We stay too.

Clint looks down at the steer for a moment.

CLINT
(continuing; a hard but definite decision)
I'm goin' to see Travers.

ROZKY
It will do no good.
Three times Mr. Beecher
and I have talked to him.
His answer is always the same.

CLINT
(determined)
He's the only one who
can help us.

ROZKY
(quietly)
It is not right . . . to have
to ask a *man* for water.

CLINT
There's no other way.

ROZKY
(nods)
Beecher and I will go
with you. Perhaps he
will listen to all of us.

CLINT
(hesitates a moment)
All right.

Rozky nods and moves to his horse. As he starts to mount, he realizes the crib is still there. Clint has already mounted.

ROZKY
(untying crib)
Oh, I almost forget.
I came to bring the crib to
your wife.

CLINT
(smiles)
Kinda' rushin' things, ain't you?
Peg's not due for two more months.

Rozky carries crib over to him.

ROZKY
(smiles, embarrassed)
Mrs. Rozky . . . you know
how she is. She worries.

He hands crib up to Clint.

CLINT
We thank you. Both of you.

ROZKY
I ride over and get Mr. Beecher.

CLINT
All right. I'll take the crib to Peg
and meet you down at your lower pasture.

He waits as Rozky mounts and rides out. CAMERA HOLDS on Clint as he watches him for a moment and then turns and rides in the opposite direction, toward his house.

(They go to visit Ol' Man Travers, who has stored most of the water, but Travers is firm—the water belongs to him, not them. He won't let them share. He doesn't care if the cows are dying. He's keeping the water. So they decide to kill Travers for his water. Clint is elected to do the deed, but he's not eager. He doesn't have it in him to kill a man for his water, and when Peg finds out, she pleads with him not to go through with it. He refuses and goes out to do the job. He takes Travers out of his house, by gunpoint, and is about to kill him. Travers offers a deal for water, but only for Clint, not for the others. Peg, carrying a rifle, rides up on her horse and orders her husband not to murder. A huge cougar comes out of nowhere.)

Fascinated, Clint watches the cougar move closer to its prey, Travers. It suddenly dawns on him that the cougar is the answer. It's almost as if the cougar were sent to kill Travers for him. He lowers his gun a bit. He ad-libs while he lets the cougar move into position.

CLINT
Travers offered us some water, Peg.
You willin' to let the others do without?

WIDE SHOT FAVORING TRAVERS
Clint in f.g. with back toward CAMERA. Cougar on rock above Travers' head—if possible.

PEG
(o.s.)
Listen to me, Clint. I'm sure
Mr. Travers would be willin'
to help us all if you'd just let him.

CLOSE SHOT CLINT
His eyes are riveted on the cougar.

CLINT
Too late, Peg.
(almost a whisper)
He hasn't got a chance.

CLOSE SHOT COUGAR
studying his victim

CLOSE SHOT PEG

PEG
(near hysteria)
Please, Clint! Please!

CLOSE SHOT CLINT
He is fighting a tremendous emotional battle with himself.

MED. SHOT TRAVERS, COUGAR
The cougar is overhead, crouching to spring.

CLOSE SHOT CLINT
His face is bathed in cold sweat. As if in a trance, he slowly raises his gun.

CLOSE SHOT PEG
Seeing him raise the pistol, she gets ready to fire.

PEG
(hysterically)
No, Clint! No!

MED. SHOT COUGAR
springs at Travers

MED. SHOT CLINT
Lightning fast, he whips up his pistol and fires.

MED. SHOT PEG
fires at Clint

FULL SHOT GROUP

Peg rushes over to Clint, who holds his shoulder . . . just grazed by her bullet. Travers, not fully realizing what has happened, stands by the dead cougar.

PEG
(sobbing)
Clint! Clint!

CLINT
It's all right, Peg.
(takes her in his arms)
It's all over now. It's not
in me to kill a man. I couldn't
even stand by and see him killed.
(tenderly)
We'll find a way . . . let's go home.

They start out.

CLOSE SHOT TRAVERS
He watches them go. There is a bewildered, puzzled expression on his face.

MED. SHOT CLINT, PEG

With his arms around her waist, Clint leads Peg home. CAMERA MOVES with them. The ordeal over, Clint's only thoughts are for Peg.

CLINT
(softly)
You shouldn't have come,
Peg. This far . . . it's hard on
'ya.

PEG
(smiles happily)
I feel fine.

She leans her head on his shoulder.

PEG
I love you, Clint
Howard.

Clint tightens his hold around her waist. Suddenly, something hits him on the cheek. He stops, not daring to hope. Peg, too, is suddenly very still. Now, another raindrop hits them . . . another . . . and another. They look to the sky.

INSERT: SKY

Heavy, black rain clouds fill the night. It begins to rain . . . hard.

They are getting drenched. CAMERA PANS DOWN to a small puddle of water at their feet. We just see their feet as they step into the puddle and walk out of SHOT. CAMERA HOLDS on the puddle . . . rapidly filling with water.

FADE OUT.

THE END

"The Unrelenting Sky" led to other *Zane Grey* scripts. I ended up writing nine more that season. After all those years of starving, I tried to make up for lost time by writing nonstop. The words just rushed out. For years, I had been unable to get credits, but finally it was happening. I felt terrific. I was consumed with a new kind of energy.

My friend Nolan Miller (now a famous clothes designer) and I would often go to La Scala for dinner, and while he searched the room to pick up pretty women, I'd look for stars. I'll let Nolan finish the story:

"He would go up to Joan Crawford and say, 'What kind of part would you like to play that you've never done before?' She'd say, 'A funky rooming housekeeper who has a lot of cats.' And then Aaron would practically write the story sitting at the table. By the time we had left the restaurant, he had cast the show for next week."

Dick Powell became the great mentor of my life. He took a liking to me and started inviting me to come to his office every night at the end of work to have a drink. "Skinny," he would say on the phone, "the ice is getting hot. Get over here." Out of those late-night chats came one of the best scripts I ever wrote.

Dick had heard that a hot young performer named Sammy Davis, Jr. wanted to get into acting, so he made me a reservation at Ciro's to go see Sammy, who was then performing as part of the Will Mastin Trio. Sammy was knocking audiences out with his versatility. He sang, danced, did impressions, and played several instruments. I was as bowled over as everyone else, and I told Dick so. "Then why don't you write a script for him?" he asked.

My story was that Dick would play a sheriff and Sammy his deputy, a man who would save his life when a heavy tried to kill the boss. Sammy loved it, Dick loved it, and I was really proud of the script. But then, three days before we were set to start shooting, Dick told me that the sponsor had nixed the story. We couldn't have a black man kill a white man, even if the white guy was a villain. "Wait a minute," I said. "The whole town is upset that Dick's hired a black deputy, but Dick wants to give him a chance. And he loves Dick so much for giving him the chance that he kills someone for him and saves the white man's life."

I couldn't believe the sponsors would kill that concept. Dick shrugged and said, "Get me another script for Sammy. We can't let this happen to him." Five days later, I handed Dick a new manuscript.

The sponsors had no problem with the new one, called "Mission," the true story of the Buffalo Soldiers, an all-black Infantry unit during the Civil War that was sent on a mission of no return. An Indian says to Sammy, "Why do you listen to the white man and fight his fight against us? He hates you as much as he hates us." And that was okay with the sponsors! They didn't censor it at all. The sponsors racist attitude really stunk, but here I was using their forum to point out bigotry and that was okay with them. It was acceptable to make the whites bigots, but it wasn't okay to have a black deputy kill a white man to protect his friend's life. Didn't make any sense. But that's the way things were done then. Thank God sponsors don't have the rights of censorship anymore.

"You're going to produce this show one day, aren't you, Skinny?" Dick Powell said to me one day. And within two years I did. I became almost adopted by Dick. I don't know why, but it was the best thing that ever happened to me.

He taught me everything I know about television. He always said, "If it ain't broke, don't fix it." I didn't know anything at the time. I thought he made up that phrase. He taught me that the secret to good television is attention to detail. He taught me to spend as much time as possible in the editing room, because that's where good film is made.

Dick Powell was a great guy, a very kind man, but you always knew he was your boss. He always said, "All I ask is that you don't leave the studio before me." He never left any earlier than 7 P.M., and when he did, he'd say, "I'm leaving now, Skinny. I'll look for your taillights behind me."

He never screamed at you, but he'd give you faint praise. If you did something wrong, he'd say, "You knew that, Skinny, didn't you?" When he was in a really good mood, he'd sing one of his old songs from the Warner Bros. musicals, usually "I Only Have Eyes for You." I can't tell you how many times he told me whether or not he liked a script or pilot by launching into "I Only Have Eyes."

You know, Dick had at least three careers. First he starred in those Warner Bros. musicals in the 1930s. When he got too old to play the boy singer, he became a hard-boiled detective. Then when television came in, he became a producer and director. Over and over again throughout his life, people in the business kept saying he was through, but he kept bouncing back. I thought of that a few years ago when I had no network shows on the air. After all these years, I still feel like Dick and I are tied at the hip.

The best script I've written was created, like so many of the best shows are, out of a production problem. We had to make an air date and a script fell out. Dick didn't know what to do. I told him I had an idea I could write in three days.

"If it's as good as that Sammy Davis script, go ahead and do it." I called it "The Silent Sentry," and it was about two opposing soldiers from the Civil War who meet by chance and end up brainstorming on ways to end the war.

Since we had no time to build any elaborate sets or cast actors, I had to write something for two people only, on the backlot with a small set. That way we could make our air date. We had Dick, and I got the director, Don Taylor, to star as the other soldier. Dick's son, Norman Powell, filled in as substitute director.

THE SILENT SENTRY

by Aaron Spelling

FADE IN:
EXT. FORT. DAY
SHOOTING DOWN on Fort under attack.

NARRATOR
At 4:30 A.M., April 12th, 1861—
Confederate troops opened fire on
Fort Sumter. The bloodiest of all
wars—the Civil War—had started.

DISSOLVE TO:

EXT. BATTLEGROUND DAY
HIGH SHOT SHOOTING DOWN on battlefield.

NARRATOR
Armies of farmers, ranchers, and
bank clerks marched into the field.
Thousands turned plows into guns
and died on the dirt they had
seeded. To the tunes of "Dixie"
and "John Brown's Body" friend
attacked friend. Brother killed
brother.

DISSOLVE TO:

EXT. BATTLEGROUND DAY
QUICK ACTION CUTS to accent narration.

NARRATOR
Chickamauga—Bull Run—Antietam
—Gettysburg. Infamous battles in an
infamous war.
(BEAT)
But there were others—
little-known dead in little-
known battles . . .

Pea Ridge, Little Round
Top—Cemetery Ridge.

EXT. CLEARING DAY
SHOOTING DOWN to an empty wooded area—on extreme end of the area, we see one YANK SOLDIER—ONE REB.

NARRATOR
And there was still another
battlefield. The mountainous
wastelands of the West. The war
of freezing cold—the war of
the solitary picket—

MED. SHOT REB
CAMERA ZOOMS into CLOSE SHOT. He is hunched in a hole, holding his rifle ready.

NARRATOR
One Reb.

MED. SHOT YANK
CAMERA ZOOMS into CLOSE SHOT. He is staring at the Reb, rifle in firing position.

NARRATOR
(over)
One Yank.

BACK TO MED. SHOT
HOLDING both men.

NARRATOR
and one must die!

(Both men end up forgetting their differences, befriending each other and drafting a document about how to end the war. Reb and Yank are proud of what they've accomplished and get ready to return to their posts to show how it can be done. But then their old hatreds come back into play, and when it comes time to leave, neither man can do it. Suddenly the two friends are two uniforms again . . . two guns. They become convinced the other will kill him when not looking. Neither Reb nor Yank will leave first, so they decide to walk out together, and go their separate ways. But both turn around and shoot the other.)

MED. CLOSE SHOT YANK
As his body stiffens in death, his fingers loosen—the treaty falls to the ground.

MED. CLOSE SHOT REB
The impact of his fall has knocked the treaty out of his tunic front. He is dead.

MED. SHOT THE TWO MEN
The whining wind is a funeral dirge for the two soldiers. As it blows over them, it whips the pieces of the treaty away—sends them flying over the snow and out of CAMERA. CAMERA HOLDS on the two men.

NARRATOR
No one will ever know what
happened here. No one will ever
read the honor and hopes of man.
No one . . . except the snow . . . the silent
sentry.

FADE OUT

THE END

After the great experience with *Zane Grey*, I decided the only kinds of scripts I wanted to write were for anthologies, which were one of the dominant forms of programming in the 1950s. They were the precursor to the TV movie of the week, usually based on a theme (science fiction, *The Twilight Zone*, Westerns, *Zane Grey*) featuring great actors and new characters every week. I didn't want to write characters that had already been created for existing series. It may sound like a stupid attitude, but it served me well, because I never got the reputation as an "episodic" writer. I just wanted to do my own stuff. Today things are different. There are no anthologies. The trick now is to make pre-existing created characters do what they haven't done before.

It was a Desilu Playhouse script that got me solely into producing. I consider it my second best script (after "Silent Sentry"), a story of a little immigrant plumber who was helped into this country by people who turned out to be members of the mob. In order to stay here, he had to deliver a favor—kill someone they didn't like, in this case a sweet Jewish tailor.

Edward G. Robinson, the great actor from the Warner Bros. gangster films, promised he'd make his TV debut as the plumber, but the studio decided to save $5,000 and get a different actor. I was heartbroken and the show was a disaster. After it aired, I went to the bathroom and threw up. "You've got to grow up," said Carolyn. "You should never write anything that you don't produce." I never did.

At first I hated producing because it took me away from writing, but I loved working with writers on story concepts and rewriting scripts. The hours were longer than when I was just a writer, but then I would never have to be second-guessed by anyone anymore.

Before moving on, I've got to tell you one last *Zane Grey* story. One of the great friendships of my life happened during that period. Dick Powell told me that his dear friend Barbara Stanwyck wanted to make her television debut on *Zane* and he asked me to write her a script—which I did, about the first female sheriff of a Western town. She liked it so much, she started calling many people of influence at other studios, telling them to hire me. She called Stan Kamen at William Morris and put in a good word. She called other actors and other producers. She was really wonderful.

Missy (her friends called her "Miss Stanwyck" and her close friends called her "Missy") became Tori's godmother and she also introduced me to Nolan Miller, who designed so many of the beautiful gowns for my shows over the years.

As I will discuss in further detail later, my marriage to Carolyn had broken up. I was dating an actress named Jackie Lane at the time, and it was her birthday, so I went to a flower shop to get her a present. I was looking around and then Missy came out with this tall, skinny guy named Nolan Miller. Nolan worked at the flower shop and put floral arrangements together for Missy.

"I want you to hire this fucking guy," she said.

That's the way she talked. Every other word out of her mouth was the "F" word. She had one salty mouth, and this was in an era when we didn't really hear that kind of language.

"What am I going to do with a florist?" I said.

"He also designs clothes," she said. "He's a terrific designer. You should use him on your shows."

So as a favor to her, I said okay and we started Nolan on *Burke's Law*. He's been with us ever since. Part of the deal for a star to appear on the show was $1,000, a ride to the studio in a Rolls-Royce, and a free Nolan Miller gown. Years later, when I asked Emma Samms to join *Models, Inc.*, I couldn't promise her the Rolls, but she got the same clothing deal—a nice salary and free Nolan Miller costumes. That's what clinched the deal.

Now that I was doing pretty well, I wanted to move my parents out here from Dallas, but they didn't want to leave Texas. My sister and her children were there and they were comfortable. I did move them out of Browder Street as soon as I could, but they were uncomfortable accepting big gifts. So I sent checks or money via my sister Becky and she would make them take it.

But, I'm proud to report, that as I moved up the ladder in Hollywood, so did my father in Dallas. He realized his dream—which was to become a "marker" in a Dallas department store. "I don't sew anymore," he told me one day. "I mark the clothes on the customer, and give them to other tailors to sew. I wear a coat and a tie now."

Dad died on the job, at 84, and I'll never forget what he said to me shortly before he passed away: "You followed your dream and you made mine come true too."

Postscript: My mother died shortly after Dad, and Becky and my brother Max are no longer with us. Danny operates a seashell business in San Francisco, and my brother Sam is retired in Dallas.

Five

In my early writing career, I felt everything I wrote should really say something. My *Playhouse 90* script was about a man who exacts a long, terrible revenge on a small Western town. The reason for his grudge: When he needed medicine for his sick wife, he couldn't come up with $1.87 to pay for it, and the townsfolk let his wife die. I guess it was pretty good because after it aired, 20th Century–Fox called to buy the script as a feature for Alan Ladd, called *One Foot in Hell.*

Why was I so interested in man's inhumanity against man? Because I grew up in a neighborhood that was full of it. When you get your ass kicked every day as a child and have a nervous breakdown at nine, it tends to stick with you for a while.

I have become much better known over the years for glitzy entertainment (although, for some reason, people always forget to mention shows like *Family* and movies like *And the Band Played On* and *Day One*) because I believe that people are looking for a release and TV should provide it. We're in the entertainment industry. It's our job to entertain. I'm always telling writers not to be ashamed of writing things that entertain people.

I hate all those silly sitcoms that litter the TV screen, but if you took them off, I think the suicide rate would jump higher than anyone could imagine. I'm glad those shows are on TV. I don't care who you are, but we all need to escape from something.

It was while writing the script for *One Foot in Hell* at 20th Century–Fox that I created my first series for Four Star, *Johnny Ringo.* At 20th, I handed in the first 35 pages of the film script to the producer, proud of how fast it was coming to me. He looked at me and said, "Don't ever do that again. That's not how we do motion pictures. I want no more than five pages a week."

I went over to see Mr. Powell at his bungalow, and I complained about how strange it was to have to write so little. He solved the problem by telling me that CBS was looking for a new Western, something different. "You have any ideas?" I thought about it and asked myself the question, "What if there was a seven-shooter gun?" All the guns back then were six-shooters and all the Westerns were then known for the kinds of weapons the hero used. It's like video games today, where inventors are always trying to come up with new ways of attack.

Johnny Ringo debuted as a pilot on *Zane Grey*, and then became its own series for CBS on October 1, 1959. It was the story of the first seven-shooter in the West and starred Don Durant as the gunfighter-turned-lawman of Velardi, Arizona. All Johnny wanted to do was forget about his violent past, but every gunfighter who came through Velardi wanted to try Johnny's draw. The extraordinary thing about Johnny Ringo and his "peacekeeper" was that when he would be in battle with somebody, he would fire his sixth shot, and the heavy would say, "Now I have you," but he didn't. He'd always get the guy on the seventh shot.

Johnny Ringo was famous for never being beaten. And I saw to it that his record stayed intact.

I wrote the pilot, we shot it, it was picked up for a series, and all the while I was still handing in my five pages a week on *The Last Man*.

And then I was producing three series at one time, with *Johnny*, *Zane*, and *The DuPont Show with June Allyson*. How did I do it? Simple. First of all, I had great staffs, and secondly, back in those days, many dramas were a half hour in length, so they were much easier to produce. I would love to do a half-hour drama again. I wish they would come back. Two acts and you're out. You set up the first act and finish the second act. (One-hour shows are built on four acts where we set up a problem in act one and keep building on the problem until we end with the resolution in act four.)

June Allyson was Dick's wife, a former Broadway chorus girl and major Hollywood star of the 1940s and 1950s, who often played a wholesome girl next door or wife to clean-cut guys like Jimmy Stewart and Van Johnson. She appeared a few times on *Zane Grey*, and got her own half-hour anthology series in 1959, at a time when most anthologies were hosted by men. (The only exceptions were *The*

Loretta Young Show, 1953–61, and *The Jane Wyman Show*, 1955–8.) She was the regular hostess and occasional star and, unlike *Zane*, she tended to attract even bigger names, since most of the stories were contemporary and not as restricting as Westerns. Stars like Bette Davis, David Niven, Joseph Cotten, and Jane Powell appeared, and on one episode, a play called "A Summer's Ending," June and Dick made their first joint TV appearance.

June was a cuteypuss. She was petite and beautiful and had two of the most beautiful lips I'd ever seen, which was part of her sensuality since she was the "girl next door." I loved her movies and I loved working with her. She was very sweet to me and we never had a problem on the set.

Dick went the contemporary route in 1961 after *Zane Grey* went off the air and his *Dick Powell Show* anthology was added to my plate. Dick figured he'd assign six producers to the show and that they would all alternate, but it didn't end up that way. He found it was easier for one person to report to him, and that job went to me. And I also continued to write the host spots for him.

The very first episode of *The Dick Powell Show* was called "Who Killed Julie Greer," and it was about a filthy rich and quite sophisticated Beverly Hills policeman named Amos Burke. The episode was so successful we eventually spun it off into a separate series, *Burke's Law*.

Amos Burke was a millionaire Los Angeles chief of detectives who lived an elegant lifestyle in a palatial mansion and drove everywhere in a chauffeured Rolls-Royce that came complete with a fully stocked bar. Burke liked to assign himself personally to the most interesting cases, usually involving the rich and famous, while two detectives did legwork and helped question the suspects.

The script was written by playwright Frank Gilroy (*The Subject Was Roses*), who had written a film for Dick Powell, and Dick wasn't sure whether or not he wanted to play this rich detective, but I talked him into it. I told him it would be a lot of fun, and it was.

Before we started production, I got this great idea about having cameos by famous guest stars to round out the show. It was the first show to use multiple guest stars. Much later we did it again on *The Love Boat*, *Fantasy Island*, and *Hotel*. And Angela Lansbury has been doing it beautifully on *Murder, She Wrote*.

We had eight stars on the first episode, and each actor worked just one day. "Why don't we see if we could get famous guest stars to play the suspects," I said to Dick Powell, "and really have some fun with it?"

"Who's going to work for just one day?"

"You've got friends."

"Like who?"

"Edgar Bergen's close to you. He'd be great."

"Like Edgar Bergen's going to do it."

"You'll never know if you don't ask him."

So we made a deal. I would cast the young parts and he'd do the older ones. I went to Carolyn Jones first, since we were married, and naturally she said yes. Nick Adams was a close friend and so was Lloyd Bridges and they both said yes. So I had three. Dick got Ronnie Reagan, one of his closest pals, as well as Jack Carson, Dean Jones, Kay Thompson, and Bergen.

Viewers loved seeing their favorite stars pop in and out of the show. And *Burke's* was so good we decided to spin it off into its own series. This time we found someone even more debonaire and sophisticated for Amos—Gene Barry, who had starred in *Bat Masterson* as the dapper ex-lawman and professional gambler who roamed the West in a derby hat and a gold-tipped cane disguised as a sword.

Gene was "Amos Burke." As good as Dick was in the part, Gene was better. He knew how to wear clothes. Dick hated wearing suits. He was a sportscoat man, but Gene looked great in a tuxedo.

We continued getting the best names to appear as guest stars (like Jayne Mansfield, Buster Keaton, and Terry Thomas) and attracted some wonderful writers, like *Columbo* creators William Link and Richard Levinson and science fiction great Harlan Ellison. I'll never forget that Gloria Swanson was our 100th guest star. This was after *Sunset Boulevard*—an unforgettable performance.

Burke's was an unusual show because the murders were so ridiculous. We never had anyone walk into a room and kill anybody. Instead, for instance, we'd have the victim drive down Sunset Boulevard, and pass a big smoking billboard. Out of the hole where smoke came out would be a gun protuding from the mouth of the billboard model and it would go off.

We coined the phrase "Burke's Law-isms" because Amos had all these great quips. There were four per show and we even published a book of them. (Some examples: "*Never waste time talking about the future—Burke's Law*" . . . "*Never bring 25-year-old Scotch to a man who drinks two-dollar corn whiskey—Burke's Law*" . . . "*Never grow up, you'll get old—Burke's law*" . . . "*Never drink martinis with beautiful suspects—Burke's law.*")

Up until *Burke's*, I wrote and produced mostly Westerns. With *Burke's* I was able to let my imagination go wild with stories of a fantasy millionaire lifestyle I had only dreamed about as a kid. And we went all the way. *Burke's* was one of my first great campy shows. The crimes tended to be very bizarre. One week we had a man-eating plant as a suspect.

Then ABC threw us a curve ball with the "James Bond" craze. Suddenly secret agents were in. We'd gone from Westerns to cop shows and suddenly spy shows were the rage. So, in 1965 *Burke's Law*, the story of a millionaire L.A. detective, was forcibly changed to *Amos Burke—Secret Agent*. He became a debonair, globe-trotting secret agent for a United States intelligence agency. I hated it, Gene hated it, we all hated it, and ABC was very wrong to change it. But that's what ABC ordered, and they were paying the bills. And they *were* wrong. Viewers tuned out and the program change spelled the end of the show. We were canceled at the end of the 1965 season.

Speaking of heartbreak, would you like to know what my biggest disappointment has been in all my years of producing television? What CBS did to the new version of *Burke's Law* that debuted in 1994. We brought Gene back, hired a young actor, Peter Barton, to play Burke's son, and got some of the great names of today to appear on the show. CBS scheduled the show Fridays at 9 P.M., and at first we averaged a 22 share, the best results CBS had seen in that slot for years. CBS was so happy, they quickly renewed us and sent me a huge trophy case, which is still in my office. It's a figure of me on the phone. Underneath, it says, "Aaron Spelling, MVP—Most Valuable Producer." Their way of saying thanks for finally fixing their Friday problems.

Burke's began when a talented CBS executive named Jonathan Levin called me and suggested we do a remake. The experience went so well, I ended up hiring Jonathan as the president of our television division at Spelling Entertainment Group.

Everything changed for *Burke's* in May 1994 when Jeff Sagansky, then president of CBS Entertainment, resigned, and was replaced by Peter Tortorici. He renewed *Burke's*, but kept it off the schedule for midseason. The management change brought on a new policy of pursuing younger viewers at all costs, even if it meant going from a 22 share to a 13, which is what *Burke's* replacement, *Under Suspicion*, was averaging.

It seemed that once Jeff Sagansky left, everyone at CBS was determined to kill *Burke's*. We made our 14 episodes and they held us and held us and held us. Finally, we had a timeslot. Tuesdays at 10 P.M., opposite ABC's *NYPD Blue*, one of the biggest hits on television. Obviously we were going to get killed, and we did. We lasted one week. Then *Burke's* reappeared a few weeks later, Fridays at 8. We did okay, but only got two weeks there. The next thing you knew we were on Saturdays at 9 P.M. For two weeks. And then back to our old timeslot, where we didn't do 20s, like before (Could all the juggling have had anything to do with it?) but we did 15s, which was still better than *Under Suspicion*.

Then we moved to Thursdays at 8 P.M. Have you ever heard of a show with five different timeslots in two months? Any time I'd call to complain, they'd just change the subject. They didn't want to hear about *Burke's Law*.

It was a very sad and humiliating experience. Our executive producers, Duke Vincent and Jim Conway, did a great job and Gene Barry and Peter Barton were great. I keep remembering Dick Powell's line. I wish I had said it to CBS: "If it's not broken, don't fix it!"

When I look at the late 1950s and early 1960s, it's amazing to think of all the long-term relationships I made that had such a big effect on my career. I'm talking about people like Dick Powell, Alan Ladd, Preston Sturges, Jack Webb, Abe Lastfogel, Stan Kamen, Leonard Goldberg, and Larry Gordon.

Leonard and I became partners in the 1970s and had probably the greatest run of any TV production team in the history of Hollywood. *The Rookies*, *Starsky and Hutch*, *Family*, *Charlie's Angels*, *Hart to Hart*,

S.W.A.T., *Fantasy Island*, *T.J. Hooker*, and *Chopper One*. It was hit after hit, with nine shows and only one flop.

Len began his career at the BBD&O advertising agency, the agency that bought commercials on Four Star shows for their clients. He came out to Hollywood in the early 1960s to visit all the studios, which was something the agencies did every year, because at the time the agencies had more power than the networks. If they liked a show, it aired. Period.

Len came over to Four Star and introduced himself, and he seemed like a nice guy, so I called him later at the Beverly Hills Hotel to see if he'd like to have dinner. He seemed lonely and I thought he might enjoy the company. "I don't have any plans tonight," Len said. "In fact, I don't know a single person in the state of California. I'd love to have dinner."

We went to my favorite restaurant, La Scala, and at this point, I'm going to let Len finish the story:

"In those days, La Scala was the hottest place in town. We walked in and in one booth was Natalie Wood and in another booth was Yvette Mimieux and I thought, I could die right here. It was another world. Aaron was very dapper, meticulously groomed, and very well dressed. Don't ask me why a guy from Texas and a guy from Brooklyn hit it off, but we did.

"It came time to order, and I said, 'I love Italian food, but you know what's good here—why don't you order?' I'll always remember the first thing Aaron said. 'We'll have a Leon salad.' (That was the house salad.) He paused and added, 'Half-chopped.'

"I thought, wow, that's fantastic. What a place this is. There's a guy in the kitchen who picks up lettuce and slices half of it down, and if there's a piece of cheese, he half-slices that too. I thought if I ever wrote a book about Aaron, I'd call it *Half-chopped*."

Dick Powell had been offered many opportunities to go into politics and was very popular. The rumor at the time was that if Dick's best friend Ronnie Reagan didn't decide to run, Dick was the Republicans' choice to run for Governor of California. Who knows what might have happened?

It was never meant to be. As *The Dick Powell Show* began its second season, his health began to deteriorate rapidly. The year was quite rough for me, because Dick was indestructible, as far as I was concerned.

Dick first got an inkling that something was wrong when he went to New York with June to attend a network affiliate meeting. He put on his tuxedo shirt, but it was too tight. So he had the valet bring over another one, this time a half size bigger, but that was also too tight. They tried again with a shirt that was one full size bigger, but it didn't make any difference. The experience was so weird he decided to see the doctor when he got back to L.A. He was diagnosed with throat cancer. "Don't worry, Skinny. I'm going to beat it," he told me.

He lasted about a year, continued to act, and spent a lot of time on his boat. His final acting role on the show was in "The Court-Martial of Captain Wycliff," which aired on December 12, 1962. His last appearance as host was on New Year's Day 1963. He died the following day.

His family then asked that all the filmed introductions he had already prepared be deleted, and so a succession of guest stars like Robert Mitchum and David Niven appeared as hosts for the remainder of the season.

Without Dick Powell at Four Star, I didn't really want to stay there. But I was still under contract and remained another two years. Tom McDermot, an advertising man from Benton & Bowles, was asked by Niven and Boyer to take over, and I continued to oversee *Burke's Law*.

Carolyn and I separated before the Four Star association came to an end. By this time, my career was thriving and her movie career was slowing down. After she got the part of Morticia on *The Addams Family* in 1964, we got a divorce. She was a smash on the show with a whole new TV career ahead of her, so I felt less guilty about the divorce.

I was producing all day, and she'd be on the set all day, and we hardly saw each other. But we remained good friends after the divorce; we even used the same lawyer and split everything right down the middle. I also gave her our house on Beverly Drive. She certainly deserved it.

In truth, I don't think either of us was ready for marriage. We both wanted to be in the industry and found that it was cheaper living as two. What brought us together wasn't love, but our interests. I wish we could have been like Tom Hanks and Rita Wilson. His ascension to huge stardom hasn't affected his marriage. I wasn't ready for Carolyn to be nominated for an Academy Award. I was excited for her, but when you're an actor you can't help but think "What about me?" I'm sure her attitude was the same about my career. Why did I get to produce all those TV series?

We never really had a chance. Our whole lives were predicated on when our next job would come along.

I never really knew what love was until I met Candy. I don't consider one moment of my time with Carolyn to be wasted, but it's so different now. They say in the song that love is better the second time around and that just fits me to a tee. The second time I was ready.

Now let me tell about the pal we used to call "Gooter."

I was dating Mary Ann Mobley in 1963, right after she was crowned Miss America. After our fourth date, she told me she had a buddy in town and wanted me to meet him because he wanted to get into show business. "Maybe you could find something for him to do at Four Star," she said.

This suited guy from the south named Larry Gordon came in and met me on a day neither of us will forget. Not only was a young and very stunning Raquel Welch waiting outside my office for an interview for a show, but all of a sudden the studio came to a halt. John F. Kennedy had been shot, and I was given the task of shutting Four Star down and sending everyone home. I brought Larry with me, and since the studio's gates were about to close, we went over to my hotel to talk. We hit it off immediately. He was from the south and as eager as I had been ten years earlier when I arrived in Hollywood.

While we were talking I got this terrible pain on my right side. I called my doctor and he rushed me to the hospital for an appendectomy. Larry came with me and stayed there for hours, and then kept returning. He visited me continously.

When I got out of the hospital, I asked, "Do you really want to learn the business?" He did.

"I'm not going to be able to drive for a while, so why don't you drive me?"

So Larry worked for me as my general assistant, and we became such good friends that he eventually moved in with me at the hotel and shared my two-bedroom suite. I was newly divorced and really into the bachelor lifestyle. There was a group of starlets called "Burke's Girls," and every show would open with them. We'd have a party at the hotel, and we'd call our buddies and say, "Hey, we've got six ladies and two guys, come on over."

I told Larry that he was going to have to start writing. "You know the show," I said. "You're with me every day." Larry wrote his first script for *Burke's*—"Who Killed the Wrestler?" about female mud wrestlers—and it was really clever.

It may sound strange that we became so close so quickly. That's easy. He was there when I needed him. Anyone who was nice enough to come visit this guy in the hospital and stay there night and day was a terrific friend. He still is and always will be. No one is prouder of Larry than I am. He's one of the top motion picture producers in the business, with movies like *48 Hrs*, *Field of Dreams*, and *Die Hard*. There is no way I can express what an important role he's played in my life.

Larry and I saw a lot of Leonard whenever he came out to the west coast. As my career took off, so did Len's. I kept adding more shows to my portfolio and Len moved to ABC, where he became director of development, New York, working for the vice-president of the department, Douglas Cramer, who, ironically, became my new partner on *The Love Boat* and *Dynasty* after Len and I went our separate ways at the end of the 1970s.

ABC promoted Len to vice-president of daytime programming, where Len really made a name for himself with shows like *The Dating Game*, *The Newlywed Game*, *Where the Action Is*, and the Saturday morning *Beatles* cartoon.

Len says that when he accepted the daytime job, one of his associates said to him, "You're crazy—you'll never have dinner with Aaron Spelling at La Scala again," but he saw his way around that by hiring

Larry Gordon as head of talent for the west coast. He put Larry in charge of *Where the Action Is*, a daytime music show that featured a lot of go-go dancers. That kept us all together, since we all loved to party and go to the hot clubs of the day.

Larry and Len used to play gin together all the time, and in fact Larry once won $25,000 from him. "You're clearly a better gin player than I am, and I had a ball playing with you," said Len to Larry. "But not only don't I have $25,000 . . . I don't even have $1,000." We didn't have any money back then, but we sure had a great time.

After *Burke's Law*, I did two more series for Four Star: *Honey West*, starring Anne Francis as prime-time's first female private eye, and the first *Smothers Brothers Show*.

Honey was first introduced on an episode of *Burke's Law*, because we didn't have time to make a pilot. We met with ABC to tell them our idea about this sexy female private detective, and I had Nolan Miller draw sketches of this very slinky, beautiful Honey for them. In one she carried a whip and the other she was sitting with a tiger. "And that," I said, "is the show." Like James Bond, it was based on a series of books and ABC bought it immediately.

The Smothers Brothers Show predated the variety series that made them household names a few years later. Our sitcom featured Tommy as an angel (Who knew that 35 years later angels were going to be so prevalent in our business?) who returns to Earth two years after his death to watch out for brother Dick, a rising young executive.

I created the show with Richard Newton, a buddy of mine from SMU. The Smothers were just starting out then, and making a name for themselves with their "Mom, always liked you best" act at college campuses, the old Purple Onion folk club in San Francisco, and on comedy albums. Their manager, Ken Kragen, brought them in to see me, and I was really impressed. I liked their repartee. They were like a young Martin and Lewis. Tommy had this great deadpan expression, where Jerry Lewis was all facial and falling on the floor.

The show lasted a season on CBS, but didn't make much of an impression in the ratings. It was different. It wasn't a "ha-ha-ha" sitcom, but instead had a great deal of warmth. A year and a half later, CBS signed up the boys for *The Smothers Brothers Comedy Hour*, the show that made them household names and launched such young performers as Steve Martin, Rob Reiner, Bob Einstein, Pat Paulsen,

Jennifer Warnes, and Mason Williams. I felt like saying "I told you so" when the boys finally hit. I knew they had something.

One last word on *The Smothers Brothers Show.* Nickelodeon pulled the sitcom out of the vault a few years back and reran it for a while on their terrific Nick at Nite lineup. I had profit participation on the show, and recently received a royalty check from Four Star (now owned by New World Entertainment) for the sum total of $30. Now you can understand why I decided to form my own company.

I left Four Star in 1966 after some idiot decided to wipe Dick Powell's name off the masthead. I didn't want to work there anymore, and just walked out, not knowing where my next job would come from.

Six

AFTER I left Four Star, Mr. Lastfogel set me up with Harold Mirisch at United Artists, because the studio was going into television, and they were interested in having me head their TV division. I was paid $75,000 a year at Four Star, but the offer was $100,000 for UA and, naturally, that was great money. All I had to do was go to New York, meet with execs there, and sign the contract. I left on a train the next day, arrived in New York, signed my contract, and went to their meeting.

I called Mr. Lastfogel to find out how the meeting went, and he told me it went great, but there was just one problem. UA had a change of direction and decided not to get into the TV business after all.

"But don't worry," he said, "you've got a signed contract. They have to pay you anyway. If you don't find a job, they'll still pay you."

I moped around for a few days and felt guilty about making all this money doing nothing. I decided I would go back to writing full-time and create another series. A few nights later I went over to La Scala to have dinner. I was sitting at the bar having a drink first, when someone yelled from across the room.

"Hey, partner!"

I ignored it. The man yelled again.

It turned out that the guy was none other than the great entertainer and TV producer Danny Thomas. I had known Danny socially over the years, and had first come into contact with his family when I wrote an episode of *Zane Grey* for Danny and his daughter Marlo, who made her TV acting debut on the show.

"Hey, partner," he said, and he gave me a big hug.

"Hi, Danny, how are you?" I replied.

"What do you think, partner? What do you think? Are you excited?"

He could tell from the look on my face that I didn't know what he was talking about. "Uncle Abe hasn't told you yet?"

Mr. Lastfogel had left a message for me at the hotel where I was living, but I hadn't called him back.

"You're my new partner. Fifty-fifty." And Mr. Lastfogel got me another raise, this time to $110,000 a year. I was back in business. With Thomas–Spelling Productions.

Like Dick Powell in drama, Danny Thomas was one of the great TV sitcom pioneers, starting with his *Make Room for Daddy* series in 1953, in which he starred and produced with Sheldon Leonard. From there, they built an empire of sitcom classics, including *The Dick Van Dyke Show*, *The Andy Griffith Show*, and *Gomer Pyle, U.S.M.C.*

After *Make Room* (later retitled *The Danny Thomas Show*) went off the air in 1965, he and Leonard split up, and Danny decided to shift gears and expand into dramatic television, which is why he selected me.

Danny was on the road most of the time performing, so I had complete freedom to do what I wanted. And we started the company off with a bang, selling three shows right off the bat for our first season.

The first show was a format Danny was known for—the sitcom. I knew very little about comedy, but I knew how to laugh, and Tim Conway sure knew how to make me chuckle. After his hilarious second-banana stint on *McHale's Navy* as bumbling Ensign Charles Parker, Danny wanted to create a series for Tim when McHale sailed off into the sunset in 1966. So we built *Rango* for his unique talents, which debuted January 13, 1967.

Rango was a lawman who couldn't do anything right, the accident-prone son of the commander of the Texas Rangers in the 1870s. He had been assigned to the quietest post in the state, in an attempt to keep him out of trouble, and his assistant was Pink Cloud, an Indian who hated to fight. He discovered that reading an interesting book in a comfortable bed was much better than skulking around the plains. In language that we would never use today, he would say lines like, "Rango say him return when sun high over teepee. By that, I presume he meant he would be back by noon."

Rango was the first of the Tim Conway sitcoms that for some reason failed to capture his brilliance. However, now Tim is highly successful in those *Dorf* videos. He's all on his own, and he's sold millions of those tapes.

Tim's one of the funniest men I've ever met, and *Rango* wasn't bad. The format just didn't work. I learned something on *Rango* that I've said a million times since. You can't make fun of a Western. Western fans won't stand for it.

My next series with Danny was a serious Western, also for ABC, *The Guns of Will Sonnett*. The idea was that here was Walter Brennan, a three-time Academy Award winner (*Come and Get It*, *Kentucky*, and *The Westerner*) who the audience still loved. Why not put him together with a younger sidekick?

Danny had produced Walter's *The Real McCoys*, TV's first rural sitcom, which led to *The Andy Griffith Show*, and other shows of its type, such as *The Beverly Hillbillies* and *Green Acres*. In *McCoys*, Walter played Grandpa, an old codger who liked to meddle in his family's affairs. On *The Guns of Will Sonnett*, he starred as a gruff old ex-cavalry scout who took care of his grandson (Dack Rambo). Together, they searched the West for the boy's father in the 1870s. James Sonnett had disappeared 19 years earlier, leaving the infant Jeff in Will's care. And the boy had also been left with one goal in life—to find his father, who had become a notorious but very elusive gunfighter. Like *The Fugitive*, each week they traveled to different places and met different people who had come into contact with James Sonnett, but they never did find him, until the final episode, when they met the man who claimed to have killed him.

One thing I tried never to do during the making of *Guns* was to talk politics with Walter Brennan. He was very, very conservative, to the right of Rush Limbaugh. Our politics were diametrically opposite, but it didn't affect our relationship. We actually got along great (even though I had to bite my tongue when the subject of politics came up), and after *Guns*, which ran for two seasons, I cast him in both of our *Over the Hill Gang* movies.

Another quick note about Brennan: He did every show with cue cards. At seventy-three, he couldn't remember his lines, but when I would watch the dailies, I was amazed—he never missed a line. Never saw anything like it.

While doing *Guns* we also produced a new Danny Thomas anthology for NBC, based on a commitment he already had with the network. Danny introduced various dramas, as well as musical comedies (in which he appeared) and an occasional full-length comedy. I produced the dramas, but devoted most of my time to *Guns*.

Then *The Mod Squad* was born. It changed my life forever.

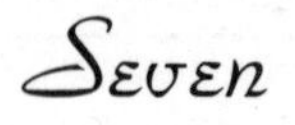

Seven

THE MOD SQUAD

EXT. A SUNSET STRIP HOT DOG STAND—NIGHT

SHOOTING across eight or ten motorcycles bunched at curb. In b.g., hot dog stand is loaded with teenagers. A few outside lounging, with FOLK-ROCK BLASTS from a jukebox.

NEW ANGLE—MOVING SHOT

to favor three kids' . . . "show-bating" on bikes in parking lot . . . PETE COCHRAN, a rugged, attractive surfer; LINC (LINCOLN) HAYES, a good-looking Black man; and JULIE BARNES, a stunning teeny-bopper with sharp flair.

FULL-INTERCUT

A squad car wheels to curb sharply. Out of it comes Lieutenant WHEELER, a mild, easygoing detective . . . followed by two Uniformed Policemen. Kids in hot dog stand see him head for Pete, Linc, and Julie.

Wheeler reaches the three . . . shows his identity. Pete grins.

PETE
What we do?
Run a red light?

The other kids move in, gather round the fringes of scene, follow it. Trio "plays" to them, gets laughs throughout. One kid turns on a transistor . . . more ROCK clashes with ROCK FROM juke, as:

WHEELER
Get off those bikes . . .

LINC
Bikes are made for
ridin', Daddy.

WHEELER
(harder)
Not here! Not this time of
the night! Now . . . do we take
you or the bikes?

JULIE
Hey, dig that police brutality!

(*Pete, Linc, and Julie meet Captain Adam Greer, who hauls them into his office and reads them the riot act.*)

ADAM
I made a deal with you
and I expect you to see it through—
all the way! Now you *know* how these
kids act. You've *been* there.

There is a very slight beat.

ADAM
(continuing; rides over, glares)
The whole idea's to meld *in* with
'em. You stand *out*, you might as
well wear your badges!

Beat . . . Trio looks grim, uncomfortable. FREEZE FRAME, start *MAIN TITLES* mid-harangue. From infinity, OPENING TITLE bursts out at us . . . "MOD SQUAD" . . .

FADE OUT

The Mod Squad was born at The Daisy, a hip, sophisticated Beverly Hills club on Rodeo Drive where EVERYBODY used to go to be seen and meet others. Jack Hansen, who owned the JAX Boutique, was also the proprietor of The Daisy. They had catered food, two pool tables, and a dance floor. It was a real industry hangout, and you'd always find big names like Ryan O'Neal and Natalie Wood there. Jack played soft romantic music so you could meet people, and you couldn't get in unless Jack knew you or had personally invited you.

It was at The Daisy that I got to know a former cop named Buddy Ruskin. He and a friend of his, Sam Hess, told me about how the L.A. Sheriff's Department had their own undercover narcotics squad composed of young officers.

"You ought to do a show about them," he said. The more I listened, the more intrigued I became. In fact, I bought the idea from Buddy that night, gave him a "created by" credit and started reworking the concept to pitch to ABC.

I thought it would be interesting if instead of just young cops, they were juveniles who had done something wrong in the past. As I saw it, the Police Department would form this secret unit and no one on the force except for the Captain would know these kids were cops. The kids had a choice. They could serve time in jail, or be part of the undercover unit. This to me was more interesting because the kids didn't really want to be cops, but they had no choice.

The show, very simply, was about three hippie cops, Pete, Linc, and Julie, one white, one black, and one blond, who had each dropped out of society after their own brush with the law. Pete was the reject from a wealthy Beverly Hills family, Julie the runaway daughter of a prostitute, and Linc (the one with the sunglasses) was the brooding black rebel, raised in Watts and arrested during the riots.

All three were on probation and were offered a chance to redeem themselves by working on a special "youth squad," whose purpose was to infiltrate the counterculture and do something about the adult criminals who were always trying to take advantage of the young. Under the guidance of Capt. Adam Greer, they had a chance to make a difference and help everybody "get it together."

We came up with the name "The Mod Squad," I pitched the concept to ABC, and the network bought it immediately. They were a "youth" network, and here was the first cop show with an attitude. It was a million light years away from *Dragnet* and the other cop shows of the day. Nobody had ever done a young cop show before.

We premiered in the fall of 1968, the height of "flower power" and the youth movement. Michael Cole, Clarence Williams III, and Peggy Lipton played the three members of the Mod Squad. They were all unknowns at the time, and the show turned them into instant stars. (Tige Andrews played Capt. Greer.)

The son of an electronics salesman in Madison, Wisconsin, Michael traveled around after college, going to Chicago, Las Vegas, and San Francisco before settling on Los Angeles and an acting career. Along the way, he worked in a bookstore, a pizza parlor, and as a dishwasher, a busboy, and a bartender, and then in L.A. he decided to study acting. After two years of working with an acting coach, Michael went on to get one-time shots on *Gunsmoke* and *Run for Your Life*, and an interview with me for the part of Pete Cochran at Paramount, where our offices were based.

I thought he had just the right look and attitude for the role. I had started telling him the concept when he stopped the conversation and said, "I don't want to do this shit."

"Why don't you let me finish telling you what the show is about?"

I explained that Pete was a rich kid who got into trouble with his family for what he had done and they had disowned him. Michael cut me off again and said he didn't want to be a part of a show that was about trapping kids. "Why don't you let me finish?"

He was getting pissed and so was I. But I finally was able to complete the description and Michael suddenly took a different attitude. Once he heard the whole thing, he realized that Pete wasn't a fink at all. And "The Mod Squad" would never arrest kids . . . and would never carry a gun or use one.

"Wow," he said. "Count me in."

I was willing to put up with Michael's attitude because it was just what I was looking for in Pete. Off camera, Michael was very inside himself and quiet. We used to call him the "brooder" of our group. Which, of course, was perfect for Pete.

Peggy was born in New York City, the daughter of a lawyer and a professional painter, and she was already a successful model by the time she reached her early teens. She started taking acting classes when her family moved to Los Angeles, and she broke in on an episode of *Bewitched*, where she had all of two words: "You're late."

She went on to appear on such shows as *The Virginian*, *The Invaders*, and *The John Forsythe Show*, and by the time our paths crossed, she was under contract to Paramount, and I had seen her on the lot.

She came in to read for us, and there was just something about her that was so vulnerable and beautiful and soft. She wasn't the vision of an undercover cop at all. I always said that what we were looking for was a canary with a broken wing and Peggy personified that to a "T." She had the greatest vulnerability of any actress I've ever worked with. I don't think we ever read anybody else but Peggy. She was meant to be Julie.

Clarence Williams III grew up in New York City and started acting as a child at the Harlem YMCA production of *Dark of the Moon*. After a two-year stint in the service, Clarence returned to New York and appeared in several Broadway plays. The one that really established him was *Slow Dance on the Killing Ground*. Bill Cosby went to see the play and was knocked out by Clarence's performance.

I had gotten to know Bill at Paramount, since *I Spy* was based there. We got to be buddies, and Bill came over to my office one day and told me about this young actor who knocked him out in *Slow Dance*. We were looking for an African-American actor for the part of Linc, so, naturally, I was quite interested.

We flew Clarence to Los Angeles and gave him a small role on *The Danny Thomas Hour*, to serve as a screen test. Here was the setup. Some young people were robbing a store, and Clarence played the driver of the getaway car. He didn't want anything to do with it, but he also didn't want to let his buddies down.

So we filmed the scene, Clarence made his little speech about how wrong it was, and then the guys went in and robbed the store. They jumped in the car, Clarence drove away, and ended up smashing the vehicle into a telephone pole—which wasn't called for in the script.

We were all quite scared and ran over to see what happened.

"I don't know how to drive," said Clarence. "I've never driven before."

"Then why did you do the role?"

"I didn't want to lose the gig. I want to be in *The Mod Squad*."

I cast him in the part that night.

Clarence was a real pistol and very serious about his work. He was the most accomplished actor of the trio and always wanted to stretch in his work. His wife, Gloria, was a Broadway actress, and since she was in New York while he was in L.A., Clarence and I palled around a lot, most often at The Factory, a new club off Santa Monica Boulevard.

Clarence was so angry, and rightfully so, about the treatment of African-Americans in our business and the world, and I loved his passion. I learned from him that even at the height of the Civil Rights movement there was still bigotry in our business, which I didn't realize until I saw things through his eyes.

I remember being asked about bigotry in Hollywood during an interview and I said there was less in our business than others, because we were a more liberal industry. The reporter followed up by asking, "Have you ever seen any bigotry in Hollywood?"

"Let me answer you in my own Texas way," I said. "You don't have to see a bullfrog to hear it croak." People don't wave a flag and say, "Hey, I'm a bigot," but when you look back at the TV schedules of the time and see that only two stars were African-American—Clarence and Diahann Carroll (*I Spy* had already gone off the air)—the bigotry of the era was pretty self-evident.

A good title is sometimes so important to a show's success. It's the hook that first gets people interested enough to tune in. *I Love Lucy*, *Charlie's Angels*, *Beverly Hills 90210*, *Melrose Place*. All inviting titles that tell you a little about the show. And of all the shows we've done, I've got to say that *The Mod Squad* is probably the best title we've ever come up with. It tells you everything you need to know about the show in three words. A series about a bunch of hip kids.

ABC came up with their own title, but it had no style whatsoever. Again, I defer to Len to finish the story:

"I was now head of programming for ABC, and we were getting ready to put *The Mod Squad* on the air. The only problem was that the higher-ups at ABC were very nervous. They thought *The Mod Squad* was too radical a title, and that it would alienate viewers. The network did all this research and it all came out overwhelmingly that a much better title would be 'The Young Detectives.'

"I took Aaron to La Scala to deliver the bad news. We had a lot of wine and then I sprung it on him. I told him about what the research said, and the title that ABC wanted. He said he'd rather not do the show at all than to call it 'The Young Detectives.' 'I can't do a show that's supposed to be hip and cutting edge and call it that.' He got up and suggested that if we wanted the new title, then perhaps we should have Danny Thomas produce it. Aaron didn't want any part of it. I told Aaron to sit down. I agreed with him. And I went back to ABC and said Aaron refused to change the name, and that was that.

"We premiered a few weeks later, and no one complained. There have been lots of youth dramas since, but *Mod Squad* was the original. I remember the ad we put into *The New York Times* the day the show premiered. We had the silhouettes of the three kids, and they looked great. The ad copy said—'If you see these three people in an alley, don't run. They're cops.' "

One of my biggest thrills was three years later when the Los Angeles Dodgers got Steve Garvey, Davey Lopez, and Bill Russell and called them—what else, The Mod Squad. It really means a lot to you when things you do are put into real life. Everyone says art imitates life; well, life imitates art sometimes too.

The Mod Squad was my first really big hit. Whenever you have a show that's taken in by young viewers, it's going to be bigger, because young people react much more vocally.

Interviewed during the *Mod Squad* era, I talked about how being relevant paid off. "At least it's a show of today," I told a reporter. "The only way to convey ideas today is through dramatic action. Documentaries can't do it anymore. We have to be emotionally involved. I think the real purpose of TV is to entertain, and within that entertainment you can at least report on what's going on. I think every episode should convey an idea." . . . A message for young people, but not laid on with a trowel!

Look at the shows of the time—*Petticoat Junction*, *My Three Sons*, *The Red Skelton Show*. They didn't appeal to the young generation. Those shows had no sense of reality about them. If you were young, were you going to watch Red Skelton? No way. Sure, *My Three Sons* was a hit, but it was the corniest interpretation of family life I'd ever seen. That's why I think young viewers found *The Mod Squad* so quickly. It proved to me there was an audience out there for a young show if we honestly depicted what was happening.

I tried to build up the contrast between our show and the older model of a cop show, the one where I got my start, *Dragnet*, which had returned with a new version called *Dragnet '67*, with Jack Webb and Harry Morgan.

They were right-wing, we were liberal. They thought everybody under 25 was a creep, we thought everybody under 25 was misunderstood. And, more importantly, *Mod Squad* had an ingredient called "soul."

Linc had the truest line we ever had on the show in describing his life: "Our house had one bathroom and wall-to-wall people." And I think that just about said everything. I wonder how I came up with that line? See, even the crap I went through on Browder Street was good for something.

The Mod Squad, as I say, was instantly embraced by young people, but we didn't crack the top 20 until our third season on the air, when we finished at number 11. A lot of it had to do with ABC at the time. Perennially the number three network, ABC, the year we premiered, only had two shows in the top 20: *Bewitched* (number 11) and *The FBI* (number 18). The first year of *Mod*, we were only carried by 139 stations; that went up to 192 for year two.

I didn't realize how successful we were until ABC brought us to New York to do promotion for the show after our first six episodes. I took a train to the city, and met the cast at the airport. We cabbed into town and Clarence made a big deal about taking us downtown, so he could show us around. The only thing is, people wouldn't let us move. It was total pandemonium. We got down one block, and we couldn't go any farther. We had to run into a department store and hide, and they had to put us in the freight elevator to get us out. I had never seen anything like it.

There was never a week in five years of *The Mod Squad* that I didn't have lunch or dinner with Peggy Lipton, Clarence Williams III, or Michael Cole. They were my buddies. The four of us became close in a way I had never experienced with any of my other actors. I owe them a lot, and I'll never forget them.

One experience I'll never forget about *The Mod Squad* is an early episode where Linc gives Julie a friendly kiss at the end of the show, and ABC asked me to cut it. "You can't do that," I was told. "You can't have a black man kissing a white girl."

"This isn't a sensual kiss. This is a kiss of affection and loyalty and bonding. They're buddies."

I won and ABC agreed to let it in, but they warned me I'd receive thousands of complaint letters. I didn't get one.

The point is that *The Mod Squad* wasn't just a cop show, it was about people. Most people don't realize that for five years of *The Mod Squad* I kept my promise to Michael. No one ever carried a gun and no one ever fired a shot. We protested the war we were in, we made social statements about drugs, we said it was okay to have a black kid as your best buddy. Now that may seem like a silly statement today, but it sure wasn't then.

Another thing I learned during the making of *The Mod Squad* was to always think ahead about title sequences. When we were on our final night of finishing the pilot, I realized we had forgotten to do the title sequence. It was 6 P.M., we were scheduled to shoot until 10 P.M., and I was frantic. I used to zoom around the studio in a little golf cart, and as I cruised the Paramount lot I passed the alley where Clarence had crashed the car. Just perfect for the main title sequence.

We moved the crew over, rehearsed it, and shot, and it turned out to be one of the most interesting main titles we've ever had. It said exactly what the show was about. One lonely kid ran down the alley, and he was joined by another kid who darted out from a little shelter, and then another kid joined in.

It was three kids either running from something or to something and they were together.

The Mod Squad still holds up today. Some 25-plus years later, it's still playing somewhere every day. And I'm amazed that people still talk to me about the show. Whenever they come up to me, they say, "I've been a fan of yours since *The Mod Squad.*" They don't usually mention *Burke's Law* or *Zane Grey*, but they always bring up *Mod Squad.*

Peggy Lipton, who was nominated for an Emmy four times for her role on *Mod*, went on to marry Quincy Jones, and spent most of the 1970s and 1980s retired from acting, as she raised her two daughters.

After she and Quincy divorced, Peggy started working again, appearing on *Twin Peaks* (a show our company partially financed and distributed through our Worldvision unit) as Norma, the owner of the bizarre town's diner, and on a short-lived CBS series, *Angels Falls*. Clarence Williams remained quite active in theater and also appeared as Prince's father in *Purple Rain* and in the films *Sugar Hill* and *Tales from the Hood*.

You probably haven't noticed, but there's been a Julie in every one of my shows. Jane Wyman played a Julie in *Twenty-Dollar Bride*, my first sale, and the name's been my good-luck charm ever since. It worked with *Burke's Law* (the first script was entitled "Who Killed Julie Greer?") and on *The Mod Squad*, and so I've always tried to figure a way to work a Julie into all my shows, even if the Julie was a minor, walk-on character.

Some of my notable Julies: Julie McCoy (Lauren Tewes) on *The Love Boat*, Julie Gillette (Shari Belafonte-Harper) on *Hotel*, Mr. Roarke's goddaughter Julie (Wendy Schaal) on *Fantasy Island*, and Julie Rogers (Tanya Roberts) on *Charlie's Angels*.

My last show with Danny Thomas was an attempt to do another young show, since that was my new niche. Larry Gordon and I came up with the idea, and we gave it to the great Rod Serling (*The Twilight Zone*) to develop it into a series, one that was really ahead of its time.

The New People made headlines in 1969 as TV's first 45-minute drama. It was a great concept about a group of college kids who've gone on a cultural exchange tour of Southeast Asia during the summer, only to have their plane crash on a mysterious Pacific atoll en route home. It turns out that the island was an abandoned U.S. atomic test site, complete with all the buildings and other trappings of a modern world. *The New People* was *90210* on an island, and our kids had to go about building their own "new" society.

Rod was one of the all-time greats of television. Besides creating and hosting the still-relevant and most successful TV anthology, *The Twilight Zone*, he also was one of the best and most prolific writers television has ever seen. He penned many of the best *Playhouse 90* scripts, such as "Requiem for a Heavyweight" and "The Comedian" and also lent his services to such "Golden Age of Television" series as *The Kraft Theatre*, *Studio One*, *Suspense*, *General Electric Theater*, and *Desilu Playhouse*.

In between *Zone* and his return in 1970 as host/creator of *Night Gallery*, Rod wrote for other series (like *The Loner*), turned up as an actor occasionally (he guested on an episode of *The Jack Benny Show*, in which the comic tried to convince Rod to write for him), and occasionally developed shows, which he did for me.

I was in awe of Rod. "How can you write so many scripts for *The Twilight Zone*?" I used to ask him. "Simple," he would say. "I don't have to have a third act to explain anything. All I have to do is say 'And that's the way it was in the Twilight Zone,' and I'm home free."

We gave Rod our idea for *The New People* and he went off and wrote it. It was a perfect first draft, and we didn't have to give him any notes or ask for any changes. You'd have to be an idiot to try and rewrite Rod Serling.

When we sold *The New People* to ABC, I had no idea at the time I'd never be able to syndicate it or sell it to foreign TV stations, due to the crazy 45-minute format, which was incompatible with virtually every other TV show of the time. *New* went on the air because of the success of *The Mod Squad*, but it was so different and only lasted four months, mostly, I believe, because of the odd scheduling.

ABC had this radical idea about having a 45-minute variety show (*The Music Scene*, hosted by Lily Tomlin and David Steinberg, among others) airing from 7:30 to 8:15, and then having *The New People* follow to 9 P.M. It was neither a half hour nor an hour, and you had to remember to tune in at 8:15, which was hard to do when you were on opposite *Rowan & Martin's Laugh-In* and *Gunsmoke*. It didn't make any sense to go from music to an adventure show.

The New People is one of my favorite flops: I'll always remember it fondly. It was so unique, the idea of landing in a place that was scheduled to be blown up and starting a new life together. Like *The Mod Squad* and *90210*, the kids had to bond together because there were no adults. But it wasn't like *Lord of the Flies*, it dealt more with the kids' personal problems—loneliness and things like that. More importantly, they had to invent new rules and new mores. We've often talked about bringing the show back and trying again with a new contemporary version. I'd love to see that happen.

Rod Serling and I worked together twice again after *The New People*. First, he wrote a pilot for us called *The Oath*, which didn't sell, and he also did a quick rewrite for me on a 1975 TV movie. He only worked two days on the project and wouldn't accept any money. "Just buy me some fruit," he said. So we filled a truck full of grapefruit, oranges, and apples and had his lawn covered completely with them!

Sadly, when he called to thank me, he also gave me some sage words of advice: "Slow down, Aaron. Take it from me. You're working too hard. I thought I was immortal too, but I'm not."

A few months later he died of complications from open-heart surgery.

Eight

IN THE late 1960s, I was feeling low. Dick Powell had died. Alan Ladd was dead, my marriage with Carolyn had broken up, and I wasn't wearing success all that well. I look back at this time as my mad playboy era. The columnist Harrison Carroll from the *Los Angeles Herald Examiner* used to have a regular feature he called "Aaron's Girl of the Week." Some might think it was bachelor's heaven. Believe me, it was bachelor's hell! I think a lot of it had to do with guilt about leaving Carolyn. I didn't want to hurt her by settling down and marrying again.

For about two years, I went to every party, event, and opening imaginable. And then one night I met this gorgeous girl named Candy Marer. She came from a very good family in Beverly Hills and her mother was dead set against her seeing the wild man she'd read about in the newspapers. But we persevered and I went from a crazy swinging nut who went out every night to a quiet guy who realized that the only life worth living was to love and be loved. It's corny but true.

I met Candy at my favorite Beverly Hills hangout, The Daisy. I was double-dating that night with a friend of mine named Mark Nathanson, shooting pool and ignoring my date. She wasn't very happy about it, so I asked Mark to do me a favor and take her home. When he returned, I saw this cute blond sitting with some friends. Mark knew one of the ladies who was with her and I asked him to go over and introduce me to the blond. But she had read the gossip columns and wasn't at all interested in meeting me.

I wouldn't take no for an answer. I walked over and said, "I'm not going to bite you. How about a dance?" Let's have Candy finish the story.

"We went on the dance floor and they were playing 'My Funny Valentine.' The song ended, but we kept on dancing. In fact, it seemed like we danced all night. We just stood out there and talked about everything under the sun. As we were dancing, Aaron told me he was going to marry me one day. I thought, 'Oh sure. This guy must use that line on all the girls.'

"It turned out that we had danced for six songs in a row, something I discovered when my date got so upset he left The Daisy without me. We stopped dancing and Aaron asked for my phone number, but I wouldn't give it to him. But Aaron refused to accept that. He went to my girlfriend, who I was staying with for the weekend, and begged her to have me call him when we got home. I don't know why I called him, but I did. We ended up talking on the phone until around 4 A.M. And we made tentative plans to date the next night."

Those plans were thrown off kilter the next morning when the mother of Candy's friend called and told her and Candy to hop a plane to Las Vegas and join the family there for the weekend. Candy called me to break our date, and asked me to drive her to the airport. I didn't know how to get there, so I had my associate producer take them, and invited Candy to visit me on Sunday at our celebrity softball game. I played with Peter Falk, Ryan O'Neal, and other celebrities every Sunday at Barrington Park, and we always had a barbecue afterwards at my pad.

Candy ended up calling me from Vegas on Saturday, saying she was bored and would definitely be back in time, and she returned the next day to help me host the barbecue.

At the time, Candy (she was born Carol, but everybody called her Candy) was 18 years old and had just graduated from Beverly Hills High School. She was attending an art institute part-time and her father was successful in the furniture business. Candy's fellow students at BHHS had elected her "the body" when she was a freshman because she had a model's figure. She was just stunning. Besides her beauty, I loved that she wasn't an actress. I was tired of socializing with people from the industry all the time.

While she was in Vegas I went out and bought her an engagement ring on consignment. Was I serious? No idiot buys an engagement ring on consignment and is serious. But I was infatuated with her.

From that baseball game on, I never dated anyone else for the next three years. This was pretty radical of me, considering what a wild idiot I had been. How wild? Consider this. The week before I met

Candy I had been to an ABC affair riding on the back of a motorcycle driven by a starlet. Does that sound like me? I must have been nuts in those days.

In fact, when Candy's parents returned to L.A. and heard that she had not only dated me but that I had given her a ring, they were furious. "You went out with that playboy!" they said. "Return the ring." She returned it and laughingly said, "I'm sure you'll offer it to somebody else by the end of the week."

But I did finally seriously ask Candy for her hand in marriage during one of our baseball games. "By the way," I said to her, "you've got to marry me," and she replied, "Okay."

That was stupid of me because I wasn't very serious about my proposal. Sure, we went out and got a marriage license, but I got cold feet, and after a year I let the license expire. Candy waited and waited and finally told a friend of ours that she had had it. She wouldn't wait anymore. So she packed her bags and moved to New York, where she was offered a modeling contract.

I was sorry to see her go, but also kind of excited about the prospect of going back to The Daisy and back into those swinging days. But, you know, men are really stupid. Once Candy left, I was suddenly so bored that I stayed home and watched TV a lot. My friends Mark Nathanson and Larry Gordon kept trying to get me to go out. "What are you," asked Larry, "a recluse?"

I told Larry I missed Candy. "Then why didn't you marry the girl?"

He was right. I was really in love, and I had blown it. I called Candy in New York and apologized. "Honey," I said, "you're right. I've been a jerk. Please come home. I realize I can't live without you. I love you. Please marry me. I mean it."

Six weeks after leaving me for the Big Apple and a new life, we were finally wed in a small ceremony at Candy's parents' house. We said our vows and danced to "My Funny Valentine." It's been our song forever. I don't care where we are, when we go to parties we seldom dance; but if they play "My Funny Valentine," we're on the floor.

Don't laugh, but every time I'm depressed about a show or a pilot, Candy sings "Valentine" to me. It always breaks me up, and I realize what's really important in my life.

* * *

Candy's parents got over their initial distrust of me. I grew on them. And her father eventually came to work for our company, handling our insurance affairs.

Candy taught me something called gentility. I would take her to those big ABC dinner parties, and I'd see which fork she was going to use first, because growing up poor in Texas, I had no idea about such things.

As this book was being written, Candy and I have been married for 26 years. I consider a lot of people to be dear friends—and that list includes Duke Vincent, Frank Mancuso, Larry Gordon, Lew Wasserman, Nolan Miller, Bill Haber, Sumner Redstone, Steve Berrard, Ray Stark, Eric Roth, Joel Schumacher, and Henry Gluck. However, Candy is really my best friend. She's everything to me.

I've said that I never knew what love was until I met Candy. To find true love, I think one has to stop loving themselves. By that I mean you can't keep your innermost thoughts and dreams to yourself, because that's not sharing. Candy's the only one I've ever shared with. I've cried in front of her and not been ashamed. She's the only one I've ever shared my fear of failure with and the joys of success. If you really love somebody, you have to reveal yourself. You can't hide behind masks, which is what I always did before. I was always play-acting. I didn't want to be me. I wanted to be anyone else. When Sammy Davis, Jr., came out with the song "I've Gotta Be Me" I realized something. I was always afraid to be me until Candy encouraged me to drop the mask.

The second time around, I was really ready to be married. In my first marriage, I was younger, much more ambitious, and afraid of failure. With Candy, I finally realized that my work must be secondary to my marriage.

I love to surprise Candy by buying her jewelry, and we're teased as much about her jewelry as we are about our house. Okay, I admit it, I like to buy her things—it's just one more way I can say, "Thank you, Honey."

We have something else in common. I'm an incurable romantic, and so is Candy. I have dated, I've been married before, and I will tell you, sometimes your romanticism can get laughs from other people. But I'm a big believer in that Elizabeth Barrett Browning poem—

"How do I love thee? Let me count the ways." Nothing typifies my relationship with Candy more than that. I don't think a month goes by that I don't write a poem to Candy expressing my love. She is my partner, my wife, my life . . . and always will be.

These days, besides running our household and being very active in charitable causes, Candy is a regular celebrity on the QVC home shopping cable network, where she goes on air to sell the dolls she's created. I don't know if you've noticed, but when Candy goes on her shows, her set looks a little brighter and roomier, a little more Hollywood. That's because when she told me she was going to go on QVC, I had one of my designers build her a set. I just wanted her to have something special, because her "Fantasy" dolls are special. It's not just because they're beautiful, but all the profits go to Centro de Niños, a charity Candy loves that provides free daycare for the working poor. What could be more special than that?

We had been married for two years and lived in a little house off Coldwater Canyon that cost $75,000, completely furnished. On my birthday in 1970 when I was blowing out the candles, Candy said, "Make a wish." I did and she asked me what it was.

"Dick Powell was my mentor," I said. "Now Danny Thomas is my mentor. I need to know whether I can do it on my own."

"Then let's do it."

"How can we afford it?"

Candy's answer was simple. "I'll go back to work. We can do it."

I talked to Danny, and he was quite dear and let me out of my contract. He understood. In fact, he wrote a cute song as a good-bye present for me when we split, to the tune of "Thanks for the Memory."

> *"Thanks for the Memory,*
> *of all that we've been through*
> *a Lebanese and a Jew*
> Rango *went astray*
> *with Tim Conway*
> *I lost a million two*

so thank you so much

Aaron, thanks for the memory
of the noise from Sonnett's gun
Brennan looking for his son
cried in Goldberg's ears
and ran two years
I only lost a million one
so thank you so much

Many's a show that we ground out
and many's a blow that we found out
oh hell
what a swell
new people fanned out
but i didn't cuss
we had cost plus

and thanks for the memory
of our Mod Squad *school*
the ratings, they are cool
we've parted now
but with the vow
you gave me (ABC exec) Elton Rule
thank you so much

After the singing and good-byes came the hard part. Now, all of a sudden, we had to hire secretaries, get an office, install telephones, and all those other things I never thought about. How would I pay for it all? It seemed impossible.

But a few days later I got the answer to all of my seemingly insurmountable problems when I received a call from Leonard Goldenson, the chairman of ABC. I had first met Leonard at Four Star, when he used to ask us to sell our shows to ABC. And of course we'd made *The Mod Squad* for ABC. Anyway, Leonard said he was sending Elton Rule, the president of the company, out to see me.

We met at the Polo Lounge, and Elton offered me a whopper of a deal: a three-year contract, exclusive to ABC, calling for four series. "We'll pay for those damn offices you seem so worried about," he said.

At the time, ABC was way behind CBS and NBC. As the saying went, ABC was fourth among the three commercial networks. Milton Berle's famous line was: "Put the Vietnam War on ABC and it will be over in 13 weeks," but I didn't care. I loved the people there and the opportunity. And the network certainly was good to *The Mod Squad.*

Not only were they guaranteeing series on the air, they were also paying for those phones, secretaries, etc. The deal was eventually sweetened to also include made-for-TV movies. One year we made 12 of them, and over the life of the deal a total of 138, with such well-known titles as *The Over-the-Hill Gang, The Boy in the Plastic Bubble*, and *Little Ladies of the Night.*

None of this would have ever happened if Candy hadn't said to me, "Follow your dreams." My wife never gets enough credit for my success. To me, she is everything. Without her, I'd still be working for somebody. She's a cute, ditzy little blond, but she's my real strength. If I'm becoming redundant talking about Candy, please forgive me. Redundancy becomes her!

And I also can't say enough about Elton. He became one of my closest friends during this period. After we made the deal, he said something to me that day that I'll never forget—"Aaron, you can always trust me." And he kept his word.

Elton treated me like a member of the ABC family. He invited me to ABC think tanks in Palm Springs, to pilot presentations, to affairs most producers couldn't get into. Elton and I were great together and I miss him terribly—another one of my great mentors and friends who's no longer with us.

Silent Force was my first show for Aaron Spelling Productions, and it starred Ed Nelson (who was then hot off *Peyton Place*), Percy Rodriguez, and Lynda Day (she later added the "George") as government agents assigned to fight organized crime. And since I was striking out on my own, I felt the need to do something I had never done before. Go to New York in May to sell the show to network executives, an annual tradition that still continues to this day.

Under the terms of the ABC deal, they had to pay a penalty if they didn't pick up one of my shows, but I didn't want the money—I wanted to be on the air. And here I was, the only producer in Hollywood with an exclusive contract with a network, and if I didn't go back to New York, it would be like I was thumbing my nose at everyone.

A strange thing happens back there. Every company and every studio is there. They all hang out at 21 and the Ritz and the Regency hotels, trying to somehow get the ear of a network exec. In ABC's case, first that would have been company chairman Leonard Goldenson. If they couldn't get to him, they'd try for president Elton Rule. Everybody was fighting for dinner and lunch engagements and getting in to see the big board in the war room, where potential pickups of pilots were posted. You had to find out if you were on the board. If you were, you had to kick the crap out of everything that was against you, or you wouldn't stay on the board. And if you weren't on the board, you were dead.

In my case, I had dinner with Elton and he casually told me *Silent Force* was on the board, but not to tell anybody. I was a happy camper and got on a train the next morning to come back home.

Today, it's not the scheduling board that kills you, but the testing process. The networks love to test shows with sample audiences to, as they say, see how it plays in Peoria. The problem with that process is the minute you ask someone to see a show, they're suddenly a critic and looking at ways to knock your show.

I once made a movie for 20th Century–Fox, a little $6 million picture about a guy who loses his job, stays home, and does housework while his wife earns a paycheck. The testing was very poor on that film, so Fox only released it in 16 theaters. But then a marvelous thing happened. People liked what they saw and started telling their friends. So Fox went from 16 theaters to 22 and 35 and eventually 1,000 theaters. And this little $6 million movie went on to gross $64 million. It was called *Mr. Mom*. So now you know what I think of testing, especially for television.

When we write a pilot script, we don't test the concept or the script. We put our money where our mouth is. Today there's a deficit every time you do a pilot, usually $300,000 to $1 million. We believe in the project, so we invest our money in it. And if they don't buy it, we lose.

Back in 1969, Len Goldberg and Barry Diller created a novel alternative to network series when Diller was head of programming at ABC.

They called them "Movies of the Week," and the 90-minute features were a regular staple of the ABC Tuesday lineup. They weren't the first MOWs (NBC started the trend in 1964 with *See How They Run*, starring my pal John Forsythe), but ABC was the first to schedule them on a weekly basis, guaranteeing that viewers would get a "World Premiere" motion picture every Tuesday.

They wanted to show different kinds of characters. Not everybody had to be a Marcus Welby–like hero. They wanted characters with flaws, ones who didn't have to return the following week, and they wanted to attract actors, writers, and directors who didn't want to commit to five years of a series.

Plus, they had 90 minutes to fill in between *The Mod Squad* and *Marcus Welby, M.D.*, and made-for-TV movies seemed like a good bridge between the two shows. They got ABC to pony up $15 million for 26 movies, and they gave Danny and me a production order to make ten of them.

The first I heard about it was when Len came to my house and told me they would be starting something like *Playhouse 90* on film, different dramatic anthologies every week. It seemed like a great idea at the time, and it obviously created a cottage industry.

The Over-the-Hill Gang was the first ABC MOW we put into production. Walter Brennan, Pat O'Brien, Chill Wills, Edgar Buchanan, Jack Elam, Andy Devine, Ricky Nelson, and Gypsy Rose Lee starred in a story of a town under the rule of an unscrupulous mayor and his crooked sheriff. A former Texas Ranger sent out a call for help to his old outfit and got more than he bargained for with the Over-the-Hill Gang.

Although we were the first to go into production, Milton Berle's *Seven in Darkness* beat us to the air as the first film shown by ABC. *Seven* was a drama about people trapped on a subway after an accident.

Why kick off our MOW program with a Western? Well, if you're going to do a movie, you pick on what you're most familiar with. I started with *Zane Grey*, so doing a Western with old-timers just seemed like the right thing to do.

And it was exciting to do anthologies again. It was like going back to the *Playhouse 90* days, except that ABC was paying us $450,000 for 90 minutes, which was a huge amount of money back then.

We produced some really interesting work back then, like *The*

Ballad of Andy Crocker, which starred Lee Majors as a kid who returned to his small town in Texas after serving his hitch in Vietnam, only to discover that the war was so unpopular that nobody wanted him. This was the first of those kinds of movies, and people weren't telling these kinds of stories at the time.

Sammy Davis, Jr., starred for me in a film about a private eye called *The Pigeon*, and we did a movie about an African-American unit during World War II called *Carter's Army*. It featured a young comedian named Richard Pryor and a new discovery named Billy Dee Williams.

One movie I'll never forget was *Run, Simon, Run*. We made it in 1970 and the film starred Burt Reynolds, who was then also headlining in one of his early TV series, *Dan August*. *Deliverance* hadn't happened yet.

Burt costarred with Inger Stevens in a story of an Indian who returned to his tribe after a prison term and swore vengeance on the man who really murdered his brother. Inger had been best known as Katy Holstrum on *The Farmer's Daughter* (1963–6), but hadn't done much afterwards. Burt and Inger fell in love during the making of *Run, Simon, Run* and you could feel their affection for each other on the screen. She was so beautiful and vulnerable, we created a series for her, *The Most Deadly Game*, and we really felt like we had a winner.

Inger, George Maharis, and Ralph Bellamy starred as a trio of great criminologists who dealt only in unusual murders (i.e., the most deadly game). After we completed the pilot and sold the show, Burt and Inger broke up, and a few days later, Inger, who had a history of personal problems and had attempted to commit suicide in 1959, tried again, and this time she was successful.

We recast the part with Yvette Mimieux, reshot the pilot, and missed our September air date, premiering instead a month later than usual, but we were dead on arrival. The show just had a feeling like it was damned. We couldn't recover from the negative publicity.

I went on to make over 100 TV movies for ABC while exclusive to the network, films like *The House That Would Not Die*, with Barbara Stanwyck; *Love, Hate, Love*, with Ryan O'Neal and Leslie Anne Warren; *Satan's School for Girls*, with Kate Jackson and Cheryl Ladd, in a pre-*Charlie's Angels* teamup; *The Best Little Girl in the World*, about anorexia at a time when no one was talking about it, and *The Boy in the Plastic Bubble*, which starred John Travolta, then appearing as one of the Sweathogs on *Welcome Back, Kotter*. He played a sick boy who lived in an enclosed bubble.

We had a really hard time convincing ABC to let us do that one. They only knew John as a Sweathog, but finally they relented and John was brilliant in his first dramatic role for television. ABC was brave to let us do it, because networks weren't doing those kinds of films. They were interested in action, comedies, and horror pieces, and they weren't presenting the kinds of serious topics that are explored often today.

Back in 1977, Len and I produced a film called *Little Ladies of the Night*, and to this day it still remains the second highest-rated made-for-TV movie of all time, with a 36.9 rating. (*The Day After* is number one and Farrah Fawcett's *The Burning Bed* is number three.) *Little Ladies* starred a very young Linda Purl as a teen runaway who comes to Hollywood and starts turning tricks to survive. Carolyn Jones played her mom and David Soul was a social worker.

The movie wasn't about teen prostitution, as critics said, but it was really about runaway children. It wasn't an exploitative film. We got interested because there were so many runaway kids out here living in empty buildings. We wanted to explore why they ran away, what they were running from, and what they wanted to do with their lives.

It's amazing what's happened to the made-for-TV movie business since it first got started. Back then there was one night of TV movies a week. Now it seems there's at least one movie a night on the big networks, and if you factor in cable networks like HBO, Showtime, USA, and Lifetime, there are as many as 200 TV movies made a year.

We still make TV movies, but we stay away from the topical "true story" presentations like the Amy Fisher and the Menendez Brothers stories. We feel they're dangerous. When you say it's a true story, you get copycats. I don't think viewers empathize when they know it's fiction.

Nine

DESPITE MY interest in working for myself, after two series and ten MOWs, I found the workload to be absolutely overwhelming. Barry Diller convinced me that I needed a partner, and that my old friend Leonard Goldberg was the perfect candidate. We got together after I shot *The Rookies* pilot and formed Spelling–Goldberg Productions.

At the time Len and I joined forces, he had been head of production for Screen Gems, the division of Columbia that produced such series as *Bewitched* and *The Partridge Family*. Len hated the job, because after being the top programming boss at ABC, he found that he had to answer to too many chiefs at Screen Gems. He couldn't wait to get out of there.

Having Len with me really did lighten the load, because he's a storyteller like me. We met at the end of every day to make sure everything was going smoothly, and made all big decisions together. We basically created some of our shows together, even though we gave credit to writers. We felt we had to do that, in order to attract top writers.

Our first hit under the ABC deal was my pilot *The Rookies*, which started Spelling–Goldberg off with a bang. We debuted in 1972 and the show starred Kate Jackson, George Stanford Brown, Michael Ontkean, and Sam Melville as three young rookie cops, all single except for Mike (Melville), who was married to a young nurse, played by Kate.

Like *The Mod Squad*, our trio of cops were young and fresh out of the police academy. They were dedicated to a new, more humane way of law enforcement, which, naturally, put them at odds with their tough mentor, Lt. Eddie Ryker, played by Gerald S. O'Loughlin. Where the traditional cop would shoot first, ask questions later, our Rookies preferred to first try and solve disputes amicably.

I've always been fascinated by the police academy. What kind of people apply there and why? Why do they want to be cops? That seemed like an interesting premise for a new young show. I like people who don't have an attitude about what they're doing yet, who are learning, who make mistakes, and who have bonded together. At the same time, they were a little afraid of being on the dangerous streets because they'd never been there before.

I also thought it was a good way to show that cops are people too, and that they bleed both physically and mentally. You can get angry at a cop for giving you a ticket, and some cops can be overbearing and do things they shouldn't, but they go out and risk their lives every day and that fascinates me. Who would want to do that when they get so little credit for what they do?

I met somebody from the LAPD police academy who told me I would be able to shoot some of the show there, and I was excited about being the first person to bring his cameras into previously unseen territory.

Rookie cops, it turned out, get street assignments with older cops for training, and ABC liked that part of the show more than the academy, so we only went there once in the pilot.

The Rookies was the first time I worked with Kate Jackson, who would later become a household name in *Charlie's Angels*. Kate was born and raised in Birmingham, Alabama, studied in Mississippi and New York City, did some theater and modeling, and began her television career as Daphne on the spooky ABC afternoon serial *Dark Shadows*. She did some guest spots on *Bonanza* and *The Jimmy Stewart Show*, and by the time our paths crossed, she was under contract to Paramount. I saw her there and she struck me as perfect for the part of Jill Danko, the nurse. She was beautiful and strong, and I thought she had the vitality and strength to be with all the guys. I asked Paramount to let her out of their contract to do our show, and they agreed.

(Interesting side note: Kate Jackson and Michael Ontkean later went on to costar as a married couple who break up when he discovers he's gay in the 1982 film *Making Love*.)

Rookies holds up today, but I must admit that the show never had the soul of a *Mod Squad* or *90210*. But for a 1970s cop show, it was pretty different. If you look at the cop shows of the era, you may have seen where the characters lived, but you knew very little about them. To this day you can't tell me what home life was like for Sgt. Joe Friday of *Dragnet*.

That's why viewers took to shows like *The Rookies*, and later to Steven Bochco's *Hill Street Blues* and *NYPD Blue*. They began to investigate the private lives of police professionals, and people really responded to getting an inside look.

We introduced our next series, *S.W.A.T.*, on an episode of *The Rookies*. *S.W.A.T.* was about the Special Weapons And Tactics police unit, who handled the kind of cases too unusual or violent for normal cops. S.W.A.T. units responded to cases with their high-tech weaponry. The show starred Robert Urich, Rod Perry, Steve Forrest, Mark Shera, and James Coleman as the members of the S.W.A.T. team, and it was based on real-life S.W.A.T. teams that had been formed in several large cities following the civic disturbances of the late 1960s.

The S.W.A.T. squad, all Vietnam veterans, dressed in semimilitary attire and sporting powerful weapons, toured Southern California combat zones in a specially equipped van (a tank just wouldn't have been right). When the force was so strong that the normal police couldn't respond, it was time to call the S.W.A.T. team. They were the ultimate peacekeepers.

The show started when one of our *Rookies* writers, Rick Husky, found out about real-life S.W.A.T. teams, and suggested there might be a show there. The real ones kept their S.W.A.T. gear in their trunk, and when they got the call, they had the option of going S.W.A.T. Obviously we couldn't do a show that way, so we made them a separate team. But once the show became a hit, the real-life cops imitated art and set up individual S.W.A.T. teams and gave them a van like ours.

It was on *S.W.A.T.* that we first teamed up with Robert Urich. At the time, Bob was a virtual unknown, despite his short-lived role on the TV adaptation of the film *Bob & Carol & Ted & Alice*.

Bob grew up in Toronto, Ohio, and played football for Florida State, going to the 1967 Gator Bowl. (FSU tied Penn State 19–19.)

While working at WGN Radio in Chicago in 1971 as a sales account executive, Bob decided that he really wanted to be an actor, and started getting roles in local theatrical productions. During an Arlington Park Theater production of *The Rainmaker*, Bob met another Florida State University alumnus, Burt Reynolds. They became friends, and Burt asked his agent to fly to Chicago and see Bob perform. Bob was signed to the agency, and Burt helped get him roles on such series as *Gunsmoke*, *Kung Fu*, and *The F.B.I.*

By 1974, Burt had become a superstar in movies, thanks to the film *Deliverance*. And he was still helping Bob. I was at the office one day when my secretary told me Burt Reynolds was on the phone. "Hey, I hear you're casting *S.W.A.T.*," he said. "There's a young actor I want you to meet from Florida State. He did some great work there. You've got to meet him."

I was happy to. "Let me see what my schedule is."

"Can you see him today?"

"Oh wow, Burt . . . I don't know . . . what time?"

"Right now. We're in your outer office."

And the next thing I knew, Burt and Bob walked through the door. Bob was tall, muscular, very attractive, with a great smile. He read a scene for us, and it was obvious Burt was right. Bob was perfect. He didn't get a lot to do in the show, however. The action was the star. But Bob really came into his own for us a few years later when we cast him as Dan Tanna in *Vega$*.

S.W.A.T. only ran for a year and a half. It was very violent (more on that in a minute) and there was great pressure to get it off the air. When it first premiered, the show went straight into the top 20, but when we returned the following year, the numbers fell dramatically. *S.W.A.T.* was a very difficult show to find stories for. How many times can you have bad guys kidnap somebody and need to call the *S.W.A.T.* team?

Len and I both have gold records hanging on our walls, which is the one thing we'll always remember about *S.W.A.T.* The theme song went to number one on the Billboard charts. Barry DeVorzon cut a quickie instrumental on ABC Records and it shot straight to the top. Amazing.

Back then our cop shows followed a formula. A piece of action in the first scene showing a crime being committed, another piece of action at the end of the second act, and then the final piece of action at the end of the fourth act.

There was so much violence on TV at the time, and we weren't any more violent than most shows. But after you have children, you begin to realize that you have a lot more responsibility as to what you put on the airwaves. I swear to you, I would never, ever do a show like *S.W.A.T.* again.

Violence does exist and sometimes it's necessary to show it so kids can see how bad it is. (If a kid puts his pet caterpillar on the street in New York, it's going to get squashed. That teaches the kid a lesson. If you shoot a closeup of the caterpillar being squashed, that's unnecessary violence.)

Speaking on the subject of TV violence, which has been debated since the beginning of time, I have a hard time agreeing with some of those people who believe that violent acts on television encourage viewers to go out and mimic the act. However, as I said before, I am worried about portraying true stories on TV that contain violence. I think audiences know the difference between fact and fiction and I believe those true violent stories could result in "copycat" reactions.

While *S.W.A.T.* is my least favorite of the 50-plus series I've been associated with, one of my all-time favorites, which we launched in 1975, is *Starsky and Hutch.* It was the first buddy cop show, and went on to inspire such films as *Lethal Weapon* and *48 HRS* and just about any other buddy cop movie.

I've told you how important I felt it was to show the private side of cops' lives. We started to explore that on *Rookies*, but we took it to a whole other level on *Starsky and Hutch.*

Starsky and Hutch were two plainclothes cops who were also both swinging bachelors, and we like to refer to the show as TV's first heterosexual love affair. Paul Michael Glaser played Det. Dave Starsky, the streetwise member of the pair; David Soul was the soft-spoken Det. Ken Hutchinson ("Hutch"), and Antonio Fargas was the hysterical comic relief Huggy Bear, the flamboyant snitch. Unlike the stiff cops with no feelings on shows like *S.W.A.T.*, Starsky and Hutch truly cared for one another and it showed. As one critic wrote, "Spelling put authenticity into TV Westerns and when viewers tired of guys falling off horses, he gave cops heart. Cops like Starsky and Hutch unashamedly hugging each other. They showed fear, pain, concern."

I always believed that the last scene of the pilot episode said it all. Starsky and Hutch had been set up and almost killed, had fallen into a pool, and were sitting in a laundry room drying off. They realized someone in the police department had tried to set them up. "Who can we trust?" said Starsky. "The same people we always trust," said Hutch, "me and you."

Writer William Blinn created *Starsky and Hutch* for us when ABC asked for a "cool cop show." The first *Starsky and Hutch* show opened in a gym, where we met Dave Starsky. Bill described him as being in his late twenties, thin, "with a face that's constantly in motion, taking it all in with a sardonic smile. He's garbed in faded Levis, T-shirt, windbreaker that's seen better days, and a knit Los Angeles Rams warm-up cap. Had he gone into literature, he'd be James Jones. Baseball: Maury Willis. Football: Greg Puritt. Politics: Pierre Trudeau."

Hutch was clean-cut with a clear gaze and "the kind of look that screams for some imperfection we can identify with, some flaw that places him with the rest of us schlepps. Had he gone into literature, he'd be William Goldman. Baseball: Mickey Mantle. Football: Frank Gifford. Politics: John Kennedy."

Hutch was lying on a weight bench finishing a morning workout when Starsky entered.

HUTCH
You're late.

STARSKY
Don't want to hurt your feelings,
but coming down here to watch
you sweat is not the high point
of my day.

(opening sack)
I got coffee and danish. Want to share?

HUTCH
Have I ever?

STARSKY
No, but I keep hoping.

They eventually leave the gym to start the day and Hutch changes into slacks, turtleneck sweater, and a sportcoat, and Bill says the two look like an "oddly matched set of bookends."

STARSKY
Your car or mine?

HUTCH
Mine. That suspension
of yours makes that thing
ride like a rock on a washboard.

STARSKY
(untroubled)
Okay.

EXT. STREET—RUN BY—DAY

Hutch at the wheel, the sedan moving into the "slow" lane, the better to observe the passing parade, such as it is, and the danger inherent there.

CLOSER—MOVING SHOT—STARSKY AND HUTCH

Hutch at the wheel. Both men glance this way and that, taking it all in without seeming to hold on to any one of the myriad things going on about them. They converse with little eye contact.

HUTCH
How'd it go last night with Cindy?

STARSKY
Acceptable, acceptable. You still seeing what's-her-name?

HUTCH
Still seeing what's-her-name,
yeah. Took her to whatchamacallit
and asked her to wear my thig-a-majig.

STARSKY
Didn't know it was that serious.

Bill Blinn suggested casting David Soul, with whom he had worked on the short-lived series *Owen Marshall, Counselor at Law*. (David had also been seen as the hooded "Mystery Singer," on the Merv Griffin Show, had done an episode of *Star Trek*, and received his big break as the costar of *Here Come the Brides*, the show that turned Bobby Sherman into a teen sensation.)

Len and I saw Paul Michael Glaser in the film version of *Fiddler on the Roof* (he played Perchik, Tevye's revolutionary son-in-law) and we felt then that we had found our Starsky. We auditioned Paul and then brought him to read for ABC. Besides *Fiddler*, Paul had done a lot of theater, appeared on two daytime soaps (*Love of Life* and *Love Is a Many Splendored Thing*), was in the Broadway and film version of *Butterflies Are Free* with Goldie Hawn, but was nervous as hell for the network reading because he had never done anything like that before. So the director came up with an idea. He rushed out and got Paul a bag of popcorn, and asked him to do the whole reading with David while munching on popcorn.

Well, believe it or not, that did the trick, and Paul wasn't nervous anymore. He got the job. Truthfully, the moment the two of them stood together and read their scene, it really didn't matter how nervous Paul was. They just clicked.

Paul brought a real wild-ass attitude to Starsky, who was in direct contrast to David Soul's cool. They became real buddies off the set as well, and it showed on-screen.

We used a lot of squealing car chases on *Starsky*, but that was to coincide with the energy of the actors. They talked fast and moved quickly. Cop shows don't have a lot of chase scenes now, but back then they were mandatory. The guys were famous for driving around town in the red Ford Torino, but I don't think *Starsky and Hutch* is known for its car chases. It was a show about their relationship.

One of the most memorable scenes we ever did, the one that always sticks in my mind when I think of the show, is the one where Starsky fell in love with a girl for the first time and Hutch knew she was bad for him, but didn't know how to tell his partner. At the end, he had to prove the girl was using Starsky, that she didn't love him and was going to break his heart. Hutch finally told him, and Starsky responded by beating the crap out of him. Hutch never defended himself; he just let Starsky pound away.

By the end, it was proven that she was indeed bad. The tag of the show focused on the two guys together, sitting around Starsky's apartment, getting bombed, and laughing. They decided to chuck it all and become football players. So they called the Canadian league to ask for tryouts, they started laughing over the phone, and the league ended up hanging up on them.

Starsky and Hutch looked at each other, and began to cry and hug each other. It was one of the most memorable moments I've ever seen on TV because these men weren't afraid to show their emotions. It's something men still rarely do today on television. They could be laughing one moment, getting drunk, each trying to forget what happened, and when the laughter stopped, the truth began and they realized how much they meant to each other.

We've worked with David Soul again on several projects, and tried to give him a solo shot in a pilot that should have sold, *Harry's Hong Kong*, about a private detective in Hong Kong. We didn't realize it at the time, but Paul never enjoyed acting very much. As big a star as he became, he just didn't enjoy acting—but he loved being behind the camera and he's now a terrific director, with films like *The Running Man* and many others.

How Paul Michael Glaser kept his sanity over the last few years is beyond me. Other men would have crumbled after all the tragedy he's been through. Paul met his late wife, Elizabeth, on the set of *Starsky*. She was a teacher at the Center for Early Education and was there to watch over underage children. They met and fell in love. Paul was taken with this quiet, beautiful woman. Unlike other TV stars who were dating starlets, he chose a normal, sweet person. He was wild, funny, and very rambunctious, just like Dave Starsky, and she was very quiet and dear.

When Elizabeth was pregnant, she got a transfusion of AIDS-tainted blood at a hospital and not only developed AIDS, but she and Paul lost one child, and the other child now has AIDS. Elizabeth spent the last few years of her life trying to raise public consciousness about the subject. Who can forget the moving speech she made at the Democratic Convention in 1992? She probably did more than anyone to dispel the myth that AIDS is just a gay disease. It can affect anyone. Her death was one of the great tragedies of our time.

Ten

FOR SOME reason, whenever critics write about my work, they always bring up *Charlie's Angels*, but somehow they always neglect to mention *Family*, one show I'm so very proud of. And both programs premiered the same year, in 1976, even though *Family* was actually born a few years earlier.

Family had the simplest of premises. It was a drama about an ordinary middle-class family. No car chases, crime solvers, or sexy detectives. Just life for the Lawrence family, the mother, Kate (Sada Thompson), father, Doug (James Broderick), teenage son, Willie (Gary Frank), teen daughter, Buddy (Kristy McNichol), and Nancy (Meredith Baxter-Birney), the elder daughter in her mid-twenties.

Family was the story of a family: the problems of growing up and keeping a family together. We didn't realize it at the time, because you never heard the expression "family values," but the show worked because it was so relatable and a true alternative to everything else on at the time.

Jay Presson Allen, who created the series for us from an idea Len and I had, described *Family* in the pilot script as the story of the "trials and tribulations of family life." One of my favorite episodes was the one where Buddy was concerned about not getting her menstrual period while all of her school chums had already entered that stage.

INT. LAWRENCE LIVING ROOM—DAY

It's now about 3 P.M. Kate is writing letters.
BUDDY comes in with her school books.

KATE
Buddy . . . School out already?

Buddy looks rather glum.

BUDDY
Yeah . . . I couldn't have stood it
another minute.

KATE
What's up? You look like something the cat dragged in.
(beat)
Was the sleepover at Audrey's fun?

BUDDY
No. It was crummy.

Kate puts her things down.

KATE
Want some milk and fruit?

BUDDY
It won't help.

KATE
Want to talk?

BUDDY
(sitting at the table)
Mom, did you ever hear of hormones?

Kate smiles dimly.

BUDDY
(continuing)
Well, I've got some missing.
(beat)
It's not a joke.

KATE
Buddy . . . I told you . . . I was flat as
a board till I was about
fifteen . . .

BUDDY
That's the least of my problems.

She looks at Kate.

BUDDY
(continuing)
I was the only girl at Audrey's
who hasn't started yet.

KATE
Started. Buddy, I know this is a
freer age than when I was a kid,
but you're only fourteen, and . . .

BUDDY
It's not about boys . . . it's about
girls. Everyone there already started
her periods . . . and there
I was. Nothing.

Kate breathes a sigh.

KATE
If it's any consolation, you got
your teeth late, too.

BUDDY
I feel like an outcast. In
hygiene, everybody else knows
everything, firsthand. Not me . . .
I only know what we've talked
about.

A long beat . . . Kate looks at her warmly.

KATE
Honestly, I don't think there's
anything to worry about.

Buddy gets up.

BUDDY
Suppose it never happens?

KATE
I promise you . . . it will.

BUDDY
Okay . . . but just to be sure, would
you check things out with a hormone
specialist? I'd like another opinion.

KATE
(smiling)
I'll do that.

Buddy takes her books and starts upstairs.

You didn't see a lot of television like that back in the 1970s, when, at the time we first started talking about the show, the most popular dramas were *Hawaii Five-O*, *Kojak*, and *Police Woman*.

Family was born in my kitchen. Len Goldberg and his wife Wendy were over for dinner, and while Wendy and Candy were in the other room, Len and I were sitting around the table talking about life. He told me a story about a visit to see his parents in Brooklyn. When he got up in the middle of the night to get some water, he found his dad leaning on a chair, looking out the window, upset.

Len's father owned a business in the garment district and it was about to go bankrupt. "What am I going to do?" the elder Goldberg asked. "I'm 60 years old. How am I going to earn a living?" As Len told that story, we talked about what an emotional image that is for a family, and how you never saw anything like it on prime-time. "Nowhere on television can you see stories about your father losing his job," we said. "Those millions of little moments that make up real life."

And that's how we came up with the idea for *Family*. That led to a discussion of writers, and I don't know how Jay Presson Allen's name came up, but it did, and we didn't think we'd ever be able to get the gifted playwright and screenwriter (*The Prime of Miss Jean Brodie*, *Marnie*, *Cabaret*). Her agent, Jeff Berg, however, told us she was interested in doing something for TV and set up a meeting. We met her at La Scala, told her our idea, and she liked it.

We pitched the idea to ABC's Barry Diller, who gave us the go-ahead to have Jay write the pilot. She spent two weeks at the Beverly Hills Hotel, knocked out a script, gave it to us, and we immediately fell in love with it. It was touching and had marvelous moments of compassion. It was the type of show we hadn't done before, and Jay's script was exactly what Len and I had talked about in my kitchen.

But ABC didn't buy it. Barry called us and said the network wouldn't go forward with producing the pilot. "This is what I'm afraid of," he said. "You'll make a great pilot but ABC will never put it on the air. It's too good for television. I don't want to make any more heartbreak for you. So take the heartbreak at the script stage."

And *Family* was dead.

That is, until two years later when Mike Nichols entered the picture.

ABC had made a production deal with Mike, the director of such classics as *The Graduate* and *Silkwood*. ABC had presented Mike with three projects, but he turned them all down. But he wanted to do *Family* after his Connecticut neighbor Jay Presson Allen showed him the script. ABC's Michael Eisner, then the top programming exec, called to tell us the news. "Why don't you call Mike Nichols and see if you can make a deal with him?"

We went nuts. "We, who have given you all these hits, we love the show, and that's not good enough?" Len said to Eisner. "But Mike Nichols, who has never done anything on TV before, says he wants to do the show, and now you can't wait to put it on the air?"

"Just calm down and call Mike," said Eisner, and we did.

Mike Nichols was thrilled to work with us, because he couldn't be out here all the time overseeing the show. He was instrumental in helping us cast the show, design the sets, and obtain the services of feature film director Mark Rydell (*On Golden Pond*) to direct the pilot. It was quite an impressive lineup: Nichols, Allen, Rydell, and Spelling–Goldberg, the kind of credits you weren't used to seeing on television.

And then Mike Eisner left ABC and was replaced by Fred Silverman, who found *Family* on the shelf and scheduled it for midseason. Finally, we were on the air. And after all the naysayers, we found a solid audience Tuesdays at 10 P.M.

Let's talk about the casting of *Family* for a moment.

Mike came up with the idea of Sada Thompson as Mom, because he knew her from Broadway, where she had won many awards, including a Tony. We all knew James Broderick from the TV show *Brenner*, so he was an easy call for Dad, and Gary Frank, who had done a small role on the short-lived drama *Sons and Daughters*, came in and read for the role of son Willie and we loved him.

Mark knew young Kristy McNichol, and he brought her to our attention. Kristy was born in Los Angeles, the daughter of a former actress, and made her professional debut at age six in commercials. By nine she had done her first TV show—an episode of *Love, American Style*—and by fourteen she had a regular role on the TV series *Apple's Way*.

Mark brought Kristy over to my house on a weekend, where Len, Mike, and I looked at her, and knew on the spot that she was Buddy. Without a shadow of a doubt. She had that cute, pixie, tomboyish face we were looking for. A real kid. We didn't want a gorgeous, young model-type.

There were few shows at the time that exploded the hurts and desires of a young teenage girl like Buddy. The only place you saw young kids on TV were in comedies, not in dramas where you really got to know a character. Buddy was the forerunner of the kids on *Beverly Hills 90210* and I'm sure viewers related to Buddy because every family has a kid just like her. She wasn't sexy or beautiful, just an average girl.

Viewers had an immediate rapport with Kristy. She became the break-out star of *Family*, a teen sensation who went on to win two Emmys for her work, to costar with Burt Reynolds in the film *The End* and with Tatum O'Neal in the film *Little Darlings*.

A few years later, Kristy returned to television on the sitcom *Empty Nest*, but had to quit the role in the middle of the run because she was suffering from depression. I was very sad to hear about it. I certainly saw no signs of her suffering from anything when she was on *Family*. In fact, back then, I always got the feeling that Kristy was happier there than anywhere else. Every Monday she would come in, all revved up and ready to go, like it was the Fourth of July. She seemed so excited to start on a new episode.

The hardest part to cast was that of Buddy and Willie's older sister, Nancy. We had to recast the part twice until we finally got it right with Meredith Baxter-Birney, who at the time was best known for her one season on 1972–3's *Bridget Loves Bernie*. Meredith was a joy to work with and audiences loved her. I don't know why having Meredith as Nancy worked, but it sure did. She just blended in the right way and was exactly what we needed. Chemistry is everything on a TV show.

Of all the series we've ever done, *Family* received the most critical acclaim and swept the Emmys in every category except one—producers. Kristy won two statues; James Broderick, Sada Thompson, and Gary Frank got one each.

We used to say that if any other producer did *Family*, they would have won an Emmy every year. We even said that if we were the only nominee in the category and they opened the envelope, it would be empty. We were known for producing mass-market commercial hits, which were not in favor with Emmy voters at the time. Their feelings about us probably had something to do with another popular show we had on the air at the time about three female detectives and a guy named Charlie.

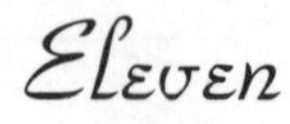

CHARLIE'S ANGELS still stands today as the biggest hit of my career. Here's how it all began, from the pilot script *Charlie's Angels*, by Ivan Goff and Ben Roberts.

FADE IN:

SERIES OF SHOTS—DAY

These are designed to introduce JILL MUNROE. Jill looks like an angel, and is—one of Charlie's. She is naive, warm, romantic. Jill wears her heart on her sleeve, and since her heart beats within a lovely bosom, men all over the place are eager to be the recipients of those ready emotions. We see:

EXT. BEACH—DAY

Jill is riding a Hobie 14 on a curling wave toward shore. The beeper pinned to her lifejacket BUZZES. PULL BACK as the twin hulls hit the sand and we see in f.g., on the bulkhead of a small beach house somewhere between Coral and Trancas, a telephone whose small red light is blinking. Jill reaches across the narrow beach, is breathless when she picks up the phone.

JILL
(into phone)
Hello . . .

CHARLIE'S VOICE
It's Charlie, Angel.
Time to go to work.

CLICK. FREEZE FRAME.

SERIES OF SHOTS—DAY

Behold SABRINA DUNCAN. Sabrina also looks like an angel . . . mm-hm, one of Charlie's. She is radiantly beautiful, silkily sophisticated, born to be a princess. As a matter of fact, whenever you bump into Sabrina you might wonder if Prince Rainier knows she's missing from the palace. We see:

EXT. MOUNTAIN EQUESTRIAN TRAIL—DAY

Sabrina, aboard a beautiful chestnut, jumps a few natural obstacles—a fence, a fallen log—comes at a gallop TOWARD CAMERA. DRAW BACK to show a stable area where a young groom answers a RINGING phone and holds out the receiver to Sabrina, who dismounts, takes phone.

SABRINA
(into phone)
Hello . . .

CHARLIE'S VOICE
It's Charlie, Angel.
Time to go to work.

CLICK. FREEZE FRAME.

SERIES OF SHOTS—DAY

Meet KELLY GARRETT, the third of Charlie's angels. Kelly is a fresh California beauty, tall, lean of limb, with long, tanned legs and a today sense of humor. Her glance is level, her manner clearheaded.

INT. GYMNASIUM—DAY

Kelly, in a leotard top, works out on the parallel bars. The phone on the wall RINGS. Kelly drops off the parallel bars, goes to it.

KELLY
(into phone)
Hello . . .

CHARLIE'S VOICE
It's Charlie, Angel.
Time to go to work.

CLICK. FREEZE FRAME.

EXT. CHARLIE'S OFFICE—DAY

It stands, aloof and old-fashioned, on a block in Beverly Hills. A dark couple drives up and parks in front, and SCOTT WOODVILLE gets out. Woodville is the only person in our particular set who has ever laid eyes on Charlie. He carries an attache case, enters the building, CAMERAS FOLLOWING, then PANNING as he goes inside to examine the very discreet bronze plaque beside the high doors. Etched into the plaque are the words—no more, no less—"PRIVATE INVESTIGATIONS."

INT. CHARLIE'S OFFICE—DAY

We are in the high-ceilinged entry hall, furnished, as is everything else in the building, with exquisite taste and little regard for money. Woodville enters, as JOHN BOSLEY, fiftyish, cheerful, round-faced, with a dryly devastating sense of humor, comes down the stairs.

BOSLEY
They're inside.

WOODVILLE
Good. Charlie'll be calling any minute.
(hands him slide-photo cartridge
from attaché case)
Will you set up the projection
machine, Bosley?

BOSLEY
Right.
(a bit pettishly)
I suppose I'm to be left behind
again—for the really heavy stuff?
Look after the office, answer the
phones, pick up the mail—

WOODVILLE
Sorry, Bosley.

THE INNER SANCTUM
It is lush, beautifully appointed, with antiques and impressive art. Kelly is, as indicated, at the dartboard. Sabrina is drinking something cool and frothy and she has mixed in the Waring at the bar. Jill is on the deep couch, leafing through a magazine. There's not much she could learn. All the girls look as though they belong in the magazine. Kelly is working a wooden Chinese interlocking puzzle. They look over as the door from the hallway opens. Woodville enters with Bosley, who goes to set up the projection console during the following:

WOODVILLE
Good afternoon, ladies.
You're all looking very
chipper. Ready for the
launching pad?

SABRINA
Any idea what this one's
all about, Woodville?

WOODVILLE
Charlie will let you know when he calls.

JILL
Why does it always have to be
on the phone? Why can't we
ever *see* Charlie?

WOODVILLE
I believe that was very clearly
spelled out when you were hired.
Nobody sees Charlie except me.
He's a very private person.

JILL
I know. But to work for a man you've
never laid eyes on. It seems so—impersonal.

WOODVILLE
And you, Miss Munroe, would you
like to make it—personal?

JILL
Be a pal. I've spent I don't know
how many hours lying in bed, staring
at the ceiling, trying to put a face and
a body on that voice.

WOODVILLE
(unmoved)
Beats watching the Late Show,
I imagine.

He moves to the projection console, next to which is a telephone-squawkbox combination. (The phone, naturally, is red.) Sabrina passes Jill on her way to her easy chair.

SABRINA
Don't tell me you're falling for Charlie?

JILL
A voice on the telephone?
Don't be silly.

The phone RINGS.

WOODVILLE
Here we go.

Woodville picks up the phone.

WOODVILLE
(continuing; into phone)
All present and accounted
for, sir.

(They watch slides and learn that their client believes a wealthy man named Vincent LeMaire, missing for seven years, was murdered and that his second wife might be responsible. He wants the Angels to visit the estate and the daughter, who lives in England with the first wife.)

CHARLIE'S VOICE
Woodville will brief you.
He has every scrap of information you'll need.

JILL
Where will you be, Charlie?

CHARLIE'S VOICE
Where I always am—with my
nose to the grindstone.
The waters run deep in this case,
and I'm up to my hips right now.

EXTREME CLOSE SHOT

Charlie is up to his hips, all right—in a whirling Jacuzzi. We can see, across Charlie's shoulder, his hand holding the poolside phone. We cannot, of course, see his face; we will never see his face. He hangs up. In b.g., a BEAUTY in a bathing suit has been approaching with a cool drink.

GIRL
Here you are, Charlie.

CHARLIE'S VOICE
Bless you, my dear.

When I started in this business, it was a rule in the industry that no actress could "carry" an hour-long show. It was okay to have a female lead in a sitcom, but for some reason, executives were convinced that viewers wouldn't buy into a drama unless it had male leads. Hence, back in 1960, the dramatic lineup consisted exclusively of dramas featuring men: *Perry Mason*, *Dr. Kildare*, *Ben Casey*.

I tried several times to break down the ignorance: in 1965, with *Honey West*, TV's first drama about a female private detective, starring Anne Francis as the female equivalent of James Bond, a trench-coat—wearing, karate-kicking P.I. But ABC didn't know what to do with the show. They scheduled it Fridays at 9:30 opposite *Gomer Pyle*, which was then the number two show in the country, and we were doomed from the start. But at least we were headed in the right direction.

The next season, Barbara Stanwyck returned to television in *The Big Valley* and it was a hit, but she was also surrounded by men. Still, it was a start. We got a few dramas with female leads—*The Girl from U.N.C.L.E.*, *The Snoop Sisters*, and *Amy Prentiss*, but it wasn't until

Police Woman in 1975 that TV started to turn the tide. Even then, with Angie Dickinson in the lead role, she still had to have Earl Holliman by her side as her boss.

And then there was *Charlie's Angels*, the show about three beautiful private detectives named Sabrina, Jill, and Kelly. Instead of taking messages for their male bosses, these women really did the legwork, fighting and collaring each episode's villain. In doing so, they developed the type of buddy relationship previously reserved for male heroes. So even when one of the angels did end up in jeopardy and needed to be saved, it was another angel, not a man, who did the rescuing.

Still, we were crucified for this show. Female critics thought we were exploiting women, but you really can't have it both ways. They scream that there are not enough women on TV, and when you put them on, they say, well, what we really want to do is show them as brain surgeons or running for president! We could never figure out what the griping was about. Was it because we were the first show with three beautiful women? I don't know too many men on TV who are unattractive. Was it because they were sometimes in bathing suits? When my kids go to the beach, they see more bikinis in one day than anybody saw on the series.

How did *Charlie's Angels* happen? At the time, action/adventure shows were dominated by inner-city realism with such gruff types as *Columbo* and *Baretta*. Len Goldberg and I thought a change would be nice. We were brainstorming in our office one day, looking for something new for Kate Jackson, since *The Rookies* was coming to an end and we didn't want to lose her. We thought, "Why not do something outrageous—a cop show with women?" We'd had every other variation on the cop show formula. "Let's put some stunning beauty into the genre and see what happens."

We came up with something we called *The Alley Cats*, about three karate-chopping, leather-attired female detectives named Alley, Lee, and Catherine (get it—the All-Lee Cats) and pitched it over breakfast at the Polo Lounge to ABC's Barry Diller and Michael Eisner. "That's the worst idea I've ever heard," said Michael. Added Barry: "You guys should be ashamed of yourselves."

They refused to even let us write the script, but they did buy a movie from us that morning called *Murder on Flight 501*, which would feature a young actress named Farrah Fawcett.

Anyway, the next wrinkle in the story is that Michael Eisner called us a few months later to discuss a problem. To get Natalie Wood and Robert Wagner to agree to star together in our TV film, *The Affair*, we had agreed to jointly develop a TV series with Wagner and Wood that they would co-own with us. ABC had set aside $25,000 to develop a pilot, but we had never come up with the right property. Michael called because the deadline was about to expire, and if we didn't submit something, ABC would have to forfeit the $25,000.

"Why don't we write a script for *The Alley Cats?*" we said.

"That's a terrible idea," said Michael. "Do something else."

"We want to do *The Alley Cats.*"

Michael gave up fighting. The deadline was looming, and he'd rather have a script he didn't like than no script at all. "I don't care what you do," he said. "Just do something."

So we went to RJ and told him the concept for the show, and he responded just like Barry and Michael. "That's the worst idea I've ever heard." He laughed. "But what do I know about TV production? You guys are the experts. Go do it."

So the script got written, but Michael and Barry's tastes didn't change overnight. When it arrived, they passed. *The Alley Cats* sat on the ABC shelf, gathering dust.

Lap Dissolve and cut to a year later, when Fred Silverman was brought in to head programming at ABC. Freddie was looking for new shows to put on the air to get ABC out of third place, and he went through the development report. He called me after reading the description for our show. "That thing you have about those three girls . . . you still want to make it? Let's do it."

As Fred recalls: "I found the script and it just sounded like a cute concept. Three sexy women, running around and solving murder cases. Sounded like there was something there."

Indeed.

So now came the hard part—casting. We knew we wanted Kate Jackson to play Sabrina. She would be our brunette, the smart, semi-leader of the troupe. Our TV movie *Murder on Flight 501* brought us our Jill. We had used Farrah Fawcett to play an airline hostess on

Murder as a favor to her then-husband Lee Majors, who was my buddy when he worked at Four Star on *The Big Valley*. We ended up cutting her fifteen lines down to five. But then we made a U-turn as we got to know her better and decided to give her more to do. She was very nervous and not great yet, but there was something about her that was just fantastic. And from that experience, we decided to team Farrah with Kate. We were looking for the California beach-girl type, and Farrah was perfect for that. She was drop-dead gorgeous and the living image of the beautiful L.A. blonde in tennis shorts or a bathing suit.

Like Kate, Farrah was also from the south, born and bred in Corpus Christi, Texas. She came to Hollywood in 1969 via a photograph of the "Ten Most Beautiful Coeds" from the University of Texas that ran in *Cashbox* magazine. A Hollywood agent saw it, called Farrah, and urged her to come west.

Farrah did a lot of commercials and had small roles in the films *Myra Breckinridge* (the same 1970 movie that also featured the debut of a very young Tom Selleck) and *Logan's Run* in 1976 before we joined forces for *Angels*.

For the part of Kelly, we were looking for a "sophisticated" type and Jaclyn Smith was just the kind of woman we had in mind. Jackie was also from Texas—Houston—and she studied acting at Trinity University in San Antonio. She eventually decided to try her luck in Los Angeles, where she appeared in 75 commercials (she was "The Breck Girl") and also did one-shots on such series as *Switch*, *McCloud*, and *The Rookies*.

Jackie came in and read for us and, by her own admission, was very nervous. She left the audition convinced she had blown it, and left for a second reading at Universal, only to find at the end of the day that she had two offers waiting for her. Luckily, she accepted *Charlie's*.

It's funny how we came up with the title. Len and I were brainstorming in my office and Kate joined us. None of us was happy with the title of the show. Then Kate saw a picture I had on the wall of three angels. "Maybe you could call them the Angels." Bingo, Kate! Initially, it was going to be *Harry's Angels*, but at the time, ABC had another Harry show, *Harry O*, so instead we became *Charlie's Angels*. And our next move was to find our "Charlie." I had known John Forsythe for years, and we had worked together on a TV movie, *Death Cruise*, and had become friends. We called and talked to him about the project. He laughed and said, "Sounds like fun." And we had our Charlie.

We made the pilot, but it didn't sell. Fred loved it, but his boss, New York–based ABC president Fred Pierce, had some story problems. So we requested a meeting. "Look guys," he told Len and me, "I think the girls are marvelous, but it doesn't make any sense to have these beautiful girls working for a guy over a telephone. How do they know what to do? Where do they come from?"

I looked at Len and he looked at me, and I did my best to talk us out of the situation. "Well, I guess I should tell him, Len. Fred, you haven't seen the main title yet. It says, 'Once upon a time there were three young ladies who graduated from the police academy and were given outstanding jobs. One is a traffic cop helping kids across the street. One is a girl typing in the office, and one is a meter maid. I took them all away from that. Now they work for me. My name is Charlie."

I made that up on the spot and it did the trick. Fred was excited. "Oh, they went to a police academy? Great. Let's go."

And then ABC tested the pilot with sample viewers. Most people don't know this, but *Charlie's Angels* was one of the worst testing pilots in the history of ABC. The average score on good pilots was 60, and *Charlie's* was way, way below that. ABC was convinced they had a real loser on their hands, so they didn't put the show on the schedule and aired the *Charlie's* pilot in June.

There was no promotion for the show, and certainly no big stars in the cast, but the show attracted a huge 59 share, comparable to the kinds of crowds only attracted today by mega-events like the Super Bowl. Wouldn't the networks kill for those kinds of audiences now?

ABC quickly added *Charlie's* to the fall schedule, where it continued its winning ways. The show was so strong, it helped turn ABC around. The perennial number three network went to number one for the first time in 1976, thanks to *Charlie's Angels*, *Happy Days*, and *Laverne and Shirley*.

Charlie's Angels made megastars of Kate, Farrah, and Jaclyn, and they started dominating magazine covers and commercial endorsements. The show was a national phenomenon.

Men tuned in to see the girls and women tuned in for the exact same reason. Each Angel had eight costume changes per show, and we bought them $20,000 worth of clothes every week. We hired Nolan Miller to design the clothes and give each woman her own look. As soon as a new fashion was out, such as thigh-high suede boots, we made sure the Angels were wearing them. Nolan always said that men watched to see the ladies, and women tuned in to see the clothes. He may have been right.

And Farrah's hairdo, well, it had a life of its own. Did we help her come up with that great hairstyle? Not at all. Farrah's gorgeous, flowing blond hair was Farrah's. Who knew it would become a national obsession? We thought about changing it for a moment in the beginning, and had we been doing a traditional cop show, we would have. But her hair helped make the show. It became one of our signatures.

"When the show was number three," Farrah told *TV Guide* in 1977, "I thought it was our acting. When we got to be number one, I decided it could only be because none of us wears a bra." We were a bit stunned when we read that comment. Can you imagine TV producers going to actresses and saying, "We'd rather you don't wear a bra on our show?" Never happened. Had it occurred, it surely would have been in every newspaper in the world.

Critics hated the show. I remember one woman complaining to us at a press conference that *Charlie's Angels* wasn't "credible."

"If you really think," we said to her, and I've said it many times since, "that three of the most beautiful ladies in the world would work for a guy on the telephone who they've never met, make $500 a week, and wear $5,000 Nolan Miller gowns, then you don't understand what we were trying to do." The show was camp. Fantasy. We were just trying to have fun. *Charlie's Angels* was exactly what it set out to be: light, escapist entertainment. A glamorous, upbeat, and colorful fantasy.

Look at the situations they got themselves into. The scalding steambath capers, the cruise ship with the homicidal maniac aboard, the time the facelift farm was taken over by mobsters. Reality? Come on.

On-screen and off, Jaclyn was, as I've said, the personification of a lady. Had she been born in an earlier time, she could have starred in *Gone with the Wind.* She was always beautifully coifed and dressed. She never was seen in jeans, and I never heard her curse once. If someone said the "F" word around her, Jackie would turn red.

Kate received an unjust reputation as a tough actress to work with. She was actually great fun to be around. People began to misjudge her over the years because she's a strong woman. In fact, she was probably one of the first strong young women I'd ever met, like a young Barbara Stanwyck. She told you what was on her mind, and people weren't used to that. But she never threatened to pull a star trip by walking off the set or anything like that. She just had ideas on how to make the show better. She knew her craft and was very professional.

Kate and Jackie sat on the sidelines initially when Farrah exploded as the huge breakout Angel, but we never had to talk to Farrah about it, because she handled it very well. We never felt that Kate or Jackie were jealous of what Farrah was achieving. Like Heather Locklear on *Melrose Place*, Farrah never flaunted her covers. In fact, she was kind of embarrassed about it. I do think, however, that Farrah's success went to the heads of the people who were managing her.

David Caruso got a lot of headlines when he quit *NYPD Blue* to make movies. But that was nothing compared to when Farrah, a much bigger star at the time, did the same thing, saying she wanted to go off and be a movie star. That was strange. No one had ever done that to us before. I think Farrah was very badly advised. You know, everybody eventually wants to go into motion pictures, but to try and do it in the first year of a series isn't how it's done.

We were stunned when we heard on the radio that Farrah was quitting. I might add, it was a terrible blow. We didn't want her to go. She was very important to the show, and we tried hard to enforce our contract. Her manager at the time found a technicality that put her contract into question. We went to court over the issue, and settled when she agreed to appear in six *Charlie's* episodes over a two-year period. Farrah went off to make films like *Sunburn* and *Somebody Killed My Husband*, but her initial projects weren't very successful. I believe it was because she upset so many of her fans. They loved her on *Charlie's Angels* and didn't like the idea that she quit the show. So why didn't we continue with the case and enforce the contract? For the same reason that Steven Bochco let Caruso walk from *NYPD*. What are you going to do, force somebody to do a show she or he doesn't want to do?

Still, it sets a really bad precedent when an actor quits a series in the middle of a run. I admire people like Ted Danson, Tom Selleck, and Michael J. Fox, who stuck with their series to the end while they were doing motion pictures. The days when they said if you're doing television you can't do movies is very much past. There's no reason actors can't do both.

Still, there's no denying that many of today's movie stars see television as a training ground, with their sights set on movies. Mickey Rooney once said to me about his ex-wives, "What's wrong with me, Aaron? I put shoes on them and they walk away." And that's the way it's beginning to feel in TV. We put shoes on the young actors and they walk away.

Kate Jackson was offered the Meryl Streep role in *Kramer vs. Kramer*, and was quite upset with us when we couldn't rearrange our shooting schedule and let her off to do the film. When TV actors get offered great movie roles while doing a series, of course it's heartbreaking for the actor when they can't do it. However, the other side of the coin is that we have a signed contract with them and we have a show that we have to deliver to the network. Most important, the show made them stars in the first place!

In replacing Farrah, we had the toughest casting decision of our life. We're not talking about replacing just anyone. Farrah was a national obsession. Her pinup poster was everywhere, her smiling face was beaming off lunchboxes and T-shirts. Young girls imitated her long, layered hairdo. They wanted to be her. Men of all ages wanted to be with her. Everybody told us that if we lost Farrah, the show was over. However, we didn't believe the naysayers. We never thought *Angels* was just Farrah. Had the show been about two women like *Cagney & Lacey*, and the show lost both of them at the same time, then it would have been all over. But on *Charlie's*, we still had Kate and Jaclyn and viewers also loved them.

Still, we knew we couldn't just find another actress and have her play the part of Jill. That would have been suicide. So we decided to make the new character Jill's sister. How could anyone hate the sister of a loved one? You couldn't. We got Cheryl Ladd, who had appeared in a TV movie for us, *Satan's School for Girls*, and had once tried out for the Meredith Baxter-Birney role on *Family*. Viewers loved her and, amazingly, we suffered no backlash from losing Farrah, though we were certainly petrified about it at the time.

Let's talk about what happens to young actors when they become stars "overnight." Before the show goes on the air, they're young actors who haven't had much success or made much money. We start them off at a low salary, which, if you want to go back to the *Mod Squad* days, would be like a few thousand dollars a show. We shoot 11 shows in advance. They work their tails off, and then suddenly the show goes on and it's an instant hit.

Now they walk down the street and more people ask for their autographs than they would of any movie star. Remember, they're seen by millions of people each week and movie stars aren't. Television isn't like motion pictures where even Marilyn Monroe had to do seven or eight pictures before she was really a star. *The Mod Squad* and *Charlie's Angels*, and, more recently, shows like *ER*, *NYPD Blue*, and *Friends* were instant smashes.

So then the agents come in and the managers come in, and every agent says if you leave your agent I can get you more money. And it's really tough for those kids to cope with that, and I don't hold them at fault. The truth of the matter is that they see a show that's in the top ten and they feel the networks are making a lot of money and the producers are making a lot of money, so why aren't they making a lot of money?

I wish people would differentiate between stars and instant stars. TV, that gigantic loving monster, creates instant stars. The true stars can cope. The new stars are so easily hyped by their agents. They make demands as if they had totally paid their dues.

What most of the new stars don't understand is that unless a show's on for four years, and gets into syndication, it doesn't make any money. But let's face it, for them it's very difficult. The agents and publicity people and all the media wanting to interview them turns their heads.

As producers, we have a responsibility to counsel them on how to handle fame, but so do the agents and lawyers.

It appeared that Farrah received some very bad career advice from her then-manager during the *Angels* era. When the movies didn't work, she moved to New York and worked on Off-Broadway to escape the image he had set up for her. Now, of course, with work like *The Burning Bed* and *Extremities*, Farrah has gone from playing a cute blond on *Charlie's Angels* to becoming a fine dramatic actress. I'm very proud of her.

A strange thing about *Charlie's Angels* is the sort of "Angels' jinx" that seemed to follow the actresses' love lives. When we started the show, Farrah was married to Lee Majors, who, as I said, had been a good friend of mine ever since his *Big Valley* days. Jaclyn was going steady with a guy she eventually married, and Kate also wed during her *Angels* tour.

I don't know if it was the curse of *Charlie's Angels*, but their romances and lives off-screen were much more convoluted than the romances on-screen. They all got married and all got divorced during the run of the show.

Charlie's Angels was so huge that naturally the press wrote hundreds of stories about the show. They always seemed to be looking for dirt. The women were ultra-competitive and hated each other . . . the cinematographers had to use different camera angles for each angel. All of that was pure untrue trash.

Sure, some things got testy once in awhile, but we were all friends then, and we're still friends today. When rumors hit the papers, Len and I always pointed out that *Charlie's Angels* was a really tough show to make. Each week we undertook a big action adventure, and that's not easy to pull off. Building a show around three beautiful women is difficult because they were usually in every scene together, and since the show was built around their beauty, we had to spend many more hours than usual on making sure their hair, makeup, and clothes were all perfect. So a lot of time on the set was waiting. Plus, they would start the day at six A.M. in makeup and many days we would have to shoot until nine or ten P.M. It's hard for someone who's been at it all day to still look gorgeous at ten P.M., but they somehow managed to pull it off.

On June 24, 1981, after 109 episodes, we solved our last case. At our height, we were viewed by hundreds of millions around the world every week, and who knows how many kids brought their Angel lunchboxes to school and played with Angel dolls at home?

One of the happiest moments of my life was when three of the Angels—Jackie, Kate, and Cheryl reunited in 1992 onstage to present me the People's Choice Awards' Lifetime Achievement honor. Coming from them, it really made the evening special.

Speaking of *Angels* reunions, we tried to bring the show back when Fox called, pitching the concept for a new sequel called *Angels* '88. We had a huge nationwide search for our new women, and eventually cast Tea Leoni, Claire Yarlett, Sandra Canning, and Karen Kopins, but then the writer's strike happened and the whole project got scrapped. But it seems *Charlie's Angels* will never die. It's still airing in reruns every day, and Len and I are developing a theatrical film of *Charlie's Angels* with Sony Pictures.

It was during the *Charlie's Angels* era that I made a very stupid remark that I find almost impossible to live down.

The reporter asked why I didn't do more thought-provoking television and I replied: "People have enough to worry about. I don't think television has to preach so much. What's wrong with sheer escapism entertainment . . . cotton candy for the mind?" I probably never should have said it. It's been printed 18 jillion times since, and some reviewers still refer to me as "the Cotton Candy King of TV" and ignore my more serious work.

To this day, when people write about my work, *Charlie's Angels* always comes first, and many totally ignore *Family*, *The Boy in the Plastic Bubble* (with John Travolta in his first TV dramatic role), *The Best Little Girl in the World* (which starred Jennifer Jason Leigh in a TV film about anorexia), *Day One* (about how we never should have dropped the atomic bomb), or *And the Band Played On*, where we really tried to say something about how the government mishandled the AIDS crisis. Both *Day One* and *Band* won the Emmy award, but somehow I'm still "Cotton Candy" to the press.

And if I'm not "Cotton Candy," I'm the "King of the Jiggle." Let's talk about "jiggle" for a moment. Any time we put one of the Angels into a bathing suit—and we would have been stupid not to—the press called it "jiggle." What is "jiggle"? Haven't reporters been to the beach before? If so, do they lasciviously leer at every young lady in a bathing suit and say, "Wow, look at that "jiggle"? I doubt that. So why damn us with that silly word?

On *Angels*, the women spent most of their time in fantastic Nolan Miller gowns. There was no more jiggle on *Charlie's Angels* than there was in Busby Berkeley musicals or among the Rockettes of Radio City Music Hall.

Charlie's became associated with jiggle not because of anything we did on the show. It was due to Farrah's wet swimsuit poster, which Len and I had nothing to do with. Her manager at the time persuaded her to go for it, and everyone wound up thinking it was our idea. But don't blame Farrah either. It was her manager's idea.

AARON SPELLING COLLECTION

That's me in a scene from the film *Three Young Texans* in which Mitzi Gaynor, Keefe Brasselle, and Jeffrey Hunter starred.

AARON SPELLING COLLECTION

Me at a very young age, with my brother, Danny, posing atop a rocking horse for a photo. I was so happy with my gift, and cried my eyes out when I found out they had paid a nickel to let me pose on the horse. In fact, I cried the entire day. When Tori was born, the first present I bought her was a rocking horse. She was two days old.

The role that finished my acting career. Here I am, dressed as a beggar for *Kismet*, in which I had only one line. After seeing me like this, my then-wife Carolyn insisted that I quit acting and stick to the typewriter.

AARON SPELLING COLLECTION

AARON SPELLING COLLECTION

Here's an all-star gathering from the very first *Burke's Law*, which was an episode of *The Dick Powell Theater*, with Dick as Amos Burke before we spun it off. *Burke's* was the first show to use many guest stars as villains and suspects and we sure had a lot of them here. Back row: Ronald Reagan, Nick Adams, Lloyd Bridges, Mickey Rooney, Edgar Bergen, unidentified man, Ralph Bellamy, Kay Thompson, and Dean Jones. Front row: Aaron Spelling, Carolyn Jones, Dick Powell, and Tom McDermott, an executive from Four Star.

Aaron Spelling Collection

Courtesy Columbia Pictures Television

The Mod Squad—Clarence Williams III, Peggy Lipton, and Michael Cole.

Paul Michael Glaser and David Soul were *Starsky and Hutch*.

COURTESY COLUMBIA PICTURES TELEVISION

The cast of one of my all-time favorite shows, *Family*—Meredith Baxter, Gary Fran, Sada Thompson, Kristy McNichol, and James Broderick.

From the first season of *Charlie's Angels*—Jaclyn Smith, Kate Jackson, and Farrah Fawcett.

Charlie's Angels—Kate Jackson, Farrah Fawcett, and Jaclyn Smith.

COURTESY COLUMBIA PICTURES TELEVISION

COURTESY COLUMBIA PICTURES TELEVISION

Spelling Entertainment

The Love Boat gang—Gavin Macleod, Ted Lange, Lauren Tewes, Fred Grandy, Jill Whelan, and Bernie Kopell.

Vegas.

Spelling Entertainment

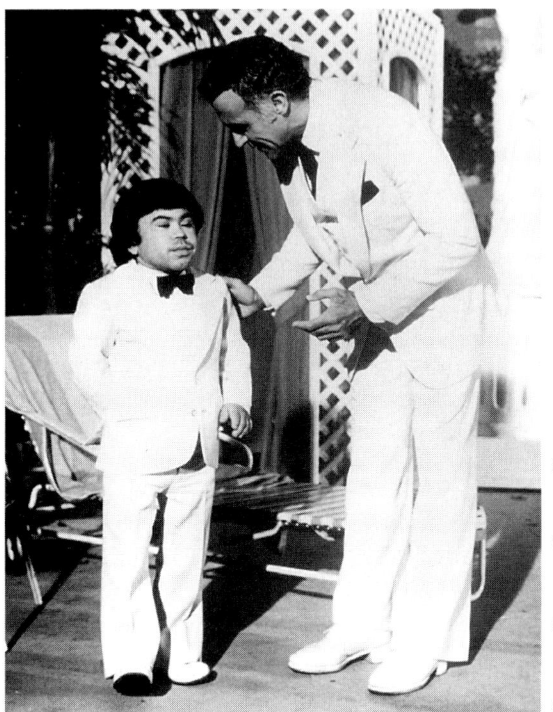

Fantasy Island—Herve Villechaize and Ricardo Montalban.

COURTESY COLUMBIA PICTURES TELEVISION

COURTESY COLUMBIA PICTURES TELEVISION

Robert Wagner and Stephanie Powers from *Hart to Hart*.

SPELLING ENTERTAINMENT

John Forsythe and the women of *Dynasty*—Linda Evans, Pamela Bellwood, Heather Locklear, Pamela Sue Martin, and Joan Collins.

SPELLING ENTERTAINMENT

Joan Collins.

SPELLING ENTERTAINMENT

The cast of *Beverly Hills 90210*, the Brenda years—Jennie Garth, Ian Ziering, Gabrielle Carteris, Jason Priestley, Shannen Doherty, Luke Perry, Tori Spelling, and Brian Austin Green.

SPELLING ENTERTAINMENT

The new cast of *Beverly Hills 90210*—Jamie Walters, Kathleen Robertson, Ian Ziering, Luke Perry, Tori Spelling, Jason Priestley, Jennie Garth, Tiffani-Amber Thiessen, and Brian Austin Green.

SPELLING ENTERTAINMENT

The cast of *Melrose Place*. *Top Row*—Marcia Cross, Kristin Davis, Laura Leighton, Josie Bisset, Daphne Zuniga, Courtney Thorne-Smith, and Heather Locklear. *Front Row*—Andrew Shue, Jack Wagner, Doug Savant, Grant Show, Patrick Muldoon, and Thomas Calabro.

Harry Langdon Photography

Me and Candy in one of our favorite pictures.

Our family on one of our rare nights out on the town together, at the Planet Hollywood in Las Vegas.

Aaron Spelling Collection

Candy at home with her dolls.

AARON SPELLING COLLECTION

AARON SPELLING COLLECTION

Randy and Tori
before they grew up.
Is it any wonder they
both decided to go
into acting?

Aaron Spelling Collection

Randy.

Aaron Spelling Collection

Tori.

Aaron Spelling Collection

An aerial view of this little house we own in Los Angeles.

PETER C. BORSARI

Me at home with a few of the awards I've been lucky to receive over the years.

AARON SPELLING COLLECTION

My star on Hollywood Boulevard. Something I never dreamed was even possible.

HARRY LANGDON PHOTOGRAPHY

Me.

Twelve

HART TO HART was created by popular novelist Sidney Sheldon. (Quick trivia question: Name Sidney's other popular TV creation. Hint: It's about a lady with magical powers.) The show was originally written back in the 1960s when Leonard was president of Screen Gems, but it never sold. Years later, we were pitching shows to ABC and we wanted to do something about a married couple who solved crimes, sort of like a contemporary *Thin Man*.

Len recalled the script that Sidney had written back in the 1960s called *Double Twist*, and the ABC exec we were meeting with, Steve Gentry, had been at CBS when it was originally presented. He remembered liking it. So we called Sidney, but he didn't remember anything about it. We had him put his secretary on the phone, and we had her find the script for him and send it over.

It was very good, although a little dated. Sidney was now a best-selling novelist and didn't have time to work on it, so we got writer Tom Mankewicz to polish *Double* and develop it into a TV series. He did a great job, and we knew we had something special.

I don't remember a drama on TV that had shown a couple could be married but still love each other very much, spend every day as if they were still on their honeymoon, be sensuous, and have fun together. The romance was a big part of the show, and that's why it worked. There wasn't anything like it on TV at the time.

Mr. and Mrs. H. (as they were referred to by their chauffeur, Max) were a super-rich Beverly Hills couple who loved to travel to new exotic places every week in their private jet, and solve crimes when they got there. Jonathan was a self-made millionaire, the head of his own conglomerate, Jennifer was an international journalist, and Freeway was their dog.

(It's interesting what viewers remember. *Jeopardy* recently honored me by devoting an entire category to "Aaron Spelling" and one of the answers was: "Freeway and Max. The question: The dog and driver from *Hart to Hart?*")

We knew immediately that we wanted Robert Wagner for the male lead. We dreamed of Natalie Wood costarring with Bob in *Hart to Hart*, but that was impossible as her feature career was thriving.

Bob started out in movies and was well-known for his TV roles in *It Takes a Thief* and *Switch*, two debonair leading men just like Jonathan Hart. Bob was the younger equivalent of Cary Grant. He came from a well-to-do family, looked great in a tuxedo, and could have played James Bond, had he wanted to. Bob was obviously the star we wanted. We were thrilled when he accepted.

Len and I were throwing out names of actresses and Bob suggested Stefanie Powers as Jennifer Hart. Stefanie had an interesting career. She was raised in Hollywood and had planned on a career in art. She tried out—and got—a small part in the *West Side Story* film as one of the Jets, which led her to a starring role in the film *Among the Thorns* and twelve others in the early 1960s, including *Tammy Tell Me True*, *Stagecoach*, and *Experiment in Terror*. She starred in the 1966 TV spin-off *The Girl from U.N.C.L.E.* and did guest spots on such shows as *Bonanza* and *Marcus Welby, M.D.* before returning to the public eye in 1977's *The Feather and Feather Gang* for ABC as part of a father-and-daughter con team.

Stefanie lived in Malibu and had visited our beach house a few times. We had also worked with her on a few TV movies, enjoyed her work, and decided to take Bob's suggestion.

Stefanie was William Holden's longtime companion and the two of them were working hard on building a big-game preserve and study center in Kenya before he died in 1981. In 1979, when we were casting *Hart*, Stefanie said she was too busy with the center to take on a series. But she fell in love with the script, and couldn't turn it down. (Interesting story about the Kenya center. Stefanie got everybody on the cast and crew—including yours truly—to donate money. My former agent, Bill Haber, went on a trip to Africa recently, and he called me from there. "Even in Africa I can't get away from you," he said. "I just saw a big plaque thanking you for your contribution. In Africa!")

After we cast Stefanie, a few executives at ABC tried to fight it.

They said she wasn't young and "current" enough. After their taste of mega-success with *Charlie's Angels*, ABC execs were always pushing now for young, Farrah Fawcett types, which was right for *Angels*, but very wrong for *Hart to Hart*.

"It will never work," one of the executives said to us. "You should have gone with a much younger married couple."

Who ever heard of a 21-year-old millionaire? Do you think the audience would have accepted that? With a 21-year-old wife? And they would be bright enough and have lived long enough to help other people? Come on.

The audience certainly took to Bob and Stefanie as the Harts. It became the roles of their careers, and to this day, they're still playing Jonathan and Jennifer in occasional *Hart to Hart* movies, which are produced by Bob's production company.

By the way, in case you're wondering, Sidney Sheldon's other TV series was *I Dream of Jeannie*. How's that for a writer being versatile?—*Hart to Hart* and *I Dream of Jeannie*.

Speaking of great leading men, the two Hollywood legends I've been most impressed with meeting have been Cary Grant and Fred Astaire. There was a time in my life when Candy and I owned a few racehorses and we used to spend our Sundays at Hollywood Park racetrack. I got to know Cary there, and will never forget the time we spent together. Look up the word "charming" in the dictionary and you'll find it under "Cary Grant." His voice and mannerisms were infectious. Every time I saw him, I would go home and do a Cary Grant impersonation.

I never got the nerve to ask him to star in one of my TV shows. I knew he would have laughed and charmingly refused. But he could have done anything he wanted. If he wanted to read the phone book, any network would have bought it.

What would have been my dream project for Cary Grant? I would have loved to do a *Burke's Law* movie starring Cary Grant. And if he were around today, I'd have him play a homeless man and see how he overcame his adversity with his sheer personality and magnetism.

The other Hollywood legend I'll never forget is Fred Astaire. I went to visit him about appearing in our sequel to *The Over-the-Hill Gang*. When I was young, my sister Becky used to take me to Ginger Rogers and Fred Astaire movies because she loved the opulence and the clothes, and later on I directed theater in a Dallas playhouse that was financed by Astaire and Rogers. (A former dialogue coach for them, Edward Rubin, formed the group.)

So meeting with Fred Astaire was like the great dream of my life. I went over to see him about my little movie, and he shocked me by telling me he had seen the first one. Then this idol of mine went upstairs, pulled out a scrapbook, and showed me pictures of him in western attire doing a dance number. I couldn't believe that the great Fred Astaire thought he had to audition for the job. I was just thrilled to be in the same room with the debonair and sophisticated Fred Astaire. Another dream come true.

Thirteen

FANTASY ISLAND

FADE IN:

EXT. THE SEA—AERIAL SHOT—A SMALL TROPICAL ISLAND

It stands alone in a vast sea. Remote. Cut off from the rest of the world.

NEW ANGLE—RUNNING SHOT
Much CLOSER now. High cliffs, deep valleys, lush rain forests, jungle, beaches, reefs.
And the SOUND of . . .

A SEAPLANE

flying over some high palms. PAN with the plane to the tower of the MAIN HOUSE where we FIND TATTOO ringing the bell. . . . Tattoo is literally a dwarf. But gnome comes closer, for there is much of the sprite about him. His size and shape—after the first look—are, if not important, irrelevant. He is just so much kinetic energy, running here, bobbing up there . . . at the moment he is quite excited by the arrival of the plane.

TATTOO
The plane . . . The plane.

Tattoo disappears from the tower. The CAMERA PANS DOWN at verandah of the building as ROARKE comes out.

ANGLE ON ROARKE

watching the plane arrive O.S. Roarke is larger than life—measured in any dimension. He runs the island. He's the reason it exists. But what he does here and why he does it is strictly his own concern. Above all, he is a man of mystery. He's bright, determined, convivial when it suits him. He can also be enigmatic, intuitive, even clairvoyant. Put another way, Roarke seems to function—now and again—on a different level than we mortals, even as would a devil—or a saint.

POV—SEAPLANE

coming in for a landing.

BACK TO SCENE

Roarke glances at his wristwatch, smiles.

ROARKE
Our guests are arriving
on time—to the second.

Tattoo comes puffing INTO the SHOT.

TATTOO
They always do and
you always act like
it's a miracle.

Roarke turns a hard eye on him.

ROARKE
My dear Tattoo—when
each guest is paying
fifty thousand dollars
for a three-day stay
on Fantasy Island, he
or she deserves miracles.

Bob Costas once asked me in a TV interview what I would say to my early heroes like O. Henry and Mark Twain if I were to meet them at a dinner party.

Well, with O. Henry I'd have to send him a huge check of royalties, because *Fantasy Island, The Love Boat*, and *Hotel* were all short stories. We didn't steal from O. Henry, but we did use his form. They were short O. Henry–style tales with a twist at the end. I owe a great deal to O. Henry.

And for Twain, I'd simply thank him for giving me a sense of humor I never had as a kid. My life was dark, with no hope, and somehow I fantasized with those kids on the raft that there would be an escape for me, too, one day.

Fantasy Island started our cycle of 1970s O. Henry–type anthologies set within the framework of a structured format. Each episode had three stories and featured guest stars. Since I had begun my career in anthologies on *Dick Powell's Zane Grey Theater*, I was delighted to bring the anthology form back in the 1970s, with a slightly different look.

Fantasy Island began as an argument. Leonard Goldberg and I were at ABC, pitching TV movie ideas, but all of our best ones were getting shot down. The execs kept telling us they didn't want "soft" stories, but ones with "heat." Finally, I kind of went crazy. I said, "You guys don't want a show. You don't want something with characters or a plot or story. You just want to have some sort of an island, where you can go and act out all your dumb fantasies. You want a show about some guy on an island to make all your sexual and other fantasies come true." And that was when they started jumping up and down and shouting, "Do it, do it."

ABC gave us an order to do a *Fantasy Island* TV movie in 1977 and we immediately thought of Ricardo Montalban as suave Mr. Roarke, the wishmaster. ABC had another idea. They saw Mr. Roarke as Orson Welles, by that time a 300-pound genius also famous for ordering nine hot dogs at a time at Pink's hot dog stand in Hollywood. Nothing against Welles. He was an incredible director and a great actor, but we thought it would be much more interesting to have Ricardo and that distinguished Latino accent of his. Welles was great, but he wasn't Roarke, no more than we would cast Ricardo to play a vampire in a Dracula movie.

I had known Ricardo for years and worked with him on several occasions. Born in Mexico, Ricardo made several films there before coming to Hollywood in the late 1940s and appearing in such MGM films as *Fiesta*, *Latin Lovers*, and *Sombrero*.

We picked Herve Villechaize for the role of Tattoo when both Len and I saw him in the James Bond film, *The Man with the Golden Gun*. We both thought he was perfect for the part. We wanted a different look and the idea of a three-foot-ten sidekick for Roarke was too irresistible to pass up.

We did *Fantasy Island* first as a TV movie in 1976 and then ABC ordered a second one. By the time we were on our third, Fred Silverman called and asked us to cut the two-hour film into two parts—he wanted to turn *Fantasy Island* into a series.

Then came the inevitable call from a lower-level network executive. "We'd like you to get rid of the little guy," he said.

"What?"

And he repeated himself.

"You're kidding."

"No, I'm not. We'd like to have an attractive, sexy girl for Mr. Roarke."

We said no, we didn't want to do that. We liked the chemistry the way it was, and suggested they do the series without us. We kept Herve.

Herve was born in Paris to a French surgeon father and an English mother. He quit school at age 11 to study art and eventually emigrated to New York to continue his studies, despite the fact that he was unable to speak a word of English. He always told me he learned the language by watching daytime soap operas. In fact, he become so infatuated with television that he decided to switch professions and began studying acting.

Despite his size, Herve got parts in many films, including *Greaser's Palace*, *The Gang That Couldn't Shoot Straight*, and *The One and the Only*. But they were small roles and didn't pay much money. When we contacted Herve about working in *Fantasy Island*, he was flat broke and living in a rather cheap transient hotel on Hollywood Boulevard.

Fantasy Island debuted as a series in January 1978 and lasted until 1984. We never strayed from the original premise. For $10,000, you could come visit Fantasy Island where Mr. Roarke would grant you one wish. A 98-pound weakling wanted to be transformed into a sex symbol during his stay. No problem. A henpecked family man wished a weekend of respect from his clan. That could be arranged. Guests were always cast with stars, and it was the first show since *Burke's Law* to use a large group of guest stars on a weekly basis.

Working with Ricardo was a joy. He was and still is a true gentleman. The only time I'd ever hear a negative word from him was if a producer had decided to put an actress into a skimpy outfit, and he'd call.

"Aaron . . . Aaron, she's embarrassed by this outfit. Does she have to wear it?"

"Of course not, Ricky. Kill the outfit."

Otherwise, Ricardo made good scripts better and not-so-good scripts work. I don't remember his ever doing any rewrites. He set a perfect example for the rest of the cast.

Love,
Exciting and new.
Come aboard,
We're expecting you.
And love,
Life's sweetest reward.
Let it float,
It floats back to you.

The Love Boat.
Soon will be making another run,
The Love Boat.
Promises something for everyone,
Set a course for adventure,
Your mind on a new romance.

And Love,
Won't hurt anymore.
It's an open smile,
On a friendly shore.
It's love.
It's love.
It's love.

The concept for *The Love Boat* was simple. The stories were set aboard the *Pacific Princess*, a luxury cruise ship which embarked each week on a romantic, sentimental, and amusing voyage. Three couples boarded—young and old, married and unmarried—and all were looking for love. Their stories were interwoven with the ship's crew.

Gavin MacLeod, best known for his roles on *The Mary Tyler Moore Show* and *McHale's Navy*, starred as Captain Merrill Stubing, and the cast also featured Bernie Kopell (he was a sidekick in such shows as *Get Smart* and *That Girl*) as Doc, the ship's medical man; Fred Grandy (he did a year on *Maude* as Carol's boyfriend, Chris) was Burl ("Gopher") Smith, the assistant purser; Ted Lange (from *That's My Mama* and *Mr. T and Tina*) played Isaac Washington, the bartender, and we cast Lauren Tewes, who at the time was just starting out, as Julie McCoy, the perky cruise director of the *Pacific Princess*. Jill Whelan joined the cast in 1979 as Capt. Stubing's young daughter, Vicki.

The Love Boat walked in my door one day, courtesy of producer Douglas S. Cramer. He was a former ABC exec (Leonard Goldberg's boss, back in the 1960s when I first met Len) who had launched the comedy anthology, *Love, American Style*, while working at Paramount. Doug had purchased the rights to a book called *The Love Boats*, a novel by former cruise hostess Jeraldine Saunders.

Doug was married to Joyce Haber, who wrote a strong and sometimes very vicious column for the *Los Angeles Times*. She was the first person to take over the mantle from Hedda Hopper and Louella Parsons. I not only knew Doug socially, but I also liked the project he had been working unsuccessfully on for two years. Doug had made two pilots of *The Love Boat*, but ABC turned both down, because, I believe, the casting just wasn't right.

When Doug and I joined forces, I went to ABC to try and convince them to do a third pilot, and Fred Silverman said, "Aaron, there's no way in the world I can get New York to okay another *Love Boat* pilot . . . unless, that is, you bring me in a great piece of casting for the captain."

The Mary Tyler Moore Show had just gone off the air, and it had been a big hit, so Fred said, "How about Gavin McLeod?" who had played Mary's friend Murray, the newswriter.

I called Gavin's agent, who said Gavin would only be interested in a comedy, and I explained that *The Love Boat* was a comedy, an hour comedy. I met with Gavin at my house and we hit it off. He signed on, and that was all Fred needed to give us the green light to shoot the third pilot.

With Gavin aboard, we had everybody, except for our cruise director. We found her on the streets of Hollywood. Bret Garwood, my executive coordinator, was taking a walk down Sunset Boulevard one day and ran into Lauren Tewes and her manager, whom he knew. At the time, Lauren had appeared in a few commercials, and was supporting herself by waitressing at a Sunset Boulevard coffee shop. After talking to Lauren for awhile, Bret said, "You have such a bubbly personality. You should try out for the role of Julie, the cruise director. You'd be good for it."

Lauren auditioned, and Bret was right, she was good. Our only problem was that her hair was all wrong, something we realized the day before filming was to start. So Candy called her hairdresser and convinced him to open up Sunday night at 9 P.M. to do Lauren's hair for the next day's shoot.

Since this was our third time at bat, ABC's budget was very tight. Doug's pilots were both filmed aboard ships on marvelous cruises. We didn't have the time or money to do that again, so we used his stock footage from the other two shows and filmed the entire pilot in Long Beach on the *Queen Mary*. We never left port.

It was still the same show—about people who find romance and comedy on the high seas; but this time, with a different cast, it sold right away, and we debuted in 1977 as the number 14 show of the year. Not too bad for a program rejected twice by ABC brass. And we ran for nine years. Douglas deserves a tremendous amount of credit for his work on *Love Boat*. He worked night and day to keep the *Boat* going and we remained partners in Aaron Spelling Productions for many years.

The appeal of *The Love Boat* was enormous. It was a show for people who couldn't afford to go on a cruise. Every week they felt like they were going somewhere exotic by watching our show. Not that we spent that much time on the water. In fact, we filmed most of the *Boat* episodes on land, on a soundstage at 20th Century–Fox, where we knocked a hole in the floor for the Love Boat swimming pool, built a stateroom, the corridors, cabins, the big dining rooms, and the huge *Love Boat* deck. It was the most elaborate set we had ever done.

We also filmed several two-hour *Love Boat* specials on two real cruise ships, the *Pacific Princess* and the *Island Princess*. We went to Mexico and on long cruises from the Virgin Islands to Alaska. Passengers were invited to participate as extras and they were delighted to take part. As the show went on, we added more and more exotic destinations, to places like Australia, China, and the Mediterranean.

On *The Love Boat*, I was able to fulfill my own dreams by hiring some of the great old Hollywood legends to guest star on the show. The studios weren't banging their doors down with offers, but these actors and actresses still had lots of talent, and I was happy to provide an outlet. We had such legends as Helen Hayes, Lana Turner, Don Ameche, Lillian Gish, Ginger Rogers, Janet Gaynor, Douglas Fairbanks, Jr., Olivia De Havilland, Alice Faye, June Allyson, and Dorothy Lamour as well as contemporary stars like John Ritter, Suzanne Somers, Loni Anderson, Andy Warhol, Patty Duke, and Bill Bixby. Over the nine years of *The Love Boat*, we used over a thousand actors and actresses as guest stars. Lana Turner was the thousandth guest.

I hate the way old actresses are literally thrown out to sea when they reach a certain age. It's criminal the way they're treated. The moment a woman's breasts droop one inch, they don't work anymore, as opposed to countries like England, where the Margaret Rutherfords work forever and are revered. But in our crazy country, once you reach a certain age, you're dead. It's a very sad statement. So if we can use an established star who's not working, it's a privilege.

I told you how we used to send Rolls-Royces to pick up the guest stars for *Burke's Law*. So did we send boats to pick up our guests on *The Love Boat*? No. People came on the show who were dying to do comedy, and when we did the big cruises, we encouraged them to bring along their husbands or wives. We found that everybody wanted to go on cruises. That's how we got some of our biggest stars.

It was difficult at first, but after the show was a hit, agents started calling us.

* * *

At no point during the production of *The Love Boat* did we realize that one of our actors would one day become a member of the United States House of Representatives. Congressman Gopher? Never in a million years.

But it happened. After *Love Boat* went off the air, Fred Grandy told us he planned to run for Congress in Iowa. We were stunned. That was like Bernie Kopell telling us he was going to challenge Mike Tyson in a boxing match. Fred never talked politics. He was always joking on the set and clowning around like Gopher. The impression he gave was that he didn't have a thought in his head, and then he suddenly announces that he's going to switch careers and run for Congress? No one could believe it.

Of course, we were thrilled when he won. He turned out to be a very good congressman and I hope the recognition factor from *The Love Boat* helped him get elected. He was afraid it would hurt his chances, but the show was so big, people knew his name instantly.

By the way, as I look over my career, I've employed one congressman, one secretary of state, and two presidents. Ronald Reagan was on the first *Burke's Law* and Gerald Ford did a cameo on an episode of *Dynasty*, along with Henry Kissinger. Are you listening, President Clinton?

One sad note about *The Love Boat.* We were forced to not pick up Lauren Tewes' contract after the seventh season. As I say, these things are always by mutual agreement, but Lauren really got stung by the dark side of Hollywood. Her marriage fell apart and she told *TV Guide* she had become addicted to cocaine. We were forced to go our separate ways.

Lauren kept to herself most of the time, and none of us knew why Lauren was having problems. I found out later on that it was drugs, and that made us all very sad. Once again, fame is a killer. Here's a woman who hadn't really done much acting before, and suddenly she was the female star of *The Love Boat.* It was really hard for her to compete with success.

We replaced Lauren with Pat Klous as her sister, Judy McCoy, but two years later, her agent called and told us Lauren had straightened out her life and wanted to come back. She returned on some *Love Boat* specials and we were thrilled to have her back. We adored her. Today Lauren lives in Seattle, where I'm told she's very happy away from Hollywood.

We also had to make a change on *Fantasy Island* with Herve Villechaize.

Again, I'm going to defer to my former partner Leonard Goldberg to finish the story: "When we cast Herve in *Fantasy Island*, he was living in the seediest rooming house in Hollywood. When he got the script, he was so happy, he started to cry. Dissolve to three years later, and I get a phone call from Herve. 'Mr. Ricardo Montalban thinks he's the star of the show? He doesn't say, "THE PLANE, THE PLANE." '

"I reminded Herve that he was getting a lot of money to do the show.

" 'Mr. Ricardo Montalban gets more. Is that right?'

"Herve used to hang a sign outside his trailer that said, 'The Doctor of Sex.' When he was in his trailer, he would turn the sign around and it would say, 'The doctor is in.' Herve started having serious problems on the set. He had terrible problems with asthma, couldn't handle fame, and started bringing a gun to the set and carrying it everywhere he went."

I don't how Len or I would have handled the problems Herve had, so it's hard to relate. We eventually had to make a change on the show. It got to the point where we couldn't go forward with Herve anymore. "Contract negotiations" was the official word for our divorce, but behind the scenes I begged Herve to get help. Unfortunately, he never found happiness, and committed suicide in 1993.

Hotel was the third in our series of contemporary anthologies with a regular cast. Like *The Love Boat*, we based *Hotel* on a book, Arthur Hailey's best-selling novel of sex and scandal, which was also made into a movie in 1967 with Rod Taylor and Karl Malden. We used the real San Francisco Fairmont Hotel on Nob Hill for exteriors, even though the entire series was filmed at Warner Bros. studios in Burbank.

Anthologies were popular at the time, so here was another case where we could bring guest stars to the show. However, on *Hotel*, we made a conscious decision to be different from the others and have the regular cast more involved in the stories and be a little less anthological than *Love Boat* and *Fantasy Island.*

Marcus Welby's young sidekick James Brolin played hotel manager Peter McDermott, and Connie Sellecca, fresh from *The Greatest American Hero*, was Christine, his assistant. But the part we were really excited about was Laura Trent, the owner of the fictional St. Gregory. With great fanfare, we announced that screen legend Bette Davis would be making her TV series debut as Mrs. Trent. But a few months later tragedy struck after we completed the pilot. Bette suffered a stroke.

Hotel was sold and we had to scramble to find a replacement. Of all the actresses in the world, would you believe that the one we settled on was Anne Baxter? I didn't put two and two together at the time, but Anne costarred with Bette in *All About Eve*, as Bette's nemesis, a young woman taken in by an aging star who eventually began to overshadow her in every way.

Anne called me after reading the *Hotel* script and said she would have to talk to Bette first and get her blessing before she could say yes. "Why?" I asked.

"Aaron," she said, "I did *All About Eve* with Bette and I don't want her to think I'm doing the same thing here, by trying to take her role."

Dumb me . . . I hadn't even thought about it. Here again was life imitating art!

Anne went to the hospital to talk to Bette, which I thought was one of the greatest things I'd ever heard, and she received Bette's approval. We revised the script and gave Anne the new role of Victoria Cabot, a wealthy aristocrat who owned the hotel. Everything worked. Anne was brilliant. Then disaster hit again. Anne died three years into the series. (Bette had died in 1983.) I had lost two great women. Two great friends.

Anne was one of the sweetest ladies I'd ever worked with, and I was very upset about her death. I didn't go to the set for months afterwards. It was so weird—first Bette had a stroke, then Anne died. It was almost as if the show was cursed. Who knew what would happen next?

Story-wise, after Anne died, we shifted from the guest-stars-of-the-week concept to more of a serial about control of the hotel. We revealed that Victoria Cabot left a 51 percent share of the St. Gregory to McDermott, and 49 percent to Cabot's family. Efrem Zimbalist, Jr., joined the show as Charles Cabot and Michelle Phillips as Elizabeth Bradshaw Cabot, the new concierge. Meanwhile, McDermott made Christine the new general manager and the romance between Brolin and Sellecca's characters became a huge part of the show.

The good news is that despite all that tragedy on the set, we did have one joyous occasion as well. Heidi Bohay and Michael Spound, who played the newlywed reservations clerk and the bellhop (Megan and Dave Kendall, respectively), met on the show, fell in love, and got married in real life in 1988. I was really happy about that. It was almost like "Thanks, God, for giving us one out of three."

Fourteen

LEN AND I sold Spelling–Goldberg to Columbia Pictures in 1977. We had a great run, but both of us felt the urge to strike out on our own again. He wanted to focus his attention on movies, and we were also at a stage where neither one of us had ever made any really big money. I made little money as an actor, did better as a writer, and then even better as a writer/producer, but when we had the chance to sell our company for many millions to Columbia, we just couldn't turn it down.

I'll tell you this, though. What Len and I wouldn't give today to have those shows back. Neither of us anticipated the growth of the networking business and cable. We'd love to still own *Fantasy Island*, *Charlie's Angels*, *Hart to Hart*, and *Starsky and Hutch*.

After Len and I split, my exclusive ABC commitments reverted back to me, and I formed Aaron Spelling Productions again. However, Len and I continued to oversee the Spelling–Goldberg shows that were still on the air, like *Fantasy Island* and *Hart to Hart*.

Len went on to become an independent producer, and then joined 20th Century–Fox as president of the film division. He's now back to producing again, and has had several big hits, including *War Games* and *Sleeping with the Enemy*.

As I said, television is a collaborative medium, and I didn't remain a solo act for long. Fred Silverman put me together with E. Duke Vincent in 1977 when Fred had this crazy idea for a contemporary version of the Bowery Boys in California. He was convinced this show would solve his ratings woes at 8 P.M. on Mondays.

Duke started as a comedy writer on shows like *The Dick Van Dyke Show* and *Gomer Pyle* and after a few years in development at Warner Bros. TV had been signed to produce shows for ABC. Fred suggested that Duke join me, and I was thrilled when he accepted. We've been together ever since and he's one of the closest friends I've ever had or will have.

Fred wanted desperately to do this Bowery Boys show, so he had Duke write it and we agreed to produce it. We called it *The San Pedro Beach Bums*. It was about five young guys who lived together on a houseboat in San Pedro, a seaside suburb of Los Angeles. We tried to come up with new versions of Slip and Sach (Huntz Hall and Leo Gorcey, respectively) with characters named Boychick, Buddy, Stuf, Dancer, and Moose, but no matter how hard we tried, we just couldn't do it. The Bowery Boys on the beach just didn't work in the 1970s. Of all the shows we've done, *San Pedro* was the most frustrating, because we tried so hard, and it just didn't work.

But the good news is that amidst all of the problems of *San Pedro*, Duke and I really hit it off and established a great working relationship. We've been together for 17 years now, longer than I had with any of my previous partners. We work well together because we're opposites. I'll let him fill you in on our relationship.

"We're oil and water but we complement each other. Aaron is quiet and shy. He doesn't enjoy conflicts, but he's brilliant when dealing with networks. I'm not. As the network executives got younger, my patience wore thin. Aaron can deal with the younger executives, writers, and producers. He's a great people guy. I'm more comfortable dealing with the Teamsters, film commissions, contractors, and location politics. I'm at home in labor union negotiations, and in Los Angeles labor is big and you have to deal with them to get anything done. I charge headfirst into conflict. Wide open. Flat out. Why? Because a conflict means there will be a resolution to a problem or a situation."

After *San Pedro*, we hit the jackpot with one of my favorite shows, *Vega$*, which starred Bob Urich as suave private detective Dan Tanna. The show was created by the brilliant Michael Mann, who later went on to executive-produce *Miami Vice*, but had also written episodes of *Starsky and Hutch*.

When Duke first read the script, he was excited about the possibilities of a show about a Vegas P.I., but he felt Michael's concept was too dark. It was about the underbelly of Las Vegas, with many scenes in dark alleys and bookie joints. Duke worked on it and added glitz and glamour, so it was more like the Vegas that people know or have heard about.

Vega$ is a very special show in my heart, because it introduced me to the fantasyland of Las Vegas, one of my favorite cities. It's like a cross-section of America and I love to watch the people while Candy gambles. We discovered something years before others caught on. There's more for kids to do in Las Vegas than people realize, with swimming pools, video games, amusement parks, etc.

Before we made *Vega$*, I had only been there once. Back in the 1950s I had been approached about writing a book for Wilbur Clark, the genial host of the Desert Inn. He was essentially a front man for the people who really ran the operation.

At the time, we were broke, and I needed the job very badly. Wilbur had us drive up for the weekend and spend two days at the D.I., where Carolyn and I, convinced the job was mine, ate freely and gambled a little. Unfortunately, at the end of the weekend, Wilbur called me and said that "other sources have advised me not to write a book." Then he hung up. He also had us charged for the room!

We had $11 left, and we had to sneak out of the hotel without paying our bill. In those days you didn't have to leave credit card imprints with the front desk. Everybody was on the honor system. I don't think I've ever been so depressed. Carolyn and I didn't say a word to each other on the drive back to Los Angeles.

Every time we go to Las Vegas now, I can't help but remember the Wilbur Clark episode and how devastated I was about not getting the job to write his book. Today, whenever we stay at the beautiful suite that Henry Gluck, the chairman of Caesars World, provides for us at Caesars Palace, I can't help but retell the Wilbur Clark story to anyone who will listen. What I really mean in my heart is I'm so glad the past is behind me.

In retrospect, of course, losing the job was actually a blessing in disguise. A few weeks after our visit, Wilbur Clark was ousted from the D.I. by the Cleveland group that really ran the show. Something tells me they wouldn't have liked the book anyway. Not what I was going to write about the Vegas of that period.

So it really was quite a triumphant return for me not only to Las Vegas, but the Desert Inn, which became home base for Dan Tanna. Tanna was described by Michael Mann as "handsome without knowing it, a strange mixture of too many Vegas lights and too little sleep," who also occasionally worked for Philip "Slick" Roth, the fictional owner of the D.I. Tanna drove around Vegas in his cool red 1957 Thunderbird convertible, which became almost as famous as Bob Urich. Tanna's team included Binzer ("Binz," played by Bart Braverman), an ex-hood who tried hard but never seemed to get the job right, and Bea Travis (Phyllis Davis), Tanna's chief aide. Greg Morris (*Mission Impossible*) later joined the show as Tanna's police contact, Lt. Dave Nelson.

At first, Duke felt he could only work with two of the hotels: Howard Hughes' Desert Inn or Barron Hilton's Las Vegas Hilton. However, Barron turned him down, because they didn't want the bother of having film crews in the casino, but the D.I. needed the publicity. They had just rebuilt the hotel and added the luxurious new wing off the golf course, and figured free exposure on a prime-time network series couldn't be bad for business.

It turned out well for the D.I. After the show went on the air, Burt Cohen, who ran the D.I., called Duke frantically. "People are going crazy here," he said. "They want to see Dan Tanna. They want to see the convertible. What do I do?"

So we had life imitate art by parking a red T-Bird in front of the hotel, and told the D.I. operator to occasionally page Dan Tanna over the intercom. In turn, we paged Burt Cohen on the show and kept the illusion alive. We couldn't have Bob Urich sign autographs all day, but at least we made it seem like Dan Tanna was running around the casino on a case.

Duke not only ran *Vega$*, but he's the one who chose Bob Urich for the part. At the time, although I didn't know it, he also auditioned young Tom Selleck for the part, but he turned him down. "He wasn't ready yet" is how Duke explains his way out of that one. He contends that Tom's voice didn't match his looks. Viewers sure didn't mind the sound of his voice (or his looks) for all those years on *Magnum, P.I.* We kid Duke about Selleck a lot. Believe me, Duke and I would give our right arms to work with Tom. Well, I'd give my right arm. Duke would negotiate and only offer his left arm.

Duke eventually happened upon Bob Urich because he was looking for big, handsome guys who could also act, and as Duke says, "That's hard to find." Duke was convinced that Bob was right for the part. "You've got the guy," he kept telling me. "You've had the guy."

"Who?" I asked.

"He's in my office," said Duke, pulling a Burt Reynolds and bringing him right into my office. "I'd like to introduce you to Dan Tanna," said Duke. I didn't argue with him.

Sometimes you get lucky, and with Bob that certainly happened. Bob was a young action hero with a sense of humor. After his stint on *S.W.A.T.*, Bob appeared in two series at the same time, ABC's short-lived *Bewitched* spin-off, *Tabitha*, and *Soap*. Bob was on the first 13 episodes of Susan Harris' daytime parody, appearing as the sexy two-timing tennis pro Peter Campbell, who was thought to be murdered by Jessica.

Bob went from playing a jock cop to being a sexy leading man. He got a lot of notice for his role on *Soap*, and we had no problem selling ABC on the idea of Bob as Dan Tanna. As far as we were concerned, he was Dan Tanna.

Well, actually, that was questionable, since there was another Dan Tana, the Hollywood restaurateur who spelled his name with one "N." We didn't see any problem, but right before we were set to premiere, our legal advisors panicked and worried that we needed Tana's blessing.

I didn't think a man who ran a restaurant on the Sunset Strip would get confused with a Las Vegas detective, but I did what I was asked to do and called Dan. He was in Europe at the time on vacation. I found him at his hotel, told him of our problem, and he said, "Let me ask you one thing. Is this a sleazy guy? Is it going to hurt me and my restaurant?"

"Not at all," I said. "It's a fun show. He has great integrity. Would you like me to send you a script?"

"No, that's okay. I trust you. Go ahead."

I can't say that we helped increase his business, but we certainly affected his name recognition. The next year, when he was vacationing again in Europe, "Dan Tana" was paged at his hotel, and everyone came rushing out to see Bob Urich.

Dan told me this story when Candy and I joined Edie and Lew Wasserman for dinner at Dan's restaurant. It's one of the Wassermans' favorite places, and Dan is a great guy. So are his steaks, too!

* * *

The only hard times Candy and I ever experienced was our inability to bring children into the world. We tried desperately to adopt, but that's not easy in Los Angeles when you're Jewish and in show business. Still, after months of disappointment, one day I got a call from a cousin of mine in Dallas who knew of a newborn baby. The mother was willing to put the baby up for adoption.

Candy and I talked about it all night. At first, we were thrilled, but Candy suddenly began to cry. "What happens if we adopt this child and someday the mother wants her back?" she asked. "What will we do then?" Since the child didn't come through an adoption agency, Candy's fears were well-grounded, and we decided to pass.

Now here's the weird part. Two months after the phone call from Dallas, Candy became pregnant with Tori and five years later again with Randy. I felt as if I had visited Fantasy Island and our fantasy had become reality.

My daughter, Tori, had wanted to be an actress since she was five, and we have to thank Robert Urich for that. Candy and I took her to Las Vegas in 1980 to visit the set of *Vega$*.

We were shooting the show at the Desert Inn and Tori was fascinated with the process. "Why don't you put Tori into the shot?" Bob said. Tori was game. We made up an easy line for her to say, and the director yelled, "Action!"

Tori entered the casino and said her first line ever as an actress—"Hi, Uncle Dan." Bob picked her up and kissed her and that was it. From that day on, she wanted to act.

I didn't want to encourage her. I never wanted Tori to be an actress, because of all the rejection, but Henry Fonda once told me, "Never say no when your daughter tells you she wants to be an actress, because you'll push her right into it." I tried to listen, but Tori's mind was made up. She was going to be an actress.

Tori was born Victoria Davey Spelling. Candy thought that if Victoria was good enough for the Queen of England, it was certainly good enough for our daughter. But after a few weeks, Candy had trouble coming up with a good nickname for her. She hated Vicki, so Barbara Stanwyck suggested Tori instead, and she's been Tori ever since.

We used to take Tori to the *Vega$* set often. Shooting a show in Las Vegas was a perfect excuse to get out of town. One time we brought along my assistant Renate Kamer, now a senior vice-president in our company, and she looked in the Yellow Pages to find something for kids to do. She came upon a listing for a "Chicken Ranch," and she thought Tori would love seeing how chickens were hatched, etc. She called to ask their hours, discovered they were open 24 hours, and then asked when the best time would be to bring over a six-year-old girl. Imagine her surprise when the man on the phone told Renate what really went on there! The "Chicken Ranch" had no chickens, but they had lots of beautiful women who were visited by lots of men for lots of money.

We returned to Las Vegas in 1990 for another show about a Vegas P.I., *Hearts Are Wild*, and this time we filmed at Caesars Palace. It was a good show, but it never found an audience. That doesn't mean we've given up on Las Vegas as a setting for a TV show. I'd do another show there again in a minute. No one has really successfully portrayed on TV the glamour of the new Vegas and the incredible new hotels like the Mirage, Treasure Island, Luxor, and MGM Grand. It's a totally different place today than it was back in Dan Tanna's era. With moving walkways like they have at the Mirage and Caesars Palace, and all the new fantasy restaurants like Planet Hollywood and Hard Rock Café, Vegas is glitzier than ever.

Our last action hero was *Matt Houston*, and that came from my old friend Larry Gordon. He was under contract to produce movies at 20th Century–Fox at the time, and he brought me this script, asked me to read it, and told me it would make a fun series.

It was similar to the *Vega$* situation. The script had a lot of problems, but within the pages lay a great concept—a rich Texas oilman's son is bored, so he becomes a part-time private eye. He has so much money, he doesn't need to take any of the cases. Only the ones he truly cares about.

So Duke rewrote it and moved the rich Texan to California so he would be "a fish out of water," a concept that works well in an action series. We sold it to ABC immediately.

We chose newcomer Lee Horsley to play Matt Houston. Lee was born in Mule Shoe, Texas, but grew up in Colorado, where he studied theater at the University of Northern Colorado. He came to Hollywood and tried out for a part on the TV series *The Gangster Chronicles*. He didn't get it, but executives at Paramount liked him and cast him opposite William Conrad in the 1981 TV version of *Nero Wolfe*.

That's where we saw him, and we thought a big, tall, good-looking fella from Texas with a full mustache was the perfect candidate to play Matt. In fact, we never looked at anybody else. However, ABC didn't share our enthusiasm. We had Lee read for Lew Erlicht, who was running ABC Entertainment at the time. Lee's a big, strong guy like Bob Urich, so we didn't think it made any sense for Lee to read an action scene for Lew. Instead we had him do a love scene. And what do you think Lew said? "Too soft."

We were dumbfounded by his reaction, and tried to explain that we had purposely selected a soft scene for Lee to read. Lew agreed to let Lee audition again, and this time we did right by Lee by having him read an action scene from *Vega$*. At the end of the scene, we instructed Lee to physically pick up the actor he was working with and to throw him on Lew's lap, which he did, marvelously.

"Okay," said Lew, throwing up his hands, "you win." To this day, we all thank Lew for giving Lee another chance. You don't get too many second chances when actors read for networks, but Lew Erlicht was pretty special.

Matt Houston has a special place in all of our hearts because it was where Duke met his bride, Pamela Hensley. She had appeared on several shows, including *Marcus Welby, M.D.*, *Buck Rogers in the 25th Century*, and *240-Robert*, and on our show she played Matt's beautiful lawyer C.J. Parsons, who assisted him on his cases.

At the time, Duke had been divorced from former *Price Is Right* model Dian Parkinson for a few years and was after Pam to date him for a year before she finally gave in. Four years later they were married. Pam is bright, beautiful, and perfect for Duke. They're still married and are very, very happy.

* * *

In 1978 we were blessed with the birth of our son, Randy. He's in great shape now, but at first, it didn't look like he would be around very long. Randy was born two months prematurely and weighed in at two pounds, 14 ounces. He had to spend two months in an incubator and doctors said he probably wouldn't make it. Luckily they were wrong. He couldn't leave the hospital for two months. It was heartbreaking to visit him and have to leave him there. I don't know how Candy got through it.

Randy's the nonvisible member of the family. Just turning seventeen as this book is being written, Randy is a writer and an aspiring filmmaker. When he was young, he used to make us laugh by saying that he wanted to be a "reducer," his version of "producer," when he grew up. Whatever he chooses to do professionally, he'll be very successful. Randy is very smart and talented. Above all, he's very sensitive to other people. I love him for that.

Randy may end up producing, but in 1996 he decided to finally take the plunge and give acting a try. By the time you read this book, Randy will have followed in Tori's footsteps with two acting projects. First, in January he made his professional acting debut on an episode of *90210* as one of Steve Sanders' (Ian Ziering) stepbrothers. He is also a member of the cast of our NBC series, *Malibu Shores*, about kids from the San Fernando Valley and Malibu. Who knows where the acting will lead for Randy, but if this is the path he chooses, it's fine with me.

One of my favorite memories of Randy as a kid was on one of our rare trips out of Southern California, when we went to the White House to visit the Reagans during Ronnie's presidency. We took a train to DC and left Randy and Tori (who were then six and eleven) downstairs at the White House with our nanny. When we went upstairs to see Nancy, she asked why the kids weren't with us. We told her we were instructed to leave them downstairs. Nancy picked up the phone and ordered her secretary to bring them to her.

Nancy offered the kids cinnamon toast. Then she said, "Hey, Randy, want to go jump on Lincoln's bed?" Randy said, "Yes, please" and headed out of the room, while eating his toast. He was dropping little crumbs all over the beautiful and spotless White House carpet, and I followed behind him, picking up the crumbs and shoving them in my coat pocket so Nancy wouldn't think we messed up the room.

Randy jumped on the bed for a while, and then Nancy went to the window. Many tourists outside were holding signs that said "Happy birthday" because it was Nancy's birthday, and she stood there and waved to people. The next thing you knew, little six-year-old Randy was standing next to her, and he was waving, too. What a picture!

Randy has a few favorite memories as well: "There was a father-and-son event at my school, and Dad and I did all the games together, like egg toss and sack hops. When he threw the egg, Dad slipped and broke his foot. We were scheduled to go to Las Vegas a week later, and he didn't want to let my mom down, so he still went, even though he was in a cast and a wheelchair. I was pushing him through the hotel, and we went over a big bump, and Dad flew out of the wheelchair, ten feet across the floor. I thought I'd killed him! Boy, was I happy when he started laughing!

"Our house was always very special around the holidays. We always had a big Christmas party for Dad's cast and staff, and Santa Claus would always be there. I never questioned why he was there, or how he seemed to know so much about me. Tori and I both thought he was real for the longest time. Every year Santa gave us presents on Christmas Eve, and I thought that it was so nice that my parents went to the extra effort to do that for us. Naturally, we celebrated Chanukah, too. Talk about being lucky kids."

Fifteen

I'VE BEEN blessed with at least one smash hit for every decade. In the 1960s it was *The Mod Squad*, *Charlie's Angels* in the 1970s, and, of course, nothing was bigger for me than *Dynasty* in the 1980s: the story of greed, lust, and unhappiness amongst the rich in Colorado. Here's how it all started on the three-hour *Dynasty* pilot, created and written by the very talented Esther and Richard Shapiro.

> EXT. ROCKIES AND DENVER SKYLINE—HELICOPTER SHOT—DAY
>
> MOVING HELICOPTER SHOT from beautiful Rocky Mountains to Denver skyline.
>
> EXT. HELICOPTER SHOT—CARRINGTON MANSION—DAY
>
> and GO IN on Blake Carrington's limousine driving from the carriage house to the front of the mansion. As the car pulls up by the front door, SUPERIMPOSE MAIN TITLE and CREDITS.
>
> NT. AN ALCOVE—JOSEPH
>
> JOSEPH, the head butler, the major domo, the man who from his impregnable seriousness, from his just slightly imperious manner, is charged with running this entire household, sits at a desk, in his shirt sleeves, sorting bills and punching an adding machine. Now the INTERCOM PHONE on his desk BUZZES. Joseph picks it up . . .
>
> JOSEPH
>
> Yes?
>
> (listens; then brusquely)
>
> Thank you, Michael.

Joseph hangs up the phone, gets up, moves away from his desk, pulling his jacket on as he goes . . .

SOME SHOTS—JOSEPH

moving along the hallways—to see this magnificent house for the CAMERA UNDER TITLES.

INT. THE LIBRARY—DOORS

A KNOCK; then the doors open and Joseph is standing there.

JOSEPH
(announces)
Michael has brought the car
around, sir.

THE ROOM

to include BLAKE CARRINGTON at his desk where he has been working all morning. (If anyone were expecting to see some pinched John Paul Getty or a corpulent H. L. Hunt . . . forget it. Blake Carrington is as handsome as a movie star in his thousand-dollar Brioni suit. If he has a significant flaw, it is simply that Blake Carrington wants what he wants . . . and gets it. Which, from his singular perspective, is hardly a flaw at all. Besides, in his view, to paraphrase yet another laissez-faire philosopher: What's good for Blake Carrington is good for Denver-Carrington Inc. And what's good for Denver-Carrington is good for everybody. Nor is that entirely cynical sloganeering. Blake is about as honest as he needs to be; generous as his tax attorneys suggest he is fiscally adroit; loyal enough to beget the loyalty he requires; crafty and dangerous as a mongoose when backed against some intercorporational wall; sexually proficient as a Masters and Johnson graduate; and taken altogether—charming as all-be-damned.)

BLAKE
Thank you, Joseph.

Blake shoves some papers into a large, already bulging briefcase—the portable office of a man whose thoughts are never far removed from his work. Snaps it shut. Joseph, with a certainty that bespeaks a familiar procedure, a congenial ritual, steps over, helps Blake into his jacket, hands him the briefcase. And the two start for the door.

SOME SHOTS—BLAKE AND JOSEPH

marching along more hallways, past priceless antiques and tapestries, Joseph a respectful half-pace behind.

EXT. FRONT OF THE HOUSE

The front door is opened by an unseen butler; Blake and Joseph march out.

THE CAR—MICHAEL

moves quickly to open a rear door for Blake. Blake slides in easily. Michael closes the door with military precision and hurries around to the driver's side.

ANOTHER ANGLE—THE CAR
starts away from the house . . .

SOME SHOTS—THE CAR
driving out along the Carrington estate's private road.

THE GATES
swing open; Blake's limousine drives through.

INT. THE CAR—BLAKE

His briefcase open, work spread out on the desk in front of him; this is a man who wastes not a moment. He speaks to Michael without looking up.

BLAKE
We'll be stopping by Miss Jennings'
apartment on the way, Michael.

MICHAEL
Yes, sir.

A moment while Michael puzzles over the instruction. Then he asks . . . carefully . . .

MICHAEL
(continuing)
Excuse me, Mr. Carrington, but . . .

that doesn't seem to be the kind
of party you'd be invited to.

BLAKE
(smiles)
I wasn't.

INT. KRYSTLE'S APARTMENT—CLOSE—CAKE—DAY
A sheet cake decorated with a cartoon automobile; groom and bride with flowing veil inside; tin cans tied to the back and a dog nipping at the tires. The inscription reads: Happy Shower, Krystle—we love you! In the room O.S., a DIN OF FEMALE CHATTER punctuated by BURSTS OF LAUGHTER. PULL BACK TO INCLUDE the room now, decorated for a bridal shower. Twisted ribbons of crepe paper run to the corners; balloons dance on the ends of strings taped to a ceiling. KRYSTLE JENNINGS sits on the floor under a suspended rain umbrella done up with pompoms and tassels.

(If Blake Carrington's taste in art is superb, his taste in women has got to be even better. Because Krystle is, by any measure, exquisite. And beauty is not even her best quality. She is bright and sensitive and decent, though with some small qualification on bright. She is also a whit unworldly—particularly in the Carrington world of high style, high society, very high finance, and not so high morality. What Krystle doesn't realize at this juncture, however, is that she has the capacity to learn all of those things. And more.)

The floor is strewn with wrapping paper and opened presents—some practical, some gaggish. Fancy underwear, a tennis racquet . . . nothing outrageously expensive. And, surrounding Krystle on the couch, on chairs, or sitting on the floor, Krystle's FRIENDS: five or six of them, working women like herself. Most of them Krystle's age; one or two older or younger. From the gifts, from the laughter, this is, in fact, more bachelor party than shower.

With the LAST CREDIT, Krystle is just taking a handmade, old-fashioned silk and lace patchwork quilt from its box; holds it up. The laughter, the chatter fall off as the women react in awe to this gift. GO IN CLOSER on Krystle, very moved as she lowers the quilt. She turns to CHARLOTTE, on her knees beside Krystle, helping with the gifts.

KRYSTLE
(near speechless)

You must have worked . . .
months . . . on this.

Charlotte, a little brassier than the others, tries—with small success, however—to play away from the sentimentality.

CHARLOTTE
Six; but who's counting?

KRYSTLE
All those weekends when you
were too busy to go to the movies . . .
or out to dinner . . . you were . . .

Charlotte gives her an embarrassed, but pleased, little shrug.

KRYSTLE
(continuing)
Charlotte . . . yo' . . .

Out of words, Krystle puts her arms around Charlotte, hugs close.

CHARLOTTE
Hey . . . you gave me bed and board
when my life was falling apart.
I won't forget that; not ever.

THE DOOR
as Charlotte steps over, opens it. Michael is standing there, cap tucked under his arm, a small wrapped package in his hand.

KRYSTLE
(a little surprised)
Hello, Michael . . .

Michael takes a step into the room, holds out the package.

MICHAEL
Miss Jennings . . .
Mr. Carrington would like you
to have this with his compliments.

KRYSTLE
Where is he?
Why didn't he come up?

MICHAEL
He's waiting for me downstairs.
(half-smile)
He thought it's safer down there.

As Krystle moves toward the window . . .

FOLLOWING CHARLOTTE

takes the gift from Michael. MELANIE comes up, eyes Michael appreciatively.

MELANIE
(just slightly lascivious)
Would you like some punch . . . a cookie?

MICHAEL
No thank you, miss.
I've got to run.

He turns to start out but Melanie blocks his way.

MELANIE
What time do you get off, Michael?

CHARLOTTE
(amused)
Leave him alone,
Melanie—he's got work to do.

MELANIE
I know; it's the uniform—
makes me crazy.

Charlotte hooks Melanie by the arm, moves her off across the room.

Michael smiles, starts out.

MARIAN
who has gone to the window with Krystle, turns back into the room, whispers, awed, to the others . . .

MARIAN
It's him. He's down there.

A hush comes over the room. The women move gingerly toward the window.

CHARLOTTE AND MELANIE

start to move to the window with the others. As they pass, PAN DOWN to Doris, the only one who doesn't seem to be interested in Blake Carrington. Or anything in the room for that matter. She is staring down into *The Joy of Sex* with scandalized fascination.

ALICE
He's gorgeous.

LISA eases up to Krystle.

LISA
Hey, Krystle, you want to trade?
I'll give you Marvin, the kids . . .
and I'll toss in six months free
diaper service. What do you say?

ALICE
(repeats)
Gorgeous, that's what I'd say.
I'd take him even if he didn't
have two hundred million dollars.

LISA
And the biggest house in Colorado.
And his own football team . . .

DOWN SHOT—BLAKE

If Blake Carrington has a weakness (and he probably doesn't), it is Krystle, whom he cherishes even beyond fast cars, fine horses, his pro football team, and—God help him—oil leases.

With Michael coming around, getting into the car, Blake leans just slightly out of his window, smiles, blows a small kiss up to . . .

UP ANGLE—KRYSTLE, THE WOMEN

in the window, working to keep at least the appearance of decorum. Krystle waves gently.

EXT. THE CAR

drives off.

INT. KRYSTLE'S APARTMENT

turns with the others from the window; reacts to Margaret who has sunk down into a chair and is snuffling. Krystle hurries over to her along with a couple of the others, puts her arms around Margaret.

KRYSTLE
Margaret . . . what is it?
what's the matter?

MARGARET
(finds her voice)
I'm gonna miss you.
We're all . . . gonna miss you.

The room turns strangely quiet. Krystle looks from Margaret to the others. And back to Margaret.

KRYSTLE
What are you talking about?
We're friends; we'll always be
friends. We're all still going to
see each other.

The continued quiet in the room says that none of them really believe it. Which unsettles Krystle.

KRYSTLE
(continuing)
C'mon . . . I'm not joining
the Foreign Legion—I'm
getting married.

More discomfort.

KRYSTLE
(continuing)
To begin with, I'll see you all
at the wedding. And then after
that you'll come up to the house,
every weekend.
(beat)
What the heck good is forty-eight
rooms if I can't have my friends over?

Dynasty was a big hit because it showed that rich people have as many problems as poor folks, and there's nothing TV viewers love more than to see rich people skewered. Isn't that why we love to read about the Kennedys and the Royal family of England?

Like *Charlie's Angels*, *Dynasty* was pure camp. Women wore fashionable hats and designer gowns and fought continuously with each other. There were long-lost sons and mothers, lost babies, kings and queens of foreign lands; illegitimate offsprings, divorces, secret pasts, insatiable sex lives, beautiful mansions, and sleek cars.

Dynasty was responsible for showing that people over forty still fall in love and have sex. We had a terrific cast, headed by John Forsythe, Joan Collins, and Linda Evans. The show was developed as our answer to CBS' *Dallas*. Prime-time serials were in then, and ABC wanted one of their own. Esther Shapiro, a former vice-president of programming of ABC, left the network with a commitment to get a show on the air and she came to us to do the show with her.

Originally it was titled *Oil*, and we hired actor George Peppard to play the lead, millionaire oilman Blake Carrington. But after a few days of filming, it was clear we had made a mistake and had to let George go. He was a fine actor, but just wasn't right for the part. He played Blake much softer than we envisioned him. George felt Blake shouldn't be strong with his children, but that's what the character was all about.

I called my friend John Forsythe, who had been the voice of Charlie for me on *Charlie's Angels*, and was best-known for movies and his role in the sitcom *Bachelor Father* as Bentley Gregg, the playboy uncle raising his teenage niece. John was a former president of the Screen

Actors Guild and wasn't eager to replace another actor, and we really had to sell him. At the time, he was starring in the syndicated nature series *World of Survival*, but John's real trouper, and got to the set for us within a day. He flew in from Arizona without even reading the script.

I hadn't seen Linda since the *Big Valley* days. Like Farrah and Jackie on *Angels*, Linda started out in commercials and did guest spots on many 1960s shows, like *My Favorite Martian*, *The Adventures of Ozzie and Harriet*, and *Bachelor Father*, where she played a girlfriend of Bentley's niece. Her big break was being cast as Audra, Barbara Stanwyck's daughter on *The Big Valley*. After that show went off the air, Linda moved to Europe for a while. In the 1970s she returned and played James Franciscus's partner on the 1977 TV series *Hunter* and costarred with Steve McQueen in the 1980 film *Tom Horn*.

When Linda came into my office to read for the part, we all knew instantly she was Krystle Carrington. She brought a vulnerability to the role that could have easily become bland, compared to others. Krystle was the heroine of *Dynasty*, the fair-haired, fair-eyed second wife, the only person on the show with 100 percent good intentions. In other words, an angel in flowing, broad-shouldered gowns.

I didn't really get to know Linda well during the *Big Valley* days, but was well aware that Barbara Stanwyck was crazy about her. I always said that Linda was a combination of flowers—she could be a rose or a sunflower. She's sweet beyond words.

The show that *Dynasty* was in the beginning bore no relation to what it became. It was originally a soap set in the Rocky Mountains, with much of the action taking place in the oilfields, and with characters like Matthew Blaisdel (Krystle's former lover, played by Bo Hopkins) and Walter Lankershim (Dale Robertson) having prominent roles. But the first 13 weeks were very tough. Audiences just didn't care until we realized we needed to shift gears and become a glossy soap about the rich and focus more on the women.

What really turned it around was the introduction of our J.R., super-bitch Alexis Colby, Blake's former wife. Viewers love a good villain, and Esther and Richard wrote her brilliantly. How mean was Alexis? Well, when her husband-to-be (an arch-rival of Blake's, of course) had a heart attack during sex on their prenuptial night, she worried that the wedding might be off and she would miss out on inheriting his millions.

Alexis and Krystle were famous for their cat-fights. During our nine seasons, they duked it out in a lily pond, a mud puddle, a beauty parlor, and a burning cabin, and once even engaged in a feather-filled pillow fight.

We originally had our eyes set on Italian legend Sophia Loren for a role on *Dynasty*, and in fact spent many weeks negotiating with her husband. But we couldn't work things out. I don't think Sophia was ready to do television, which operates at a different speed than movies. The hours spent on the set are also much longer. Sophia was still a big movie star, and it didn't make any sense for her to plunge into TV at the time.

I hit upon the idea of British actress Joan Collins for Alexis after she played Cleopatra on an episode of *Fantasy Island*. She camped up the role so beautifully that I was blown away. Others, however, didn't agree with me about Joan as Alexis. They all thought I was crazy. "She's a B-movie actress who never made it," said one. "How are you going to explain her British accent?" ABC asked. "Her children don't have British accents." Simple: Alexis went to live in England after her divorce from Blake. The Shapiros and Douglas Cramer finally agreed with me, and we finally convinced ABC, luckily for them and us.

Joan was best-known as the sexy British movie actress of the 1960s who had also appeared in the States on such shows as *Batman* (as the Siren), *Star Trek*, and *Space: 1999*. When she joined *Dynasty*, she made a smashing entrance in our second season premiere as the surprise new villainess. At the end of the first season, when Blake was accused of murdering the lover of his gay son, Steven (TV's first ongoing gay character, I might add), a mysterious, veiled woman swept into the courtroom. Not until the fall did viewers learn her identity—it was none other than Blake's former wife, the glamorous and very vengeful Alexis, who, in contrast to Krystle's white patterns, was usually dressed in black.

Our only problem, once we hired Joan, was that she wouldn't be available for four months. But we believed so strongly in her that we agreed to wait and on that first-season cliffhanger we had an extra in dark glasses standing in for Alexis. It sounds like a stupid thing to do, but it worked and it was worth it.

If anyone ever proved that life began at 40, it was Joan. In 1983, at the age of 50, she posed seminude for *Playboy*, and the issue was an instant sellout. In 1985, *TV Guide* named her the most beautiful woman on television. Those mud fights obviously paid off.

Some observations on Joan: She's a real character, very funny and carefree. The press always reported that she was tough to deal with. The truth is that if a man says something, he's strong, but if it comes from a woman, she's a bitch, and that's just not fair. Joan was a real trouper for the show, but she's also a character, and that's the fun of Joan. She has an attitude that if you don't know her may come off as haughty, but it's all an act. She puts people on beautifully.

I think Joan carries some of Alexis with her when she goes out, and who wouldn't? It's a great, campy character. People confuse Alexis with Joan because she's so damn good at it. But take it from me—she's not Alexis.

We'd love to work with Joan again. In fact, when we created *Models, Inc.*, we narrowed our choices down to two actresses to play the head of the modeling agency: Joan and Linda Gray. Fox said we could go with either one, but Joan made the decision for us. She was unavailable when we wanted to start.

Heather Locklear started with us on *Dynasty*, and became my good luck charm. We were looking for a great young vamp to play sexy Sammy Jo, who Blake hired to somehow "cure" Steven of his homosexuality. Of course, that's ridiculous, but if anyone could do that, it would be my Heather. Later, Blake accepted his son for what he was, as any father should do.

Heather, who was 19 at the time, came in and read for us in an open audition, and there was just something about her that knocked us all out. She had the classic California look—blond hair and blue eyes, which was just what we were looking for.

Before *Dynasty*, Heather had appeared in a few commercials and an episode each of *CHIPs* and *240-Robert*. She joined *Dynasty* in its second season, and became so popular that I put her into another one of our productions, *T. J. Hooker*. She became the first actress in the history of the medium to act in two shows for the same network simultaneously.

When we started with Heather, she didn't know whether or not she really wanted to be an actress, but she started working really hard and showing great growth in every episode. She just got better and better.

Hooker starred William Shatner as a sergeant who lent advice to young police rookies Stacy (Heather) and Vince (Adrian Zmed). And since *Dynasty* was a serial with a huge ensemble cast, it was easy to arrange the production schedule so that Heather could work two days on *Dynasty* and three days on *Hooker*. So doing two shows at once wasn't impossible. Hard, but not impossible.

As I said, Heather's my good luck charm. She brought me great luck on *Hooker* and *Dynasty*, and, as I'll explain later, even greater luck with *Melrose Place*. *T. J. Hooker* happened when Len and I had lunch a few years after we split up. We were sitting there talking about the old days, and Len said, "Do you think the old magic could be brought back again?"

We both decided to see if we could do it one more time, and we came up with an idea for a show about a veteran detective who worked with young recruits. We called ABC and said, "We're about to offer you something as rare as a Picasso or a Monet."

"What's that?"

"The last Spelling–Goldberg show." I laughed.

"Hurry on over."

And we sold them *T. J. Hooker* on the spot. When we made our deal to sell our shows to Columbia, we gave up our interests in all of them except for *Hooker*. Len thought we should hold onto it because of Shatner (a huge star in syndication, thanks to *Star Trek*), Heather's fame on *Dynasty*, and the fact that everyone wore a police uniform, so the show couldn't age. We've received some very nice checks for the show over the years, so chalk one up for the good guys.

But back to *Dynasty*. Another major star of the show was Nolan Miller and his incredible clothes. We spent a fortune just on the costumes alone, and no one had ever seen extravagant clothes like that on television. The principal actors would change clothes sometimes as often as six or seven times per episode.

Dynasty was filmed mostly on the 20th Century–Fox lot, but we shot interiors at a 48-room mansion in San Mateo, California, that was also used for the film *Heaven Can Wait.*

Steven Carrington is considered to be prime-time's first openly gay character. ABC was worried about that when the show began, but they didn't give us any problems—as long as there was no kissing. Tony Thomopolous was president of ABC at the time, and he had great vision. He didn't let the Broadcast Standards department interfere.

Steven had a lot of problems with his sexuality. First he was gay, then he decided he wasn't and married Sammy Jo. Then he realized he truly was gay and living a lie. This may sound farfetched now, but it wasn't then. A lot of gay men have gotten married and had children and then realized this was not what they wanted their life to be, and faced reality. You have to remember that when we did *Dynasty*, gays were afraid to come out of the closet in real life. Steven Carrington may have been the first gay man to come out of the closet on a prime-time series.

One great line summed it all up for us. Remember, this was 1981, and Blake came to see his son, who was now living with his gay lover. "I've been wrong," Blake said. "I'm glad you found someone who loves you as much as I do." That was a hell of a thing to say at the time, and we were all very proud of what we did.

Cut to a few years later, when we were making *Heartbeat* for ABC, a medical show about a group of women who operated their own clinic. One of the doctors was a lesbian, and we had a scene where she was going to dance with her lover. ABC demanded we cut the scene.

That didn't make headlines, however, like in 1994 when we wanted to end the *Melrose Place* season with our gay character, Doug, kissing his lover. The only run-in we've ever had with Fox on *Melrose* was over the kiss. We certainly weren't happy we had to cut it, and we received the blame for doing so.

We've had more than one gay kiss cut. You just never heard of the other instances. I wish we had more power, but TV is a commercial medium. It's not like a movie where you pay to enter the theater. The network buys the show from us and then has to get sponsors to pay for the show. To think that gay lovers, men or women, do not kiss is stupid. But it's not the network that rebels against showing gay and lesbian characters doing what comes naturally to them, it's the sponsors. The sales department says, "Hey, I can't sell this show," and the network has a tremendous multimillion-dollar loss, so they really have no choice. It's a rotten situation, but I do think it's getting better.

One of the big *Dynasty* moments occurred when we hired Rock Hudson to do a short stint as horsebreeder Daniel Reece, Krystle's lover. He was a great name for us, and we thought having him there would be good for ratings and publicity. We never realized it would be his final acting role and that he would be dead shortly after his episodes aired.

We hired Rock for eight episodes. He filmed them and all seemed fine. We thought he was a little too thin, but that's it. And then a few weeks after he completed his work, we read in Army Archerd's column in *Daily Variety* that Rock was dying of AIDS. Panic set in. Nobody then knew anything about AIDS. The media went crazy, and our cast and crew were obviously very concerned. It was the first time AIDS had hit so close to home for any of us. We were covered so much in the press, it was like our set was entirely contaminated by AIDS. The cast and staff were absolutely stunned because Rock was one of the nicest people in the world and we all adored him.

We had doctors come to the set and ask questions. "Did he ever cut himself? Did he kiss anybody?" Of course he did. He kissed Linda. And that shook everybody up. I'm proud to say that Linda was the calmest. She just said, "I believe in something stronger than this. If it was meant to be, it was meant to be."

Sadly, none of us ever spoke to Rock again. He flew to that hospital in France and only saw his closest friends, like Doris Day and Elizabeth Taylor. It took all of us a long time to get over this terrible tragedy.

It was on *Dynasty* that we started the trend of bringing in name actors like Rock Hudson, Ali McGraw, George Hamilton, Billy Dee Williams, and Diahann Carroll, as a way to wreak havoc for our characters or create new love interests. We thought it would be a great way to get actors who didn't want to sign five-year contracts, but who would like to work a few weeks with us. We now do that all the time on *Melrose Place*, where actors like Kathy Ireland, Jasmine Guy, Patrick Muldoon, Perry King, Antonio Sabato, Jr., Parker Stevenson, and Dan Cortes have all come in and out of that little apartment complex in West Hollywood.

Dynasty was also our first show where we changed actors midstream and had new actors replace old ones, instead of creating new characters. When we and Al Corley weren't seeing eye to eye, we had Steven Carrington sent into isolation in Indonesia, where he was injured in an explosion and forced to undergo plastic surgery. The next thing viewers knew, Jack Coleman was our new Steven, and he just looked a little different.

After three seasons, Pamela Sue Martin wanted to leave *Dynasty* to get married and we didn't stand in her way. The Steven switch worked so well, but this time we didn't feel the need for any big trips to the hospital for plastic surgery. We just brought in Emma Samms, and she became Fallon. They do things like this all the time on daytime soap operas, so it really wasn't a big deal. Viewers get used to new actors very quickly.

About this time the network asked us to do a spin-off of *Dynasty*, and *The Colbys* was born. It was a series about the side of the family that originated with Alexis' short-lived husband, the uncle of Jeff (John James), Fallon's husband.

Set in Los Angeles, the principal players included Charlton Heston as Jeff's father, corporate magnate Jason Colby; Stephanie Beacham as his beautiful young wife, Sable; Katherine Ross as Francesca, Sable's sister, Jason's ex-wife, and Jeff's mother; Barbara Stanwyck as Jason's sensible older sister, Constance, the half-owner of Colby Enterprises; and Ricardo Montalban as our Alexis type, Zachary Powers, the chief villain who was always plotting against the Colbys. And from *Dynasty* we moved John James (Jeff) and Emma Samms (Fallon) to *The Colbys* full time.

Star power wasn't enough. The Shapiros did another great job, but *The Colbys* just didn't catch on. I guess it was just too much of a good thing, but I still think it was one of the best casts ever assembled. I think *The Colbys* was too similar to *Dynasty*. Had we done a show about the downstairs maid who married the son who was then disowned by his wealthy family, we might have had a chance.

* * *

A little later, *Dynasty* finally came to an end. After nine great years it was time to sign off. Thanks to the efforts of Esther and Richard Shapiro, who had the original idea and stayed with us all the way, *Dynasty* had a fantastic run. It is still playing all over the world and just recently it debuted in Russia. I can't wait to hear John, Joan, Linda, and Heather dubbed in Russian!

I've been very unlucky with sitcoms. But in 1986, I thought I had found the surefire formula for success. Hire America's best-loved comedienne, surround her with her favorite costars and writers, and let her do what she does best. The show was the ill-fated *Life with Lucy*, and on paper, it sounded so right.

Why should America's best clown be sitting at home playing cards every day when viewers still loved her and watched her reruns every day? So, after an absence of 12 years, we put Lucy back on prime-time, reunited her with her old costar Gale Gordon (Mr. Mooney from *Here's Lucy*), and got her old *I Love Lucy* writers, Madelyn Pugh and Bob Carroll, to write the show. ABC scheduled us on Saturdays at 8 P.M.

Lucy Barker was a free-spirited grandmother who decided to take over the family hardware business after her husband died. But her late husband's partner—you guessed it, the Gale Gordon character—didn't like Lucy's way of doing business. There was plenty of slapstick, sight gags, and Lucy getting into lots of trouble. Oh, and it was also a critical and ratings BOMB!

I had known Lucy from acting on her show back in the 1950s, and Duke had worked on the Desilu lot in the 1960s. She still looked great and was as energetic as ever. Lucy was literally doing stuff she did on the old show. She'd run across the living room and kitchen in high heels at top speed and do physical comedy. And while it didn't exhaust her at all, it ended up frightening the audience. Audiences were scared that at her age she would get hurt. Instead of laughing when she climbed up a tall ladder, the studio audience would gasp in fear. When we heard that first gasp, we knew we were dead.

We all felt really badly, because Lucy wanted the show to be a hit so much. At the time, Andy Griffith had just come back in *Matlock*,

Angela Lansbury was just starting *Murder, She Wrote*, Betty White and Bea Arthur were big hits as *The Golden Girls*, and Carroll O'Connor was doing *In the Heat of the Night*, so she didn't see any reason why there wouldn't be room for Lucy in prime-time. Older actors weren't being shunned by Madison Avenue at the time as, unfortunately, they are now.

We all valiantly tried to re-create *I Love Lucy* and it was a terrible mistake. She should have played Lucy today, perhaps as an Auntie Mame grandmother. She would have been great, but once we had started, it was impossible to change directions. I loved Lucy, and I take full blame for the show not working. Well, I learned one thing in a hurry. Comedy is no laughing matter.

Sixteen

BILL HAYES, my late business manager, came to me in 1980 with a question: Had I ever thought of taking the company public? Sure, I had thought about it, but I didn't know how to make it happen. Many companies were finding it easy at the time to raise lots of cash by selling stock and this was one mountain I had never climbed. It meant the brass ring for my partners Duke Vincent, Doug Cramer, and myself. Capital to grow the company beyond our wildest dreams. However, it was just a beginning. The best was yet to come.

Bill put me in touch with Wall Street's Michael Milkin and Ace Greenburg, and the next thing we knew, they had raised over $100 million for the company. After going public, I hired two executives who had just left Viacom, Jules Haimowitz and Ronald Lightstone, in an attempt to beef up the company. But the man who really changed everything for us was Carl Linder, who owned Great American Communications of Cincinnati, the umbrella organization for the Taft TV stations, Hanna-Barbera, and Worldvision, a major syndication concern. We found that we desperately needed a syndication company, and we had our eyes set on Worldvision, which distributed ABC's shows and many of ours, including *The Love Boat*. We wanted to buy Worldvision, but we didn't have enough cash. So we merged, and Carl bought 49 percent of Aaron Spelling Productions. Carl and his son, Craig, were great partners, and I shall always be grateful to them.

And then Blockbuster walked into my life.

After we had been together a few years, Carl called me and said he was thinking of selling to Blockbuster. In my contract with him, it said that I could leave if he sold out to a new party without my approval. I was very leery about a change in ownership, but Carl and Craig flew out from Cincinnati and brought Blockbuster executives Wayne Huizenga and Steven Berrard over to my house to explain what they wanted to do. After meeting with Wayne and Steve, it took me all of 30 minutes to decide "I'm yours."

I had heard of Blockbuster, but I had no idea just how big they were or how fast they were growing. Steve and Wayne told me how they wanted to get involved in software, that there would be great synergy with us, how they could help push our new shows in their stores, where, for example, if we were launching a new show, they could promote it on in-store monitors. This all sounded great for us.

Wayne, who had made his fortune in a company called Waste Management, bought into the Blockbuster chain in 1987 when they had 19 video stores in and around Dallas, Texas. Then the company had a total market value of $32 million. By the time he closed the sale of the company to Viacom, Inc., nearly seven years later, Blockbuster's market value was $8.4 billion, a 247-fold increase in a company that added more than a billion dollars a year to its asset value. As of this writing, Blockbuster has nearly 3,500 stores in North America and plans to have over 5,000 retail outlets by the end of the decade.

Once we became a unit of Blockbuster, we had more on our mind than simply selling new shows to the networks. Now we were part of a worldwide video chain with a big hunger for movies. Then Blockbuster bought Republic Pictures in exchange for Spelling stock. We could then combine their library with ours, because, as Dick Powell always said, "the only positive thing about our business is the negative." Blockbuster also urged us to get into the movie business, and we formed Spelling Films International, where we co-financed films like Robert Altman's *The Player* and *Short Cuts* in exchange for foreign theatrical, video, and TV rights. Blockbuster also bought the Virgin Interactive video game and computer software firm and merged Virgin into Spelling Entertainment. We also own Tele-UNO, a Spanish-language satellite channel for Latin America, the Hamilton Projects licensing company, and Big Ticket Television, a production company run by former Warner Bros. executive Larry Lyttle. All told, we employ over 900 full-time employees, plus all the crews, staffs, and stars working on our shows. It seemed like overnight we had gone from a small independent company to a big conglomerate!

In September 1994, Viacom bought Blockbuster. So we became a part of the company that also owns Paramount Pictures; the MTV, Nickelodeon, and Showtime cable networks; theaters; the Simon &

Schuster publishing company and all its subsidiaries, and Paramount's Great America theme parks. I've known about Viacom Chairman Sumner Redstone for years, and we were very happy to be a part of his group.

But suddenly, a new twist was added. While we were writing this book, Viacom announced that they were going to sell our company. The press release came out August 14, 1995 and caught all of us off guard. By the time you read this, who knows who will own us!

STOP THE PRESSES

All of the above was written months ago, and we were just told yesterday that Viacom has taken our company off the market, and we will remain a member of the Viacom Family! I'm so thrilled, and I have just signed a new contract to stay with Sumner and his group.

Now back to the past. For years critics snidely called ABC "Aaron's Broadcasting Company." Yes, we were responsible for a good chunk of their schedule, but had nothing to do with that silly expression.

My relationship greatly changed with ABC after Elton Rule passed away and Capital Cities took over. I had a wonderful working relationship with Elton and fellow ABC execs Fred Pierce, Leonard Goldenson, Tony Thomopolous, and Lew Erlicht. But when they left, it was all over. A newly hired president of entertainment, who shall go nameless, told the *Los Angeles Times* upon his appointment that his ABC wouldn't be "Aaron's Broadcasting Company" anymore. After I saw that, I knew it was time for my then agent and friend Bill Haber to call ABC chairman Tom Murphy and get me out of my contract. And I must say that Tom was very gracious and fair with me.

It felt like a divorce when I split up with ABC. I'd been with them for a long time. When ABC canceled *Heartbeat* and *Dynasty* at the end of the 1988–9 TV season, I went my first TV season since 1960 without at least one show on the lineup. My seventeen-year association with ABC had come to an end, and *Variety* announced it in the cruelest manner possible: "Spelling's Dynasty Over" . . . and they didn't mean the series.

I was so depressed. I would have quit, but I like TV too much. I love the immediacy of it, the ability to reach so many people at one time. I just couldn't walk away. Besides, the company had just gone public and I wasn't about to take the money and run, deserting all the shareholders who had invested in us.

Luckily for me, I had Brandon Tartikoff in my corner.

After I announced the end of the ABC deal, then NBC Entertainment chief Brandon Tartikoff was the first person to call me. He asked me to come over and see him at NBC in Burbank. So I begged my then agent Bill Haber to drive me there because I wasn't sure where it was. I had never been to NBC before.

We drove over and walked into the reception area, where Brandon was waiting for me at the elevator. His people rolled out a red carpet and a brass band started playing "The Yellow Rose of Texas." Then we went up the elevator, and everybody in the offices stood and applauded as we walked down the hallway to Brandon's office.

The depression over the breakup with ABC ended right there. It was one of the greatest days of my life. I felt 50 feet high. In Hollywood, insecurity is boundless. No matter what you do, how little or how much, you're graded on your last show.

Ironically, my first project with NBC wasn't a TV show, but a little theatrical film called *Satisfaction*, starring Justine Bateman (of NBC's *Family Ties*) and two newcomers named Julia Roberts and Liam Neeson.

Brandon and I went over to Fox, to talk to then studio chief Leonard Goldberg (small world, isn't it?) about release plans, and I mentioned to Brandon an idea I had for a TV series about student nurses, whom I had lectured to many times in Dallas. Brandon bought it on the spot. But we did realize that the title *Student Nurses* wouldn't work. It sounded like a porno movie. So he came up with *Nightingales* instead. And my good friend Suzanne Pleshette starred as the director of the student nurse program.

In fact, we debuted at number one, just like *Charlie's* did, with a 33 share. But while the formula worked at first, it also backfired. On *Charlie's* we were spoofing the private detective business, and it's not like that's a business that many young people go into. *Nightingales* had sexy overtones and nursing groups protested the show. Loudly. They wrote letters to advertisers. We listened to the criticism, and agreed with the American Nursing Association to change direction.

"Although we will still deal with the personal lives of the student nurses, we intend to correct the things that we now realize have been offensive to the nursing profession." I said this at a joint press conference with the American Nursing Association. They quickly endorsed the show for our new direction. But it was too late. The controversy scared away advertisers and we were canceled after 13 weeks.

Looking back, I think we made two fatal mistakes. First of all, when we got a letter from the nursing association complaining about the locker room scenes, I wanted to do something about it, but NBC and my public relations people disagreed. "This is good for the show," they said. "Controversy ups ratings."

It didn't. The nursing group went to the sponsors and convinced them to boycott the show, and things just snowballed from there. I finally called the nursing association and discovered that there were things they also liked about *Nightingales*. The show had done wonders for recruiting student nurses. So I agreed to make changes, and started calling advertisers to tell them. I talked to Lee Iacocca at Chrysler and he agreed to stick with the show, but by then it was too late. Brandon checked with the NBC sales department, and they just couldn't sell the show anymore. He was forced to cancel *Nightingales*.

I wish I could tell you we did something terribly wrong outside of some locker room scenes, which we didn't really need. We didn't have huge sex scenes, but we did have romance in the show. Anyone who thinks student nurses don't go out on dates and meet men is silly. If you compare *Nightingales* to what's on TV today, including *Melrose Place*, you'd laugh.

Nightingales was axed in April 1989 and we didn't get another show on the air until September 1990 with *Beverly Hills 90210*.

During that long year of living hell, people wrote me off, but I was dormant, not dead. In this strange town of Hollywood, you notice it mostly when you don't get invited to premieres. When you go someplace, the photographers turn around and look the other way. It was really weird.

I was bored stiff and driving Candy crazy. Duke had a different attitude. Time after time, he would say to me, "Cheer up Aaron. Now we can finally relax. We'll take some time off, make a few movies, and enjoy some free time for the first time in our lives." I saw it differently: "Within three months, we'll be climbing the walls." I didn't know how to exist without lots of activity. I needed a miracle, and it happened. *Beverly Hills 90210* came into my life.

Seventeen

BEVERLY HILLS 90210

Fade In:

EXT: WALSH HOUSE—ESTABLISHING—MORNING

A Spanish-style house cheek to jowl with the neighbors in what looks like a middle-class neighborhood—except for the neatly trimmed, matching rows of trees and the expensive cars in the driveways. This is southeast Beverly Hills, where bargain prices just inside the city line start at $650,000.

INT. BRANDON'S ROOM—DAY

BRANDON WALSH, sixteen, lies awake in bed, facedown. He glances at the clock radio on the nightstand, emptied moving boxes all around. 7:15. Even as he's absorbing the time, the RADIO clicks on. STATIC only. It's still set for the stations in Minneapolis.

BRANDON
(against his pillow)
First day of school. Strange city.
New house. No friends.
(beat)
I'm psyched.

He slaps off the power, and from down the hall he hears another RADIO, turns to KLOS. Brandon brings his hand back to bed; he isn't getting up.

INT. BRENDA'S ROOM

Brandon's TWIN SISTER. She's moving to the MUSIC, a little self-consciously as she tries on an outfit. The moving boxes here have been emptied, mostly onto the floor, clothes shin deep, the result of her search for the correct first day of school outfit, assembled on the other twin bed in the room. She looks in the mirror, shakes her head.

BRENDA
I've got nothing to wear.

HOLD on her frustration.

INT. PARENTS' BATHROOM

CINDY, 42, and JIM, 44, are bumping into each other as they try to get the day started. Jim passes his fingers under the spout. He's determined to be cheerful.

JIM
It's warming up.

CINDY
The middle of a drought and we
have to run the water for five minutes.
But try to get a glass of water in a
restaurant—it's a major production.

JIM
You don't want to drink the tap water
anyway—tastes like somebody died in
it. Did you think designer water was
just an affectation? You have to buy
it in self-defense.

FOLLOW Cindy into the hallway, bumping into Brenda, holding a bunch of outfits in a frenzied state.

BRENDA
Why don't we go shopping today,
and I'll go to school tomorrow?
First impressions are incredibly important.

CINDY
You're going to make a wonderful
first impression.

BRENDA
Everybody here looks like they
stepped out of a music video.
I don't even have the right hair.

She exits to Brandon's room. Jim enters the hallway.

JIM
What's wrong?

CINDY
Your daughter has frock shock.

INT. BRANDON'S ROOM

Dressed in a different outfit now, Brenda tickles him through the sheet. He yanks it away without rolling off his stomach.

BRENDA
You're gonna make us late!
Out of there. C'mon. Up. Up!

BRANDON
Give me a good reason.

She sits on the edge of the bed.

BRENDA
Because you gotta help me
pick out something to wear.

Brandon rolls over to look at her.

BRANDON
What difference does it make?

BRENDA
Brandon, I know you were Mr. Popularity
at home, but I'm not going to miss Minneapolis.
(taking a breath)
Nobody knows me here. I could be anybody—
I can be somebody else.

BRANDON
What, homecoming queen?

Brenda looks devastated.

BRANDON
(continuing)
Why not? You're cute enough.

BRENDA
—You serious? No, I mean it—
because you've never said that before. . . .
Do you really think I'm cute?

He's surprised.

BRANDON
Don't you look in the mirror?
Yeah, you're cute!

When she smiles back at him full face, she's actually very cute.

BRANDON
(continuing)
You're just too serious.

BRENDA
I'm gonna fix that.

She snatches the sheets off him. He grabs the edge just in time to keep himself covered. She starts to exit.

BRANDON
Hey—that weird black T-shirt you
wore to Denise Baum's Fourth of
July party was very cool.

EXT. WALSH HOUSE

Brandon and Brenda exit the house and jump into their circa 1983 Honda Accord and pull away.

EXT.—BEVERLY HILLS STREETS—DRIVING

as Brandon and Brenda drive to school passing such places as Beverly Hills Hotel, Rodeo Drive, the mansions on Palm Drive and Sunset, etc., MAIN TITLE THEME PLAYS OVER as they pull in front of West Beverly High.

INT. CAR—DAY
Their mouths drop open.

EXT. WEST BEVERLY HIGH

The most incredible array of cars ever assembled in front of a high school. Jaguars, Mercedes, BMWs, Porsches, Corvettes. Convertibles and hardtops. Late models and classics. Cars we've never seen before. This looks like the L.A. Auto Show—only it's for real.

Brenda looks at her brother. Looks at the cars.

BRENDA
I think we're gonna need a
raise in our allowance.

INT. PARKING LOT
Brandon turns into the lot. Kids are trolling for spaces, checking each other out, screaming "hello's" to friends.

ANGLE—STEVE SANDERS
He scopes out the parking lot in his convertible black Corvette, wearing jeans, white T-shirt, motorcycle jacket, extreme shades. He's almost too cool.

RADIO VOICE (under MUSIC)
This is the Flash, coming to you
with over five hundred nasty jammin'
body slammin' watts on KWBH,
the voice of West Beverly High.

EXT. SCHOOL—DOWN THE STREET—DAY
A Jaguar XJ12 pulls up to the school.

INT. JAGUAR-DAY
LAUREN SILVER, very attractive, professional, early forties, chauffeurs her son DAVID to school.

David is fourteen going on forty, slightly built, and manic.

ON THE RADIO
The Flash drops his voice down to a scary growl.

RADIO
Welcome, incoming freshmen.

Lauren smiles at David.

On the radio, a door SLAMS shut. A WHIP snaps. A woman SCREAMS.

David's eyes go wide as he suddenly notices, in the rearview mirror . . .

ANGLE—NEW BMW CONVERTIBLE

Driven very carefully by KELLY TAYLOR (16), a beautiful blonde.

BACK TO SCENE

David grabs the mirror and positions it for a better view.

DAVID
I love this place!

EXT. TEACHER PARKING LOT—DAY

Ten yards and an entire social class removed from the students' lot. Mostly Japanese subcompacts and an occasional Ford Taurus.

OVER the radio:

THE FLASH
And welcome back, teachers.

(Donna doesn't get introduced until the very end of Act Two, when she yells, "Steve! Steve! Some geek is driving your car." She reappears in the next scene, answering a few lines of Spanish in Spanish class and then has just a few more lines in the show. Dylan, who was our first break-out character, wasn't in the first two-hour show at all. But he did appear in the first episode after the pilot, described as "a '90s Depp, Dillon, or Dean. Doesn't act tough. Doesn't need to." We met Dylan at TECH class at school, where Brandon was working on his computer with Scott, and two bullies try to pull Scott off the keyboard.)

DYLAN
Touch that board, my friend.
Do so and die. Please.

The bullies back off.

DYLAN
The tragedy of this country is
that cretins like you end up running it.

BULLY #2
And losers like you end up—

DYLAN
Let me tell you something so you
know in advance. I'm not in a very
good mood today. In fact, I'm feeling sort of . . .
hostile.

His eerily casual tone alarms the bullies, who back off with as much bravado as they can muster. Dylan watches them go, notes Scott's project.

DYLAN
You're doing a fine job, kid.
Keep up the good work.

He's gone. Brandon and Scott are speechless. Finally—

BRANDON
Your friend's pretty cool.

SCOTT
Friend?
(a beat)
I never saw the guy in my life.

Of all the shows I've done, the one I'm proudest of is *Beverly Hills 90210*, because it was like a new beginning for me. It all started with a phone call from my old friend Barry Diller. Then running the new Fox network, Barry wanted to do a show about kids in Beverly Hills and he asked me to produce it. "Why me?" I asked.

"You have two teenage kids, and you live in Beverly Hills."

He was right. Randy was a couple of years away from going into high school, and Tori was already there. Kids would drop by after school, and parents would pick them up, and I got to know what they were like. I heard all of their angst. Their devastation after having had a date broken, the world coming apart when a guy didn't call. One friend was worried about her parents' divorce. Whom would she belong to? It was all very helpful. You can learn an awful lot from young kids by listening from outside the door.

Fox had hooked up with a writer, Darren Star, who had written the screenplay to *Doin' Time on Planet Earth*. They asked us to work with him, which was fine, because we loved his ideas and characters for the show that became *Beverly Hills 90210*. We brought in Charles Rosin from *Northern Exposure* as the executive producer and show runner, since Darren hadn't run a show before. Fox also had us work with Propaganda Films, which at the time was one of the leading producers of music videos.

Good idea on paper, except that our expertise was stories and characters, and theirs was on the look of a production. TV shows, with the rare exceptions such as *Miami Vice*, aren't about a look, but instead are all about story and character. We divorced ourselves from Propaganda after six episodes, and then *90210* slowly began to gain a small following. How small? Fox said they'd renew the show if we could just get a double-digit share. At that time, we hadn't even cracked a ten share! Then slowly but surely, kids started talking in school the next day about this new show featuring high school teens, and these hot guys named Jason Priestley and Luke Perry, and by the end of the year, we were a bona fide hit and renewed for the following season.

I can't tell you how important that renewal was to me. We really wanted to deliver a hit to Barry, since he was nice enough to call us with the idea. *90210* was for a new network, Fox, which needed a new hit, and my company needed it too, since we'd been written off as dinosaurs after ABC canceled *Dynasty*. So, naturally, when *90210* took off, the success couldn't have been sweeter.

As originally developed, *Class of Beverly Hills* (as it was first called) was a conventional family drama about two midwestern transplants, Brandon and Brenda, struggling to adjust to life in one of America's wealthiest communities. But we found early on that there was a certain resentment to a show that dealt with people of influence, so we started to play that down and focus instead on our core characters: Brandon, Brenda, Dylan, Kelly, Andrea, Steve, Donna, and David.

Dylan became Brandon's best friend and Brenda's boyfriend. Snobby Kelly was Brenda's closest pal; Steve was her former beau, and Andrea was the editor of the school newspaper where Brandon worked. The two smallest roles were David, the young freshman trying very hard to be liked by the older kids, and Donna, the insecure friend of Brenda and Kelly.

We premiered during a season that was ripe with shows about high school life, and pundits predicted we'd be on and off the air in a second. Yet it was NBC's *Hull High* and *Ferris Bueller* that were the first casualties. Fox's *Parker Lewis Can't Lose* lasted two seasons, and we're still here.

What set us apart from the other shows was our realistic portrayal of issues. On *90210*, we entertained, but we also said a lot. We dealt with so many timely topics—drinking, drugs, AIDS, gun control, and even consensual teenage sex. We ended our first season with Dylan and Brenda going to a hotel on prom night and we really dealt with the consequences of having responsible sex at their age. We did an episode about drugs, but we didn't want to do the cliché about a kid on drugs, so we flipped it. The story was that Kelly's mom was on drugs, and we showed how it affected Kelly. This was not just a cute teen show.

Kids responded. They saw their lives being portrayed on television for the first time, and since we were making a show for a new network whose main goal was to reach teens and young adults, we were heroes at Fox. For me, it was like *The Mod Squad* all over again. Back then, kids felt *Mod* spoke directly to them. And since I made it for ABC, a network who competed with CBS and NBC by appealing to youth, it was history repeating itself by going after the same demographics. It was also déjà vu in another way. Our relationship with Fox was like our relationship with ABC in the good old days. Everything I felt for ABC then, I feel for Fox now.

The main secret of *90210*'s appeal? Bonding. You get to a point in life where you can't tell your parents everything. Parents don't understand the problems of teens the same way young people don't understand problems of aging. The kids on *90210* have to rely on each other. Their friends help them through their crises. The most frequent comment made to Tori in her fan letters is this: "I wish I had friends like you. If only my friends were as close as yours are." That's what *90210* is all about.

As I mentioned earlier, Tori wanted to be an actress ever since Bob Urich was kind enough to give her a cameo on *Vega$*. She got into every play at school and when she was nine she asked if she could spend more time studying drama. So we hired an acting coach, a nice woman named Kate Daley, and she worked with Tori for four years after school, doing scenes from shows.

Candy recalls that every night when I came home from work, Tori would immediately go through my briefcase to read the latest scripts and treatments, looking for parts she could try out for. I tried hard to separate home and work, but I did offer Tori an occasional guest spot on shows like *Fantasy Island* and *The Love Boat*.

She got a part in the movie *Troop Beverly Hills* (with Shelley Long) on her own, as well as guest spots on the TV series *The Wizard* and *Saved by the Bell*. But I can't say that being my daughter made it any easier for her. She would go on some auditions and the casting director would say, "She's Aaron Spelling's daughter. What the hell does she need a job for?" One time she went to an audition, and the casting director was really cruel to her. "I don't care who your father is," he said. It turns out I had fired him for turning up at the studio drunk.

Tori's appearance on *Fantasy Island* was a great showcase for her. She was eight years old at the time, and her character went on the island to find out why her parents were killed in an auto wreck. She wanted to have a talk with God. George Kennedy played a drunk on the island who told her he was the Almighty. By the end of the show, they had bonded and she took him home to live with her. He turned out to be a great guy who just needed a second chance.

There's an interesting story about that episode. The producer thought it would be a good idea to have Ricardo Montalban's Mr. Roarke character give Tori's character a little puppy when she came to the island so she wouldn't be lonely. There were eight puppies at the studio and they let Tori choose one of them. She immediately named the dog Pepper. The dog was supposed to be in just one scene, but the puppy started following her everywhere and responded to direction. So they kept him in every scene. On the last day of shooting, Candy and I went to pick Tori up at the studio, and Ricardo said, "I have a present for you," and gave Pepper to Tori. We already had four dogs, so Candy and I almost passed out. But how could one say no to Ricardo?

And Pepper still lives with us today.

Today, Tori is famous as TV's most prominent virgin, Donna Martin. We continue to receive more letters about that than anything else. It proves that viewers respond to what we're saying—it's okay to be a virgin; if your friends make fun of you, so what? Still, Tori jokes with me all the time: "Dad, if the show's still on in 20 years, will I still be a virgin?" I'll take the Fifth Amendment on that one!

I'll let Tori tell you some of her favorite memories about growing up. "The two most famous stories have to do with snow and seashells. We rarely travel, and when we do we go to places like Malibu and Las Vegas. So one year Mom and Dad trucked in snow for us and covered the backyard. They thought it would be fun for Randy and me to see what snow looked like. That was a real kick. The other was in Malibu at our beach house. Mom and Dad used to take us walking on the beach all the time, and they'd have Randy and me search for seashells. Somehow we always found these beautiful seashells, the kind they sell for five dollars and up in coastal souvenir shops. I didn't find out until later that Mom and Dad had the seashells buried for us.

"Later on, after I decided to become an actress, Dad worked with me all the time. He would read all my scenes with me and coach me. He came up with a saying whenever I hit it just right; he would always say it was 'plu-perfect.' To this day, when I do a TV movie or other outside projects and ask him what he thought, he still says, 'plu-perfect.' Which is what I always strive to be. Plu-perfect."

I never planned to put Tori into *90210*. Tori heard us talking in the house about our plans for the show and she decided she wanted to be a part of it.

Tori's agent called the casting director to arrange an audition. She went in as "Tori Steele," and read for the role of Kelly, but she didn't get it. There was a tiny part for a girlfriend, Donna, who had about four lines, and Tori got that role. But we didn't plan at the time for Donna to be a series regular.

However, once the show was cast, we realized we had four guys—Brandon, Dylan, Steve, and David, and three girls—Brenda, Kelly, and Andrea. We needed a fourth girl, and Chuck Rosin and Darren Star, the executive producers of *90210*, made the decision to add Tori full-time as Donna. Naturally, as her proud father, I was delighted with the choice.

I also really admired her for not saying, "Daddy, I want to be on the show." She went out and got it on her own. She read for the part, just like everybody else.

When she told me she got the part, I didn't even know who Donna was. That's how small the part was. But Tori really worked hard, and her drive paid off. Tori beefed up the role. She was cute, adorable, and learned very quickly, and it paid off for her. The writers took notice and they gave her more and more to do.

The press gave her a hard time at first, saying she only got the job on *90210* because she was working for Daddy, but let me say that I had another member of my family working for the company. I eventually let him go because he wasn't doing the job I expected. Nepotism has become a four-letter word, but that's wrong. I don't see anything wrong with giving your child a shot. But you're abusing it if he or she does a terrible job and you let it continue. That hasn't happened with Tori. Tori now gets over 3,500 fan letters a month and has been a real draw doing TV movies. As I write this, she's completed her third TV movie for NBC in eleven months while also appearing in 32 episodes of *90210*. NBC's not using Tori because she's Aaron Spelling's daughter, and I've never heard of anyone doing a series and shooting three movies in one year!

We're developing many TV movies at my company, and our executives always try to cast Tori for the leads, but she refuses. "Dad," she says, "I love you, but I just don't want to do any movies for you." She's sick of the talk that she got the Donna role because of Daddy. And even now that she's so hot she still gets knocked for being my daughter. Hollywood, oh Hollywood! When you're up, they knock you. When you're down, they knock you. And when they can't knock you, they pick on your daughter. Do I get upset when I read something that still says she got *90210* because of me? You bet your ass I do! Fortunately, since her high-rated NBC movies, that crap seems to be over.

When Tori made her first TV movie for NBC, Don Ohlmeyer, the West Coast president of the network, asked Jay Leno to have Tori come on *The Tonight Show* to plug the project, and Jay didn't know Tori, but said yes since Don's the boss. He ended up having a great time with her, and had her back very quickly. After her last visit, even though she had nothing to plug, he asked her to come back the next week. She couldn't, because she was flying to Charleston to begin filming a new NBC TV movie. When she arrived at her hotel room, she found that Jay had sent her flowers. What a terrific thing for Jay to do, and Tori says she'll never forget it.

A few weeks after Tori didn't get the part of Kelly, and before we cast her as Donna, we had a big problem. We had everybody set except for our two most important characters—Brenda and Brandon. No matter how hard we looked, we just couldn't find the right actors. We were three days away from shooting, and Fox was very concerned. Fox exec Peter Chernin called me and asked to postpone production. I agreed to hold off for a week, and came home depressed. Tori asked me why, and I told her. Little did I know that she would have the solution.

At the time, Tori read every teen magazine in the world and was also an avid moviegoer. "There's a girl in *Heathers* you should see," she said. "Her name's Shannen Doherty. And I know who would be perfect for the male part—Jason Priestley."

She showed me his picture in a magazine and told me about his role on the NBC sitcom *Sister Kate*. I watched some film on both of them and liked what I saw. We called them into the office. They read for us, and it was magic. They blended perfectly. Plus, they both had acting experience, so we didn't feel like we were taking a chance. It wasn't like they would be good in the office and then freeze on the set. We were getting professionals.

Jason grew up in Canada, where he started working in commercials at age four and by the age of eight had starred in his first TV movie, *Stacey*, for the Canadian Broadcasting Company. By the time he got his first series regular role on NBC's 1989–90 *Sister*

Kate, he had done guest spots on *Quantum Leap*, *MacGyver*, and *21 Jump Street*, and appeared in the feature films *Watchers* and *The Boy Who Could Fly*.

Jason wisely fought off the teen fandom thing, and worked hard at expanding his talents. I gave Jason a T-shirt when we started *90210* that said "QB." He was our quarterback and he took it very seriously. If there's any problem on the set, the cast will confide in Jason and he'll confide in me. Two years later he asked me to let him direct, and he's turned into one of the best directors we have on the show. Jason now also serves as a producer of *90210* and I see big things for his future. Actor, director, producer. Yep, I think he has a chance!

Luke Perry came to us after appearing on daytime television in *Loving* and *Another World*. At first, the press called him the "new James Dean," and Luke hated those references. He's not James Dean. We always thought of the character Dylan as the unpredictable loner of the show. Dylan was somebody who would rather be anywhere but school. Off-camera, Luke was always very reserved and reticent at first. I think his marriage helped him open up. He was socially shy in the beginning, but now he appears to be having fun. He made three theatrical films during his years on *90210* and has always been devoted to the show.

A lot of strange things have happened since we started writing this book. Luke Perry is no longer on *90210*, having left after the tenth episode of the 1995–6 TV season. We were hoping he would do more, but at the beginning of the season, he said he would only sign for the sixth year if he could have the option of leaving after the tenth episode. We agreed to that, and now Luke is free to work on his motion picture career. He still remains one of my closest friends, and as a matter of fact, Spelling Entertainment financed a feature starring Luke, *Normal Life*, which should be out by the time you read this book. Will Luke ever return to *90210*? I genuinely hope so.

Now I'm sure you want to hear what I have to say about Shannen, who made headlines when we were forced to not pick up her contract at the end of the fifth season. Shannen is another one of those actors who received bad career advice, and, I'm sorry to say, made a few enemies on the set. In looking back, it probably had something to do with working all those years as a child actress on shows like *Our House* and *Little House: A New Beginning*. When you work that much as a kid, and you're under constant control, sometimes you've got to break out and say "I've Gotta Be Me," and that's what I think happened with Shannen. She probably had a hard time dealing with instant stardom, her publicity, and growing up so fast.

It certainly didn't start out that way. Tori and Shannen became quick friends and hung out together a lot. In fact, Tori used to bring Shannen over to the house all the time. The Shannen I knew at that time was a very nice girl, and she was great in the show. I used to come down to the kitchen in the morning and they'd be in their pajamas raiding the refrigerator and acting like little kids who went to Beverly Hills High School. It was so cute.

It was sad to see how success affected Shannen, but let me also say this. Most of what was written about Shannen during this period has been overblown. Basically, she was late to the set at times and it upset the other actors who were ready to shoot and had to wait. But somehow those stories just grew and grew.

It's like the old story of Duke Vincent calling the production manager to report that I thought an actor's pants were an inch too long. By the time the story got told over and over, from the producer to the production manager to the wardrobe person, the pants were too long, the wrong color, and I never wanted to see the actor in long pants again—only shorts.

Yes, Shannen was late to the set, but by the time it was retold again and again the story evolved to: she was late, drunk, and had a black eye because she had stayed out all night. The story that began with a kernel of truth got turned into complete fiction.

I'm certainly sorry about what happened with her; it's not something we wanted. It's not as if she ever burned down a set or anything! She was late sometimes and that affected other members of the cast, who finally called me and said they couldn't take it anymore. So we talked to Shannen and her agent, and we all agreed it would be best to move on.

Shannen will make it. She has too much talent not to. And I wish her only the best.

After the third year of *90210*, we had to make a tough decision. Do we keep them in high school, as shows before us had done, or did we let them graduate and move on to college? It would be easier and less of a gamble to leave them in high school, but it would be totally dishonest to the audience who was growing up with them.

We made the decision to move on to college. I thought we might lose a lot of the young audience, but it didn't happen. *90210* only got more popular, and we kept the integrity of the show. The last episode of the third year was their graduation from high school. It got one of our highest ratings ever.

The majority of the cast is still in their early twenties, but I don't think *90210* is about age. It's about a group of kids who met in high school and have remained friends through college. The university isn't a big force in the show. It's their lives we're interested in, not their schoolwork.

As it stands now, the gang will graduate from college at the end of the seventh season. Who knows, maybe after that they'll get married and move on. They can do anything they want—except move to *Melrose Place*!

Come to think of it, that might be a hell of an idea!

Kidding, just kidding.

Eighteen

SOMEONE ONCE asked me to pick any of my TV settings as a place I'd want to live, and while the ranch of the Colbys would have been nice, I can't think of any place I'd rather live than in our own fantasy house in Holmby Hills. It's an escapist paradise. I can't tell you how I love feeding my fish in my fish pond every morning, taking walks with our four dogs on the lawn, playing catch with Randy outside, stretching out on the lounge by the pool. Our house is my Fantasy Island.

The *Dynasty* mansion wouldn't have appealed to me, because they didn't have dogs. How can people raise children without dogs? I love dogs. The first thing I ever wrote in school was about dogs. The assignment was to tell about something or someone that meant something to me. "Dog," I wrote, "spelled backwards is God." It may be corny, but it's true. Tiffany, Shelley, Pepper, and Muffin, like all pets, don't want anything but love and attention. They give so much and ask so little.

Of all of the productions I've been involved with, our house in Los Angeles was easily the biggest and most talked about. It's been described as the largest single family dwelling in Los Angeles County, a home with an indoor bowling alley, skating rink, and outdoor zoo. Well, it is large, but not as big as people have been led to believe. We do have a bowling alley, but we certainly don't have a skating rink or a zoo. The stories have gotten pretty wild I think because so few people have been inside. It's not because we're snobs or anything like that. Our house is a haven for our family and our friends. It's not meant to be a tourist attraction! We're very private people and don't throw a lot of big parties. I've never done an interview at our house, so journalists haven't been in to see it either. Because of that, I guess, they continue to make up things that just don't exist.

We also haven't allowed pictures of our house to get into the press.

The house has had enough publicity, and we pray for the day when it all stops.

For those of you who may want to know the truth about it, here's a thumbnail description. It has very high ceilings, because Candy and I both get claustrophobic. We have twelve bedrooms, a screening room, an editing room, so I can work at home, a nice dining room, two wrapping rooms (Candy loves to give presents), Candy's doll museum, the bowling alley, a sports bar area, a video game and pool room, wine cellar, swimming pool, and two offices (one for me and one for Candy). We have a nice art collection, thanks to Candy's good taste and knowledge, and lots of objets d'art Candy has collected over the years.

There's a cute story about our Andy Warhol paintings. Andy wanted desperately to be on *The Love Boat*, and called Douglas Cramer to try and arrange it. We were thrilled to have him, and invited Andy to a big party to celebrate being our five-hundredth star on the *Boat*. He saw Candy there, and said, "I've got to photograph that woman!" He took the picture and a few months later sent over two large paintings of Candy, one in yellow and one in blue. They are, of course, among my very favorites.

Candy started collecting dolls in the 1970s after Tori was born, and it was her huge doll collection that gave us some of the impetus to move. The collection started to take over our old house. We also had no place for the awards and honors I've been fortunate to receive over the years.

We were thinking about buying Dino DeLaurentis's house. At the same time, Marvin and Barbara Davis (he was then running 20th Century–Fox) were looking for a house. They saw the old Bing Crosby estate and told us it would be better for us than them. So we switched. We picked up the Crosby house and they bought Dino's. What made the house perfect was the fact that a big plot of land was available next door, and we'd be able to ensure lots of privacy. We have 5.5 acres, and the grounds are absolutely beautiful!

Our original intent was to keep the house and remodel it, but once we started going, we realized it would be much easier to just tear it down and start from scratch. And then we got to build our dream house. Candy said it best: "You don't fly, so we don't travel. The house should have everything you've ever fantasized about."

The bowling alley was a surprise from Candy. We used to go bowling a lot when we first met and I used to set pins in Dallas as a kid, where I used to have to line them up by hand, and hope that some drunk didn't start throwing a ball and hit me in the legs. So Candy built me a two-lane bowling alley with automatic pin setting and scoring. It's a wonderful getaway that Candy decorated with posters of all my movies, my awards, and a great picture from the pilot episode of *Burke's Law* of me, Dick Powell, Edgar Bergen, Ronnie Reagan, Jack Carson, Carolyn Jones, Nick Adams, Lloyd Bridges, Ralph Bellamy, Dean Jones, Mickey Rooney, and Kay Thompson. Not a bad cast for any pilot.

Another one of Candy's dreams was to have a double staircase leading to the bedrooms, just like the one she saw in *Gone with the Wind* when she was a kid. It took us five years to build the house. Candy spent a lot of time with the architects carefully going over the plans, and I was constantly amazed at some of her fantastic ideas. Her attention to detail amazed everyone, including me. Many people deserve credit for our home, but none more than Candy.

Me? I did nothing. Zilch. Zero. I just live here.

We were in the press frequently when the house was being built, primarily due to one neighbor, who complained to the city often. All of her calls cost us a huge amount of money because of the delays they caused. Someday we'll invite that neighbor over to see the house. Sure. When hippos can fly!

Just one more comment about our house—I promise. I have people who have worked for me who have beautiful homes in Beverly Hills, Palm Springs, Malibu, and even an island getaway. Some also have private planes and boats. We don't have any of those things except for a small beach house in Mailbu. As I've said, a big vacation for us is driving to San Francisco or Las Vegas with our kids. We love our house. It's the warmest place I've ever been in my life. And we didn't steal it or inherit it—we worked for it. End of house story.

Nineteen

WE STARTED *Melrose Place* on *90210* when Kelly (Jennie Garth) started dating a construction worker named Jake. They broke up at the end of the season, and the story line continued on the first episode of *Melrose*, when Steve (Ian Ziering), Donna (Tori Spelling), and David (Brian Austin Green) brought Kelly to the West Hollywood complex to see Jake.

Fox wanted a *90210* spin-off, and when we discussed it with Darren Star, he mentioned that he used to live in an apartment complex in West Hollywood where everyone got to know each other. We thought that was a great idea for a show. But once we got past the Jake and Kelly storyline, *90210* and *MP* stopped having anything to do with each other. They became two separate shows. The kids on *90210* were in high school at the time and all from rich families. On *MP* everyone was struggling for jobs.

Melrose turned out to be as big a hit as *90210*. I get calls every week from big Hollywood players requesting tapes of episodes they missed. Like the *Dynasty* days, when they had parties to watch the show at country clubs, college kids have *Melrose* parties every Monday night. After *Melrose* ends on Fox, millions of viewers meet in cyberspace to discuss the show on the Internet.

Do you remember how the very first show started? We introduced Alison (Courtney Thorne-Smith) as she searched for a new roommate to live and share expenses with.

EXT. LA SKYLINE—NIGHT
EXT. MELROSE PLACE—NIGHT

A YOUNG WOMAN, bent under the weight of two bulging suitcases and a backpack, hobbles quickly and silently past the swimming pool of this small courtyard building.

ANGLE—A WINDOW LOOKING OUT TO THE POOL

A set of venetian blinds suddenly part, revealing a pair of watchful eyes. Eyes that make it their business to keep track of everyone else's. The blinds open wider for a better view—giving us a good look at RHONDA BLAIR. Twenty-something, black, with hair that sends a message.

BACK TO SCENE
The Young Woman approaches the building's mailbox. A hodgepodge of names identifies the occupants of six separate apartments. She reaches for slot number one labeled PARKER/MILLER and tears off "Miller," tosses a set of keys inside, then glances furtively back at the building before making her escape.

ANGLE—THE WINDOW
Rhonda closes her blinds.

EXT. APARTMENT ONE—ESTABLISHING
WE PUSH THROUGH the door, DISSOLVING into . . .

INT. ALISON PARKER'S BEDROOM—DAY
Thrift store–chic and very feminine. Hardly any piece of furniture in this room costs more than twenty-five dollars.

A clock radio goes off at 7:30 in the midst of a weather report . . .

ANNOUNCER
. . . sunny with a high in the low eighties.
At the present time it's seventy-two
degrees under sunny skies with air
quality in the unhealthful range . . .

ALISON wakes up and glances at the clock. About twenty-three, she is pretty in a sweet, wholesome sort of way. She hides under the covers for a moment, then throws herself out of bed.

INT. HALLWAY
Alison heads toward the bathroom, which is situated between her bedroom and the second bedroom. She calls to the partially open door of bedroom #2—

ALISON
Natalie, your turn to make the coffee.

She enters the bathroom, and then after a beat, hurries back into the hallway.

ALISON (CONT'D)
Nat?

She pushes open the door of the second bedroom and enters. Then reacts, stunned at what she finds in there—

INT. BEDROOM #2
Stripped clean. Nothing left but a sagging mattress and a dresser filled with empty drawers.

Alison kicks the wall.

ALISON
Dammit!

EXT. COURTYARD DAY
Alison rushes out of her apartment, wearing a robe. Knocks on Apt. number three. MATT FIELDING, a cute, bleary-eyed kid in his early twenties answers, wearing a robe.

(Alison runs out into the Melrose Place complex and asks Matt, Jake, Michael, and Jane if they saw any intruders coming out of her place in the middle of the night. They're no help. Alison tells landlord Michael that Natalie walked off without paying the rent and asks for an extension on the rent. He's not sympathetic. Alison decides to put an ad in the paper for a roommate and a little later Billy drives up to Melrose Place. Alison isn't interested in this male roommate. Billy gives her his phone number in case she changes her mind. Meanwhile, Alison interviews other candidates, and doesn't like any of them. She goes to Shooters and runs into Billy.)

ALISON
Let's give it a shot. What the hell,
if it doesn't work out—you'll move, right?

BILLY
Too late. I already found another
place.

Alison's face falls. She's despondent.

ALISON
You didn't!

BILLY
You're right. I was just testing.

ALISON
Testing?

BILLY
To see how badly you wanted me.

ALISON
(annoyed)
Look . . . just forget it.

She turns to go. Billy grabs her arm.

BILLY
I can move in tomorrow.

ALISON
Fine. I'll take the morning off.

BILLY
Can I bring anything? A bottle
of champagne to toast our new
relationship?

ALISON
No, Billy. Just bring a check.

Fox opened *MP* brilliantly. We premiered in June 1992 when all the other network shows were in reruns. We opened with incredible hype. We were the only new thing happening on TV at the time, and everybody wanted to be a part of the phenomenon. The Gap had the *Melrose* cast pose for ads, and they plastered posters everywhere. Advertisers hyped us as a can't-miss show.

But a funny thing happened on the way to the Nielsen meter. Kids were interested in a show about the traumas of growing up, but adults couldn't care less for serious stories about what it was like to be twentysomething. At one point during that first season, our ratings were so bad that one week we were among the lowest-ranked shows on television. We had to make a change.

"Let's go for it," I said to Darren. "Let's stop trying to deny that we're a serial." Will Billy get a job driving a cab? Does the Amy Lochane character get a job as an actress? Jake breaks up with So-and-So. This was so boring. "Let's broaden our bases and get more intrigue." Looking to get new interest in the show, I called my dear friend Heather Locklear and asked her to join *Melrose* for a few episodes. Then Darren and his staff started to crank up the heat, making it more bizarre and outrageous every week. People started to take notice.

I don't know why, but when I got up one night at 3 A.M., the idea of Heather as Amanda suddenly hit me. I called her manager to ask if Heather would be interested and we set up a meeting. I told Heather she'd play the second head of an advertising agency who was very strong and wouldn't let anything stand in the way of her success. Heather relished that. We didn't describe the character as a bitch, just somebody who had a lot of fire and was as beautiful as the rest of the young people of *Melrose Place*.

Noël Coward once said that in drama "you have to put the cat among the pigeons." *Dynasty* clicked when we brought in the cat, Joan Collins, to be among the pigeons, and the same thing happened for *Melrose*. I've always said that the snake always gets the best lines. Can you remember one thing that Adam said to Eve or Eve said to Adam? I'm guessing no. But who can forget what the snake said: "Eat this apple."

Fox was excited about having Heather join *MP* for a few episodes. They're as thrilled as I am that she's been with us ever since. She's not only great on the show, but she's a pleasure to work with, and everyone connected with the show adores her.

Here's how Heather recalls coming to *Melrose Place*:

"Aaron called my manager and asked her if I would do him a favor and do the show for four episodes. Do him a favor? Who was he kidding? I didn't have a job. He was doing me a favor. I had watched *Melrose Place* and thought about how much fun it would be to be on a show like that, but I knew I was far too old for it. My manager thought that for four episodes, doing *Melrose* wouldn't help me but it wouldn't hurt me either. I was interested, of course, but I had one concern. I didn't want to be the little girl anymore. I had always been the ingenue. Everyone was older than me on *Dynasty* and *T.J. Hooker*. I was always the girl learning lessons, but I was ready to grow up now.

"I felt it was time for me to be an executive. I was in my thirties and wanted to go to the next step. And Aaron didn't disagree with me. After I joined the show, he sent me flowers and said, 'Thank you for doing me this favor.' Does he realize he's the one who's employed me for 15 years? He's the one who did so much for me."

In the beginning, *Melrose* stories were structured like the early *90210* episodes, with everybody learning moral lessons about life on each show. Once we decided to switch directions, we threw that concept out the window. Adults had no interest in watching other adults learn life lessons. They just wanted to have fun.

On the new *Melrose* we threw out my old rule—that bonding is everything. The friendly chats in the courtyard ended and the catfighting began. We started to get really far out. Which appeared to be just what the doctor and the Nielsens ordered.

Rolling Stone compared our "troubled" first season to that of the 1962 New York Mets. In their words, "*Melrose Place* changed from a slow-paced, angst-ridden, wanna-be younger sibling to *thirtysomething* into something infinitely more down and dirty and viewer-friendly."

Just like we had done with *Dynasty*, we were able to transform a slow-starting show just by adding a hot new character and spiking the storylines. Amanda dated Jake, who cooperated in an FBI sting operation to bring down Amanda's corrupt father. Michael Mancini (Thomas Calabro) took a doctorly turn toward the dark side and began dumping on his soon-to-be-ex–wife, Jane (Josie Bissett), and fooling around with her younger sister, Sydney (Laura Leighton). Billy (Andrew Shue) slept with Amanda while he was living with Alison. Kimberly (Marcia Cross) was engaged to Michael, but was killed (or was she?) as a result of his drunk driving. Sydney pursued her ex–brother-in-law Michael, discovered that his drunk driving killed Kimberly, and blackmailed him into marrying her. Matt was involved in a "Don't ask, don't tell" male relationship. Jake, meanwhile, slept with almost every female lead on the show and made every man in the audience's fantasies come true.

We also got rid of two characters when we made the changes. With Vanessa Williams, we had made the mistake of having her get married. We already had a married couple with Michael Mancini and Josie Bissett's characters, so we were being redundant there. With Amy Lochane's character, our mistake was making her a southern belle who was trying to break into show business. Her character was corny, and we found that the audience didn't care about show business. That's not what the show was about. As with most character changes, it certainly wasn't the actresses' fault. They worked their behinds off, we just didn't like the direction their characters were headed in. Both are very talented and doing well in their careers.

Grant Show was the first actor we cast for *Melrose*. Before he moved into the apartment complex, Grant was best known for his role as Officer Rick Hyde on the daytime serial *Ryan's Hope*. He also had a featured role on the short-lived prime-time series *True Blue*. Off-screen, Grant is a real guy's guy who likes to ride motorcycles and do home repair, and he brings those characteristics to Jake. Grant fell in love with fellow "Melrose-ite" Laura Leighton on the set, which isn't as unusual as it may sound. Andrew Shue and Courtney Thorne-Smith dated for about a year, and on *90210*, Brian Austin Green and Tiffani-Amber Thiessen have been together for some time.

Laura is one of our great finds. Laura plays Sydney, the irresponsible and manipulative younger sister of Jane Mancini (Josie Bissett), but before we cast her she had never acted professionally. From Iowa City, Iowa, Laura started as a singer/dancer with "The Young Americans" and then segued to acting. She was discovered by a very astute manager named Joan Green, who also handles such talents as Heather Locklear, Josie Bissett, and a young girl named Tori-Something. . . . If I were a young actress, I'd want Joan Green to work with me. She has a great knack for finding people and making them stars.

One of my favorite *Melrose* casting stories concerns the part of Billy. Andrew Shue wasn't our first Billy. The part went to another actor, who was just terrific when he auditioned in my office. But then he got on the set and something just happened. He couldn't cut it.

The director called me on the first day of shooting. "This isn't the guy we cast," he said. "Does he have a twin?"

I called Courtney Thorne-Smith, who was cast as Alison, into my office to ask her what she thought of the actor. "He's very attractive and very nice," she said, "but I don't know. We just don't seem to be reaching each other. Maybe he's nervous."

I took a look at the first day's dailies and knew we were in deep trouble. This was on a Friday. So we organized a group of actors to come over to my house on Saturday to recast the role. All the Fox executives also came. We would either need a new actor or have to stop shooting.

Andrew Shue, a former soccer star at Dartmouth and the younger brother of actress Elisabeth Shue (*Cocktail*, *Soapdish*), was one of the 22 actors who came to my house that Saturday. I had hired Andrew, who had extensive theater credits, for a cop show pilot for Fox that didn't sell. Fox wasn't crazy about Andrew in the pilot, but that was because he played a big, tough cop, and that's just not Andrew.

However, I had a good feeling about him, and had him come to the house early so I could read the scenes with him. At the end of the day, Fox hadn't made up their minds. "He didn't work on the other show," said one of the minor Fox execs about Andrew. "That's because he's not a tough cop," I said. "And that's exactly why we want him for this. We don't want a guy who's dark and threatening . . . that's not our character Billy."

We spent what seemed like hours debating it, and finally Peter Chernin, who was then in charge of Fox's programming, took me into another room to discuss it one-on-one. He said that if I felt that strongly about it, I could hire Andrew. And whenever I run into Peter, I always thank him. It's one of the best decisions he ever made. Andrew's one of the best things on *Melrose*, and his fan mail proves it.

The person Fox originally wanted was a very good actor, but he was very edgy and dark. You felt that he would have raped Alison that first night. With Andrew as Billy, you knew he would be a safe roomie, and that Alison would be comfortable enough with him that they might eventually fall in love. And he and Courtney blended together perfectly.

It's interesting when we look back at *Melrose* that the only characters who were there from the beginning were Jake, Alison, Billy, Michael, Jane, and Matt. Later on we added Amanda, Sydney, Jo, and Kimberly, four of the most interesting people in the complex.

Daphne Zuniga, who plays Jo, made her screen debut in the film *The Sure Thing*, and then appeared in several other films (*Mel Brooks' Spaceballs*, *Visionquest*, and *Gross Anatomy*) before moving to *Melrose* as a photographer and divorcée hiding from a painful past. Daphne is great at breaking your heart. When Jo breaks down and cries, she makes everyone cry! She has great windows. You can see right into her soul.

Marcia Cross, who joined us in our second season as Kimberly, is an interesting story. Her stint with us was on-again, off-again until the third season, when we finally made her a series regular. The mean things that Amanda does is because her mother left her and she must be in control. The things Sydney does is because she wants to be somebody. Kimberly does awful things just for the hell of it!

If you recall, we introduced Kimberly as the other woman in Michael Mancini's life. Jane finds out about it, throws Michael out, and Michael later decides to ask Kimberly to marry him. He's drunk, and he pops the question while driving down the Pacific Coast Highway. They kiss, and he crashes the car, leaving the impression that Kimberly is very dead.

But she returned a few months later. We made the decision to alter *Melrose* history because Marcia was just too good to lose. The actress, who appeared in a few daytime serials and tons of theater, brought a new dimension to the back-stabbing soap opera villain. Since the accident induced mental problems, you never knew what she was going to do.

We did a 1995 special for Fox on the 20 greatest *Melrose Moments*, and conducted a survey of viewers who got to vote on their favorites. The winner got more letters and created more controversy than any other. It was the scene where Kimberly made love with Michael. Afterward, she went to the bathroom, lost her composure, took a pill, washed it down, and then took a good look at herself in the mirror. She felt the side of her head and pulled off a wig, showing a huge scar above her ear and across her head.

That was my all-time favorite *Melrose* scene, too. It'll be very hard to top, but we'll try.

* * *

Why is *MP* so popular? Broken hearts. The show is about people who fall in and out of love, people whose love isn't returned, and the heartbreaks, joys, and frustrations of growing up. I think that everyone in the 18-to-49 age group has had something in his or her life that's been portrayed on *MP*. And, perhaps most of all, viewers love the outrageous things we do on the show.

Anyone who's watched several episodes of *Melrose Place* knows that these truths are self-evident: Jo and Jake and Billy and Alison are meant to be. There's no doubt about that. The biggest cliché in the world is that real love doesn't run smoothly, and nowhere is that truer than on *Melrose*. That's the motto the show runs on. The things that break these characters up can also bring them back together. And then break them apart again. The time to get them finally together, for good, will be on the series finale of *Melrose*. And we're in no hurry to start planning for that yet.

As we did with *Dynasty* and *Beverly Hills 90210*, we attempted a *Melrose Place* spin-off, but while we felt we had a success, Fox didn't share our enthusiasm for the spin-off, *Models, Inc.* It turned out to be one of our biggest hits overseas for foreign television, but Fox canceled us at the end of the 1994–5 TV season. This was a particularly bitter pill, as we had proved that with time our serials could eventually find their legs and become a signature show for Fox, as happened with *90210* and *MP*, which both started off slowly.

Models was built around Amanda's mother, Hillary, who came back into her life after many years. Hillary ran a successful modeling agency in Hollywood, and served as a surrogate mother to the young ladies in the exciting and ultra-competitive world of fashion.

We tapped Linda Gray to play Hillary and introduced her first on *Melrose*, and then, as we successfully did with *Melrose*, we worked very hard to make *Models* a separate show. The only *MP* troupe member who was seen on *Models* was Jo, a photographer who did some work for Hillary. We lasted a season of 29 hours, and, had we been given the opportunity to drop some characters and bring in some new ones, I believe the show would still be on the air today.

However, as I'm writing this book and about to tell you the exciting ending for overseas viewing, a funny thing happened on the way to the computer. The E! Entertainment Television cable network bought the show. So, if you want to see the dramatic climax, you'll have to watch *Models* on E! (Plug, plug!)

But if your local cable system doesn't carry E!, write me and I'll tell you. That's a promise.

Another postscript. Darren Star, who created *Melrose Place* for us, is no longer with our company. He left to create a series for CBS, *Central Park West*. Unfortunately, *CPW*'s ratings have been pretty low. I miss Darren, and I hope he misses us.

When we joined Fox, they were like ABC in the beginning years. Their cupboard was bare. Besides *The Simpsons* and *Married . . . with Children*, they really didn't have anything. It's been great to watch their evolution and growth. We haven't been together as long as we were with ABC, but like the old ABC deal we really feel like a part of the Fox family. Without our asking for it, they gave us a two-year renewal on *90210* and *Melrose Place*, which is something no network has ever done for us before. We're nonexclusive, but I always feel embarrassed when I sell a show to another network. I feel like I'm cheating on Fox. That's how close we are.

Twenty

THE SECRET to producing television? The ability to pick pepper out of fly shit. They both look the same. But in order to pay attention to detail, you have to be able to pick the pepper out of fly shit.

What exactly does a producer do? I can tell you what this producer does. I work with our writers to come up with story lines for our shows. And then I let them loose. When we begin, the writers and I have a concept meeting to talk about the story. Then they send me an outline. I give notes on the outline. Then I get a script, and I give notes on that too.

Next I look at the dailies—the raw footage of the previous day's production—and I also watch the rough cuts and I make the decisions on the final cuts of each episode.

On *Melrose Place*, for instance, I may move a scene around. Maybe it works better in Act Two instead of Act Three. Or we may just talk about the direction of the show.

Casting is so important. People watch TV for actors, number one. But without a good story, they'll stop watching. So both go hand in hand.

When I hire writers, directors, and actors, I look for different things. For writers, it's great ideas and concepts. With directors, it's coverage. I want to see the actor's eyes. Television is not motion pictures. It's not on a big screen but on a small box. I don't care how big that small box is, it's still a small box. I don't want directors to give us a tantalizing shot that will wander all over the screen so that we can't see the actors faces. I want to see from their eyes that they're lying or telling you their pain. Faces are the most important thing in television. If you're not showing their faces, you're out of business.

Hiring actors is much tougher. I once wrote a show for Bette Davis, and she taught me the most important thing about hiring actors. It sounds esoteric, but I swear to you it's true. When an actor reads for me, I look at their eyes. My ears hear what they're saying. My ears can tell me whether they're doing good readings or not and how they're interpreting the lines. But the eyes mean more. Eyes are the windows of the soul.

"If you see your own reflection in their windows," Bette used to say, "they're not eyes—they're mirrors. And they're looking back at you. Then they're 'play acting.' Not acting."

We stand right on top of actors when they audition, so we can get a really good look at their eyes. If I look at somebody's eyes when they're auditioning and I can see through them, then I'm seeing the soul of the actor; it works every time.

The next time you watch TV or movies, look at the actor's eyes, and see if they don't tell you more than the lips do.

I don't judge actors just on their acting talent. They don't have to be great actors and actresses. There's just a certain thing called "stardust" that jumps out at you.

"Stardust" is hard to describe. I've seen some very good actors and actresses who don't have stardust. It's an individual thing. I recognize stardust not in how actors look or how they read, but in their presence. Brad Pitt, Barbra Streisand, Chris O'Donnell, Julia Roberts, Sharon Stone, Jerry Seinfeld—they all have stardust. It's not something you can train for or buy at the store. It's just something that makes you a little different.

Sometimes you never know where you'll find your newest star.

Back in 1980, an agent came to see my partner, Duke Vincent, and urged him to audition his client for our new show *B.A.D. Cats*.

"What's she done?" asked Duke.

"She was a supermarket checker at Von's."

(Actually, she had a tiny role on the quickie TV spin-off of *Animal House*, called *Delta House*, which was on and off the air within months. Her character was named "The Bombshell," which is why the agent probably felt more comfortable talking about her role at the grocery store, which is where he had discovered her.)

Duke had the agent bring her in to me and, as he says, "It didn't take a genius to realize the camera was going to fall in love with her face. There wasn't a bad angle there." Michelle Pfeiffer had stardust.

B.A.D. Cats was a failed series. It was about two ex–race drivers recruited by the LAPD for its Burglary Auto Detail, Commercial Auto Thefts. Get it? *B.A.D. Cats*. It was one long car chase, every week, with the two guys and a lady cop named Samantha. ABC brought me the idea and we were exclusive to the network at the time, so we did it. But it's hard to make a bad idea click. We certainly couldn't make it work. The show was abruptly canceled. But there was one good thing about *B.A.D. Cats*, and that was the woman who played Samantha—Michelle Pfeiffer.

After the cancellation, I went to ABC and said we really believed in Michelle. "She's going to be a big star. Let's put her under contract so we can use her again." They said no, they didn't want her, but if we believed in her so much, we should put her under contract. "Wait a minute," I said. "We're exclusive to you. You want us to pay her, and you're not going to use her anyway? That doesn't make sense."

And so they didn't sign Michelle Pfeiffer.

Today I believe that Michelle is one of the top actresses in movies. Check her box office results, and I think you'll agree with me.

I had a similar situation with Luke Perry, one of our *Beverly Hills 90210* stars. We didn't find him in a supermarket but at a regular audition. We had cast Jason Priestley and Shannen Doherty as Brandon and Brenda Walsh, but I felt we also needed somebody who was a little off-center. The character of Brandon (Priestley) was naive, having just come to town from Minnesota, and all the other characters were nice. So we needed a dangerous guy. We read a lot of actors for the part, and then we were lucky to find Luke Perry. I made a deal with him on the spot without first taking him to Fox for their approval. I felt that strongly about him. He had been offered a soap in New York City, and I really didn't want to lose him.

Fox didn't share my enthusiasm. They said to test him on one show. We filmed one episode with Luke, Fox executives watched the dailies, and they were still negative. I was told to use him on one more show. I said, "We'll lose him if we don't sign him right away." They said, "So we'll lose him."

"I want him," I said. They replied, "We don't." So I called Barry Diller, then chairman of 20th Century–Fox studios, and told him about my problem. He said, "Aaron, I can't ask my people to pay for him if they don't like him, but if you want to pay for him, then go ahead and hire him."

This time I did the right thing. Fox didn't pay a dime of Luke's salary for the first two years of *90210*. Luke went on to become one of *90210*'s first breakout stars. I was right about Luke and I think he has definitely earned his keep at Fox.

And that certainly wasn't the first time the network told me to fire somebody based on their first day of "dailies." In 1976 ABC told us to get rid of Jaclyn Smith from *Charlie's Angels*. "You've got to shut down, find somebody else, and reshoot. We'll pay the costs. Jaclyn Smith isn't working. She's too nervous."

I took a look at the dailies and discovered there was a reason she was so nervous. Her character was supposed to be. On an undercover assignment, "Kelly" discovered her cover had been broken while talking to the bad guy (a young actor named Tommy Lee Jones). "We're not going to drop her," I said. "Don't buy the pilot, but we're sticking with her." My partner at the time, Leonard Goldberg, agreed with me, and we kept shooting.

The next day, after the second wave of dailies, ABC called and admitted they were wrong.

The networks always amaze me when it comes to casting. I think sometimes they should trust producers a little more. We have pretty good instincts. How could someone actually say that Sharon Stone wasn't sexy? Isn't that mind-boggling? Yet that's exactly what an ABC exec told me.

We were making a pilot for a detective series called *Mr. and Mrs. Ryan*. Sharon came in and read for us and we just flipped. She played the ditzy wife of detective Robert Desiderio, and they solved crimes together. We thought the show was quite good and we were very excited about it. But ABC turned us down, saying Sharon Stone wasn't sexy enough. Even if you couldn't see the sexuality and stardust of Sharon Stone, you would think that the network would have seen something there and put her under contract. But that's not what happened. She went off and made a bunch of small movies before hitting it big in *Basic Instinct*, a role turned down by many other actresses who thought the part was *too* sexy. And Sharon Stone is probably considered the sexiest actress in Hollywood today.

I'd love to assemble a clip reel someday of all the people who did small roles for us in pilots or series who went on to bigger things. Jack Nicholson on *The Guns of Will Sonnett*. Tommy Lee Jones and Timothy Dalton on *Charlie's Angels*. Louis Gossett, Jr. on *The Young Rebels*. Richard Gere in his first theatrical film—*Baby Blue Marine*. Michelle Pfeiffer on *B.A.D.* Cats. Richard Dreyfuss on *The Mod Squad*. It would be a lot of fun to watch.

Once we finish casting, we work very hard with the actors on their clothes and hair. Maybe it's stupid, and I'm probably the only producer in Hollywood who does this, but on our shows, clothes and looks play a very important role in the show's success. Remember how Linda Evans's *Dynasty* shoulder pads set a fashion trend a few years back? Or how all the teenage girls wanted to look like Brenda, Kelly, and Donna when *Beverly Hills 90210* first premiered?

I think it's wrong for a producer to sit in his office, watch the dailies, and say, "That suit is too long," or "Why is she wearing that dress?" We don't do that. Instead, I have the wardrobe department bring over racks and racks of clothes, and I ask our young men and women to come up to the office and try them on. I ask the actresses what they feel comfortable wearing, and together we come up with the right look for the show. Don't get me wrong. It's the wardrobe people who do the hard work. They have to shop till they drop, bring in multiple choices for each actress for every scene the actress is in, and that gives us the opportunity to pick what we like. I've been fortunate in working with some of the best wardrobe people in the business.

For hairstyles, I ask the young women to come to my office and show me their favorite hairstyles. We take Polaroids, and then I say that for the first five shows they can't change their hairdos. Viewers have got to be able to identify them.

I'm a big believer in consistency. When a show first starts, viewers are just getting to know the characters. I've had some shows in the past where an actress will have her hair up in the first episode, down in the second, and then bangs in the third, and the poor viewer doesn't know who the hell she is.

Back when we were making *Vegas$* in Las Vegas, I flew a barber there to give our star Robert Urich a new haircut. On TV, as Dan

Tanna, he was looking too pretty. Duke Vincent, our executive producer, and I wanted to rough him up a bit. When we do things like that, it drives actors up the wall, but it's a detail that makes a show better.

After a show is cast and the hair and wardrobe completed, we ask our new actors to spend as much time as possible together off the set. I always tell them, "I want you to hang out. I want you to be with each other and get to know each other as well as possible before the camera starts rolling. I'll even pick up your checks if you go to dinner together." Because, as I've said so many times, bonding is everything, and the camera really picks up on it.

We were talking about dailies a minute ago. I watch the dailies for all of our shows. That's every shot made by the director—closeups, masters, every angle. There are so many different ways of playing a scene that we must make sure that each scene is covered completely.

Is it really necessary? Well, when the director eventually hands in the rough cut, and we watch it, I may not like the way a scene looks, and since I watched the dailies, I can recommend an alternate shot. I don't know how, but I remember all the shots. I can't remember my home phone number or address, but I can remember film.

Also, by watching the dailies, I can find potential problems and fix them while everybody's still on the set. For instance, when we were once making a pilot for ABC, there was a scene where a woman was sneaking up, barefoot, on someone, and as I watched it in my office, I was shocked to find that the actress, who was beautiful and stunning, had the ugliest feet you've ever seen. Her veins were popping off the screen and there were several large bunions on her toes. Well, in the TV business, we try to sell glamour, and this was something that wasn't acceptable. I called over to the set immediately and told the director to find me a foot double—ASAP. And he did just that. You've never seen such beautiful feet!

My name is on the masthead of the company and I take executive producer credit on all of my shows, but I never tack on "created" or "developed" by credits, even if I dream up the concept for the show. I don't think that's fair. I think if you're running a company and you have an idea for a show you can only get good people by giving them "created by" credits. After all, they have to take the idea and fully develop it into a series. Not a lot of people subscribe to that in Hollywood, but I've always done it that way. Good writers don't want to come in and carry out a project created by someone else. They don't get the royalties or the recognition, and they deserve it. Now don't get me wrong, many writers do come in with good and very developed outlines. When they do, I lock my office door to make sure they don't escape.

Nobody does anything in television alone. It's a team effort, put together by several executive producers, line producers, writers, editors, directors, casts, and crews. You may have noticed the name E. Duke Vincent on many of my later shows. Duke's my executive producer partner and vice-chairman of Spelling Television. We've been working together since *The San Pedro Beach Bums* (*Vega$* was our first hit together). Jonathan Levin, our president of Spelling TV, is also doing a great job, and has become an integral part of my support team. Kenny Miller is executive in charge of post-production. He works with the editors before Duke, Jonathan, and I see the first cut of the film. Gail Patterson is executive in charge of production. She works with Duke and the production staffs to ensure that everything runs smoothly. Renate Kamer, our senior vice-president, has been with me for almost 30 years. She's my eyes and ears in everything that's happening in our company. Who says there's no such thing as loyalty in Hollywood.

Like any business, there are good times and bad. I'm thrilled when one of our shows is a hit, and I really take it hard when one of our shows gets canceled. I could have 50 shows on the air, but if one show fails, I'm a mess. If I come home with a certain look on my face, Candy immediately prepares the bed. She knows one of my shows has been given the pink slip, and that I won't get out of bed or take any telephone calls for three days. I get that depressed.

It's hard on everybody. When a pilot gets picked up, actors think they have a wonderful steady career in front of them, and crew members are excited about the continuous employment. To have to go on that cold stage and say, "I'm sorry, we're not going to be picked up for next year" is just the worst task in the world.

One thing I believe. If a show fails, it's my fault and no one else's. Something was wrong and I didn't catch it. I could kick my butt when that happens. It's my job and I blew it. Thank God I know I'll be coming up to bat the next pilot season, and maybe I'll get a hit that time.

Let's talk for a moment about agents. I don't think most people really realize what an agent does. Bottom line: he or she represents your interests and helps sell your project. He's also your partner. An agent doesn't just go and make a deal or sell something for you. An agent has got to know what you really care about. We don't go to a network and throw 18 ideas at the wall and hope one of them sticks. We only pitch things we really care about, and if an agent doesn't understand your love for that project, then he's not being an agent.

I've only had a few agents in all my years of show business. I started with Meyer Mishkin and then Stan Kamen at William Morris. Stan was one of the most revered agents who's ever been in this town. When he died, I was devastated. I left William Morris and didn't have an agent for a couple of years.

Then one day Michael Ovitz came to see me at 20th Century–Fox. He and Ron Meyer, Bill Haber, and Roland Perkins had just broken away from William Morris and made an impassioned plea about why I should be with them. I was intrigued, and since my business manager, the late Bill Hayes, had helped them form their Creative Artists Agency (CAA), we went with them.

That started a relationship that has continued for many years. We've never had a contract, just a very personal, warm relationship. (I got to be very close with Bill Haber, since he was in charge of the TV division. We were so tight that he never went home at the end of the day without calling me to check in, whether he was in Los Angeles, New York, Georgia, Paris, or wherever. Now that's what I call a relationship.

Agents have gotten such a bad rap. People say they live off percentages of other people and are bloodsuckers. That's such crap. If I really love a project, Bill will do something about and get it sold. You would think that I could just pick up the phone and call the networks, but I spend my days making TV shows. I'm busy with writing, casting, production, and all the other details of turning out over 100 hours of television a year.

Agents have a much better relationship with all the networks. They know what the networks are looking for and what their needs are. We can't meet socially or business-wise with the development people and heads of the networks; we don't have the time. But we rely on our agents for that. Bill Haber is not only an agent, he's one of the best friends I've ever had. Instead of pushing me to do more shows, he's constantly worried about my doing too much. The press uses every opportunity to damn agents and their agencies. Let me let you in on a little secret. They're full of shit. Ask any star who they are closest to. Most of them will tell you that it's their agents.

Speaking of agents, I should mention that while writing this book many things happened at the Creative Artists Agency. The three remaining partners, Michael Ovitz, Ron Meyer, and Bill Haber, all suddenly went their separate ways. Michael went to the Walt Disney Co. to be with Michael Eisner as president; Ron Meyer went to MCA, where he's now head of the studio working with Edgar Bronfman; and Bill Haber did something that only Bill would do—he turned his back on show business, moved to Connecticut, and is now assistant to the president of Save the Children, a major charity organization.

I guess this proves what I've said all along. Agents do have hearts.

Believe it or not, in all the years I've been in television I've only been to one Emmy show.

I've only been nominated twice. The first time was for *Day One*, a three-hour TV movie about why we never should have dropped the atomic bomb. I was convinced we wouldn't win, so I didn't go. Since Candy was in Paris, I sat home and watched the show with Randy and Tori. We were sitting there and, dammit, we won. I could have killed myself for not being there. So Duke Vincent went up and accepted for us. The nice thing was they brought it right to the house afterwards.

My second producing nomination was for *And the Band Played On*, and this time I made it a point to be there. But as the evening went on, it didn't look good. Many of our stars were nominated, as was the writer, but all of them were shut out. I was so convinced we wouldn't win that I tore up my speech and threw it on the floor. "The one time I come to the Emmys, I don't win," I said to Candy.

Angela Lansbury, who I've known all my life out here, came out to present the best TV movie award. "We're gonna win, we're gonna win," Duke said.

"Why?" I asked.

"Because the last time we won, she presented the award," he said.

"Oh that makes a lot of sense, Duke! You're really sick!" That was the first time I'd ever given him hell.

Angela announced that we had won, and I just sat there dumbfounded. Candy said, "We won, honey, we won!" All I can recall is trying to desperately remember what my speech was and who I was supposed to thank. I ran down the aisle with a camera in front of me, and Steven Bochco put out his hand for a high-five.

I have no idea what I said once I got onstage. But I can say that winning the Emmy was so sweet. Here was a project about AIDS that no one had wanted to do for four years. First it was going to air on NBC, then they dropped it, then HBO picked it up. Then we lost our director and it looked like the movie would never be made. Then, thanks to Robert Cooper at HBO, we finally did it. After the HBO run, Don Ohlmeyer, the new West Coast president of NBC, showed a lot of class by calling me and asking how I would feel if NBC could run the film after the HBO airing.

"There are a lot of people who don't have cable, who can't afford cable, who should be able to see this film," he said.

Coming from a guy whose network had it first, and then dropped it, I was very impressed. It was a courageous thing for him to do, and I'll never forget it.

To this day, *And the Band Played On* is the most important project we've ever done. Nothing will ever be closer to my heart, and I love the great cast who worked for little money to do the movie. Richard Gere, Alan Alda, Angelica Huston, Matthew Modine, Lily Tomlin, and the rest . . . I'll never forget you.

Many actors of ours have gone on to become very good directors. The list includes Jason Priestley from *90210*, Georg Stanford Brown from *The Rookies*, and Paul Michael Glaser from *Starsky and Hutch*.

Lots of actors ask me for the opportunity to direct, but we don't say yes to everyone. I decline the request if it comes up in the first or second year. That's too early. But by the third year, if they're ready, I always tell them to make sure they want to do it for themselves, and not for their ego. If they're still interested, I tell them to spend a lot of time observing the director and other actors, and to come to editing sessions to watch how we put the film together.

Having actors direct is a great thing for any series. Who knows the show better than the stars? They're the ones who are at the set all the time, and they know their character and the other characters backwards and forwards. Before we sign up any new director, we ask him or her to watch at least four or five episodes of the show. But the actors have seen them all.

Fulfilling an order for 22 hour episodes (and, in the case of *Melrose Place* and *Beverly Hills 90210*, 34 episodes) a year is not an easy thing. There are always problems associated with getting TV shows made. Unexpected rain can wreak havoc on your production schedule and you'll have to immediately switch locations. An earthquake can damage the set of a show, which happened at *Melrose Place*. An actor can get sick. An actor or actress can be very late and keep everybody waiting. Believe me, the rest of a cast who have been there since 6 A.M. can really get upset when that happens.

I once had a show with so many problems that I went to ABC and asked them not to renew it. "We just don't want to do it anymore." We took a multimillion-dollar loss because a particular actor was so difficult to deal with that we felt the inmates were running the institution.

One of the hardest parts of my job is firing actors. However, sometimes it happens, either during a pilot, or early on in the life of a series, and other times during a show's run, which is when a cast change tends to get the most publicity, as when we replaced Shannen Doherty on *Beverly Hills 90210* or Lauren Tewes on *The Love Boat*. Both of them are fine actresses and will continue to have successful careers.

I will never knock a star who has worked for us, and I will always say the change was by mutual agreement, which it usually is. It's a difficult thing to fire anybody for anything, but having been an actor I know how it feels.

From the producer's perspective, replacing a popular cast member is also murder. You always say to yourself, "How will this affect the show?" What if the audience loves the actor? In a series, everybody's expendable, but what if, for instance, the only reason people tuned into *Beverly Hills 90210* was to see Shannen Doherty? I'm sure Steven Bochco was upset about David Caruso quitting *NYPD Blue*, but Steven did the smart thing. He brought in somebody the audience already liked, Jimmy Smits. When we split up with Shannen, my first choice was Tiffani-Amber Thiessen because she had been on *Saved by the Bell* for five years. The audience not only accepted her, they were thrilled to have her on *90210*.

Making the change on *The Love Boat* from Lauren Tewes to Pat Klous was hard for me. We had discovered Lauren. However, replacing her with another cruise director meant we didn't have to rewrite any scripts. As I mentioned earlier, the switch on *Dynasty* was a little tougher. When we and Al Corley didn't see eye to eye after two seasons, we had Steven Carrington injured in an accident, which necessitated plastic surgery. Hence, a few weeks later, actor Jack Coleman was in the part. That was a lot to ask of viewers, but they accepted the change.

Sometimes the cast switches can backfire, however. We replaced an actor on *The Rookies*, brought in somebody else, and the audience just hated his replacement. We eventually had to drop the role completely. Not a smart move, Aaron!

One thing that's rarely happened at our company is firing an actor in the middle of a season. We'll just live through it and during the hiatus we just don't pick up the actor or actress, so officially it hurts the actor less. When there's a problem, the actor has ample warning. We really do try to work things out. But the old adage that one bad apple can taint the whole bushel is very true. It's also a reason we've never hired an actor named "Apple." Ugh, forgive me for that.

Seriously, Hollywood's a very strange town, and it can do weird things to people. It's not easy getting used to fame. One week you're reading for a part and six months later you can't walk down the street in peace. You're making more money than you've ever made. You're suddenly being asked for interviews, and that's hard to cope with, especially for young actors. I'm constantly amazed that we've had to make only about four changes in over 3,000 hours of television.

But when these problems start to occur, we always try to nip them in the bud by talking the problem out with the actor. Some actors start to believe the stuff their agents and managers feed them, and they'll start to tell you that the show's success is because of them. You try to convince them that they contribute to the success in a big way, but that a TV show is a team effort. You try to do the best you can to solve the problem, but sometimes it just doesn't work out.

You have to remember that actors' egos are very fragile. They're not selling shoes—they're selling themselves. When an actor is turned down for a part, it's like tearing that person's heart out. When an actor causes problems on the set, you can't always blame the actor. He or she could be having a family problem, or perhaps a personal problem. Any type of problem can affect not only their performance but their conduct on the set. Just remember, no matter what you read in the papers, actors are people too. It's damn hard to lead a normal life.

Let's take a moment and talk about music. Theme songs don't get a lot of respect from network executives these days, but they're very important to a show. The viewer can be out of the room with the TV on. When the theme starts, it's an instant signal that the show has begun. It gets them running to the set. And TV fans love themes. We recently got a new three-CD TV theme song collection from the folks at Rhino Records which included several of our themes—*The Love Boat*, *Dynasty*, and *Charlie's Angels*. We also have gold records from *90210*, *Melrose Place*, *The Heights*, and *S.W.A.T.*

Every show but one we've done over the years has had an instrumental theme (from such composers as Henry Mancini, Bill Conti, Burt Bacharach and Carole Bayer Sager, Lalo Shiffrin, and Elmer Bernstein). I've always believed that dramas needed to have instrumental themes because you had so many characters to introduce, but on comedies, a singing theme can help explain what the show is about. We had a lot to set up on *The Love Boat*. What were we going to do? Just show a picture of a ship? We did that, but we also showed pictures of the cast and had Jack Jones sing "Love . . . exciting and new . . . Come aboard . . . we're expecting you." The theme played on the radio over and over. We got lucky on that one.

The one question I'm asked the most is how does one become a TV producer. The answer is simple: Write. If you're not a writer and if you can't communicate with other writers, I don't think you can produce television. If you think of the top TV producers of today—Steven Bochco, Stephen J. Cannell, David E. Kelly, Matt Williams, Dick Wolf, Donald P. Bellisario, Chris Carter—they all have one thing in common: they're all writers. I can't think of a successful TV producer who didn't start as a writer.

The best way to start is to pick several shows and study them. Learn why they're a success or failure. And then start thinking of concepts for the characters. What hasn't Brandon ever done on *Beverly Hills 90210* that might be a fun episode for him? What would it be like if Donna and Kelly got an apartment on *Melrose Place* for an episode?

Try to get a script from your favorite show. Study it. Learn the form. Write a sample script. It will probably never get to the producer because of legal issues, but if it's any good it can serve as a calling card and example of your work. Maybe you'll get lucky as I did and a young agent might take you on and get the script out there to other producers.

A producer usually starts as a freelance writer getting an assignment to write a script. That can lead to multiscript assignments. Then you may get promotions to story editor, head writer, co-producer, producer, and, eventually, executive producer.

If you're good enough and lucky enough to become a producer, please remember how tough it was to get there. Be helpful to the young writers you'll hire. Writers, like actors, are very sensitive people. Never forget the crap you had to take in the beginning. Don't dish it out to others. I've been there, done that.

I learned my lesson many years ago, and I lost some damn fine writers. Now, when I read something I don't like, I say, "Would you please consider doing it this way?" I never say "I hate" anything about it. There are also three words you should never use with your staff: "This doesn't work." Your job is to suggest things that will make it work or help it work. Any idiot can say "This doesn't work." Is the writer supposed to read your mind as to why you don't think it works? One more thing. When you get a job on staff, remember all the bitchy things your producer says or does to you. When you're a successful producer on your own, call him in for an interview, then kick his ass out of your office.

* * *

Of the hundreds of characters we've had in our shows over the years, if I had to pick one that I most identified with, it would be Mr. Roarke, the Ricardo Montalban character from *Fantasy Island.* He made people's dreams come true. The show always ended happily. I love happy endings and whenever I can, making people's dreams come true.

I would have loved to be friends with Blake Carrington of *Dynasty* and Dan Tanna from *Vega$*. Blake gave his family love and Tanna had a great attitude about life. Brandon on *Beverly Hills 90210* is cool because he tries to help the whole gang without being preachy about it, and Amos Burke is really classy—he had the guts to drive around L.A. in a Rolls-Royce, which is about the most dangerous thing you can do in this town!

A person I wouldn't have wanted to hang out with was Alexis on *Dynasty*. Too bitchy. Remember, I said Alexis, not Joan Collins, who I like a lot. I would get along much better with Amanda of *Melrose Place*. Amanda at least shows compassion when others are in trouble. She's also devious but vulnerable. To tell you the truth, Amanda could do anything, and I would still love her. That's hardly a surprise because I happen to love Heather Locklear. She's a dear friend and my personal good-luck charm.

I was once asked to program an imaginary Aaron Spelling festival over five nights, two hours each, to show the different kinds of programs we've produced over the years. If I were to do this, I'd kick off with *Love Boat* and *Fantasy Island*, because they were both fantasies, light and compatible, then *Starsky and Hutch* and *Family* the next night, because *S&H* was a great buddy show and *Family* said something to everybody. Wednesday would be *90210* and *Melrose*, because they're our current young shows, and Thursday's the camp festival with *Charlie's Angels* and *Dynasty*. Friday night we close with *Vega$*, because the show was a lot of fun, and *2000 Malibu Road*, since it took place at the beach. You always want to end the week with the waves and ocean breezes when the rest of the country is shoveling snow off their sidewalks!

It always kills me how the media pays so much more attention to movies than television. More people will see one of our TV shows in one night than will go to a movie that grosses $200 million. I've often said that you could take three young stars of TV and walk them down the street with three movie stars and see where the crowd goes. They will always gravitate towards the TV stars. After all, those TV stars come to their house every week. They're part of the family.

There's a big difference between making TV shows and films. During the year we made the theatrical film *Soapdish* we also produced 74 hours of television. Movies just move at a really slow pace. The real excitement of TV is that you must air a show every seven days. Sure, it keeps you running, but it also keeps you young. I did enjoy the eleven theatrical films we made and we'll make more, but I'll never leave television.

In 1980 my longtime publicity man and friend Warren Cowan came up with an idea. He started to count up the many hours of television and film we've produced over the years. He realized that if you took all the movies the old studio chiefs like Darryl Zanuck, Louis B. Mayer, and all the rest produced, they were shockingly below the amount we're lucky enough to have done.

So he decided to do something about it. He put me in the *Guinness Book of World Records*. He called the London office, found out what the requirements were, and started the process, which took him nearly two years. Then he got me a blurb in one of their books, and ever since, whenever I'm introduced on television or at an awards ceremony, I'm always referred to as "the most prolific producer in history."

The power of publicity is something, isn't it?

To think that I've produced more film than anybody in the film business is just overwhelming. Randy keeps a chart in his room and updates it every year. The count is now over 3,000 hours. A magazine once printed that if you ran those shows for five hours a day, it would take you more than 600 days to see them all. I wouldn't advise anyone to try it!

On September 11, 1978, something really terrific happened to me. I was awarded a star on the Hollywood Walk of Fame. It was something I had never imagined could ever happen to me. I was the first TV producer awarded a star, and that in itself means a lot to me.

Sometimes, for kicks, Randy says, "Come on, Dad, let's go look at your star." The first time, he didn't really give me a reason, but I found out when I got there. Randy had some soaps and brushes, so we could clean up the star. That's my boy!

When I left Texas, I said if I could just be an actor in one episode of a half-hour show I could say to my family, "Look what I've done." I just wish my mom and dad were here. I think they'd be proud. Sometimes I dream of Mom and I hear her saying, "Good, baby. You're doing good!" I always thank her and Dad for the $200 they gave me to go to Hollywood. It was their life's savings.

Tag

❖

WHAT'S THE best change I've witnessed in television over the years? The addition of new Fox, Warner Bros., and UPN, networks and many new cable channels. It's great for our creative community. They've employed more writers, directors, actors, and crews. We keep hearing about this Information Superhighway and how it's coming. How will it change what we do? It won't. How can all of them find new programming?

That's what it's all about. Programming.

TV has never been as exciting and challenging as it is today. Change is constant. There's new competition and our audiences zip and zap and surf. There are new delivery methods like video, DBS, interactivity, on-line networks, and virtual reality. I don't pretend to understand how all these technologies will affect us. But I do know that there are millions of people out there who desire and demand good stories. It doesn't matter how they get them, as long as the stories involve the audience.

Dick Powell always said it, and his statement rings truer today than it did 25 years ago: "The only positive in our business is the negative." Film can play forever.

People ask me all the time: Why do you continue to work the way you do? Why not just relax and retire? I'll tell you why. I don't want to retire. It's because I can't imagine staying home and getting in Candy's hair. What would I do without my shows? I'm like a hooker on a Saturday night. I just want one more hit. Before this book is over, I'll tell you the real reason I won't quit.

I also have a fierce loyalty. I have over 300 people who depend upon me at our company. If the company was called Glamour Entertainment, I could work less. But it's Spelling Entertainment, and when your name is up there, it's your responsibility and desire to do whatever you can for the company as long as they want you.

When this book was being written, Tori was 22 and Randy was 17. And that's my only regret. Did I give them enough time? That haunts me. That's one reason I started in 1994 to take Friday off every week. To be at home with my family. I've missed too much. I just hope I can catch up.

I will eventually retire. It's inevitable. Just not any time in the near future. I can't ask the kids on *90210* to give us two more years and then leave them. I love the current group. Fox has also picked up *Melrose Place* through the 1996–7 season. There's no way I'm going to desert that group either. We all started together and we'll all finish up together.

Meanwhile, I still get the occasional snicker about being an old-timer who dares to produce TV shows for and about young people. Funny, I don't think anyone questioned Mark Twain's age when he wrote *Tom Sawyer* or *Huckleberry Finn*, or George Bernard Shaw when he penned *Pygmalion*. If you're a writer and you have imagination, why not? As this book is being written, I'm preparing a TV series for Fox about vampires. I don't know a hell of a lot about vampires, but you know what? I'll learn! There is no age barrier to imagination.

I keep saying this, but I really believe it. People who work in the television business are the luckiest people in the world. We make dreams and fantasies come true. We not only reach millions of people here in the U.S. but many more millions around the world. Tell me what other business can affect so many people.

And I still dream. Even at this stage of my career, I still believe you can never give up on your dreams. It took us four and a half years to get *And the Band Played On* made. Every network rejected it. Nobody wanted to touch a story about AIDS. But finally, after many false starts, Bob Cooper and HBO stepped up to the plate. I'm as proud of *Band* as anything I've ever done.

I'm very stubborn. If I believe in something, I stick with it. The great thing about my industry is that somebody will eventually do it, somewhere, someday. You just can't give up hope.

* * *

I'm going to tell you something that no one but Candy knows.

You know what really keeps me going?

My nightmare.

I have this same nightmare about three times a year. That I'm back on Browder Street in that $6,000 house with wall-to-wall people. My nightmare is that my entire life has been a dream, and I'm now back in that house.

I honestly believe that nightmare is what brings me back to work every day. My dreams help chase the nightmare away.

That's why I say to young people all the time, don't give up on your dream, because that's all any of us have. Following your dreams is so important. Even if you only achieve half or even a quarter of your dream, you've accomplished so much more than not dreaming at all. Who knows? You may be the next writer to sell a story. You may be the next actor or actress to be cast. And your success doesn't have to be in show business; it can be any business you choose to enter. Just follow your dream.

To all of you, I leave with one thought. It's one I've repeated to myself over and over. If you don't believe anything in this book, please believe this. Without dreams, there can be no reality. Reality without dreams is a harsh world indeed.

THE END

FADE OUT AND

ROLL CREDITS

Television Series Produced by Aaron Spelling

- *Dick Powell's Zane Grey Theater*, 1956–62, CBS: My first production, an anthology of Old West stories, hosted by Dick Powell and featuring many of Hollywood's top stars.

- *Johnny Ringo*, 1959–60, CBS: The first show I created, starring Don Durant as a gunfighter-turned-lawman in the Old West.

- *The DuPont Show with June Allyson*, 1959–61, CBS: A contemporary anthology featuring June, Dick Powell's wife, as host and occasional star. The show attracted such great Hollywood stars as June, Bette Davis, David Niven, Joseph Cotton, Ginger Rogers, and even Harpo Marx in a rare dramatic appearance as a deaf mute.

- *The Dick Powell Show*, 1961–3, NBC: Another anthology, in which the very first episode introduced a great character named Amos Burke.

- *The Lloyd Bridges Show*, 1962–3, CBS: A way-out anthology about a freelance journalist who would tell a story and then imagine himself as the protagonist. Audiences didn't know what to think. If we had just done six of them, it might have been fine, but it got to the point where the audience said, "Wait a minute, this isn't true. He's imagining all of this." And they started tuning out. But it was very exciting while it lasted and Lloyd was great.

- *Burke's Law*, 1963–6, ABC: Gene Barry replaced Dick Powell as millionaire detective Amos Burke in the first series to feature guest-star cameos. Our first episode features such guest stars as Ronald

Reagan, Dean Jones, Mickey Rooney, Jack Carson, Edgar Bergen, Carolyn Jones, and Lloyd Bridges.

- *Honey West*, 1965–6, ABC: Anne Francis was TV's first female private detective, a trench-coat–wearing, karate-chopping P.I. who lived with a pet ocelot named Bruce. She was first introduced on an episode of *Burke's Law*.

- *The Smothers Brothers Show*, 1965–6, CBS: Before there was a *Smothers Brothers Comedy Hour*, I hired Tom and Dick for a sitcom about an executive for a publishing company whose angel brother (Tom) shows up and tries to make his life better. Who would know that 30 years later, angels would be so hot?

- *The Guns of Will Sonnett*, 1967–9, ABC: Walter Brennan returned to series television after six seasons of *The Real McCoys* as an old ex-calvary scout who helped his grandson (Dack Rambo) search for the father he never knew.

- *The Danny Thomas Hour*, 1967–8, NBC: An anthology series for my new partner, Danny, hosted by the veteran entertainer. We had dramas, musical variety specials, and occasional long versions of *Make Room for Daddy*.

- *Rango*, 1967, ABC: After *McHale's Navy*, many people believed that Tim Conway deserved his own series. This was the first of many, about a bumbling Texas lawman in the Old West. Tim, as usual, was hysterical.

- *The Mod Squad*, 1968–72, ABC: My first big smash. Michael Cole was Pete, Clarence Williams III was Linc, and the lovely Peggy Lipton played Julie in the show about three young L.A. undercover cops.

- *The New People*, 1969–70, ABC: Our attempt to follow *The Mod Squad*, with another show about kids. This one was about a bunch of students who get stranded on a desert island in the South Pacific and have to begin a new civilization. TV's first (and I believe only) 45-minute drama.

- *The Silent Force*, 1970–1, ABC: Another trio of undercover cops, starring Ed Nelson, Percy Rodriguez, and Lynda Day (later known as Lynda Day George). This was my first series for ABC under my 17-year exclusive arrangement with the network.

- *The Most Deadly Game*, 1970–1, ABC: A great mystery about three criminologists who dealt in unusual murders. We cast Inger Stevens, George Maharis, and Ralph Bellamy in the pilot, but never recovered after Inger committed suicide after the show was sold. Yvette Mimieux took over the role when we went to series.

- *The Rookies*, 1972–6, ABC: Georg Stanford Brown, Michael Ontkean, and Sam Melville played young LAPD cops, and Kate Jackson was Ontkean's nurse-wife Jill. The first of the nine Spelling–Goldberg TV series that got huge ratings in the 1970s.

- *Chopper One*, 1974, ABC: Jim McMullan and Dirk Benedict played two helicopter cops keeping the city safe from rooftop snipers, park muggers, etc. Great action with a helicopter instead of the usual police cars.

- *Starsky and Hutch*, 1975–9, ABC: One of my all-time favorites. The first buddy cop show. The first before there was a *Hill Street Blues* or *NYPD Blue* to show cops who really cared about each other. Paul Michael Glaser was Det. Dave Starsky and David Soul was Det. Ken Hutchinson, two undercover cops. And their costar was a squealing 1974 Ford Torino.

- *S.W.A.T.*, 1975–6, ABC: One of my least favorite shows. A cop series about an elite unit of the police that handled the cases too tough for ordinary cops. Lots of fighting, explosions, gunfire, and that sort of thing. Way too violent for today's television. Robert Urich, Steve Forrest, and Rod Perry starred.

- *Family*, 1976–80, ABC: The series critics always seem to forget.

A classy, quality drama about an average middle-class family that introduced Kristy McNichol and also starred Meredith Baxter Birney, Sada Thompson, James Broderick, and Gary Frank. In spite of all the awards Len and I received for the show, it's hardly mentioned in our credits.

- *Charlie's Angels*, 1976–81, ABC: The biggest hit of my career. We premiered with a 59 share, which is a bigger chunk of the audience than sometimes watches NBC, CBS, and ABC combined these days. Farrah Fawcett, Jaclyn Smith, and Kate Jackson were our original Angels, and we later added Cheryl Ladd, Shelley Hack, and Tanya Roberts to the mix. David Doyle was Bosley, the assistant to Charlie Townsend, the head of his own detective agency, who was always heard but never seen. John Forsythe was the voice of Charlie.

- *The Love Boat*, 1977–86, ABC: Every week three couples boarded the *Pacific Princess* and found romance and fantasy on the high seas. Gavin MacLeod played Capt. Stubing and the rest of the crew featured Bernie Kopell (Adam Bricker), Fred Grandy (Gopher), Ted Lange (Issac), Lauren Tewes (Julie), and Jill Whelan (Vicki).

- *The San Pedro Beach Bums*, 1977, ABC: Fred Silverman wanted a contemporary version of the Bowery Boys, and this is what we gave him, about five kids sharing a houseboat.

- *Fantasy Island*, 1978–84, ABC: "The plane, the plane!" Our companion to *The Love Boat*, a show about how $10,000 could buy your favorite dream on a South Pacific island. Ricardo Montalban played dapper white-suited Mr. Roarke, the man who made the fantasies come true. Herve Villechaize was his faithful, diminutive assistant, Tattoo.

- *Vega$*, 1978–81, ABC: Robert Urich was private eye Dan Tanna, who drove around Las Vegas in his 1957 red convertible Thunderbird and kept watch over the Desert Inn.

- *Hart to Hart*, 1979–84, ABC: Robert Wagner and Stefanie Powers were (and still are, as a matter of fact) Jonathan and Jennifer Hart, that great, loving, globe-trotting couple who solved crimes as a hobby.

- *B.A.D. Cats*, 1980, ABC: Michelle Pfeiffer doesn't talk about it in interviews, but this was her first big role on a series about two ex–race car drivers who worked for the L.A.P.D.'s Burglary Auto Detail, Commercial Auto Thefts, squad. She played Officer Samantha Jensen. I think she has a future!

- *Aloha Paradise*, 1981, ABC: Our attempt to do *The Love Boat* in Hawaii at the Paradise Village resort. Debbie Reynolds starred as the Paradise manager.

- *Dynasty*, 1981–9, ABC: Our big hit of the 1980s, the show that made Alexis Carrington and Joan Collins household names during the decade of greed and excess. John Forsythe, who provided the voice of Charlie's Angels, starred for us as Blake Carrington, with Linda Evans as his suffering wife Krystle. Joan played Blake's ex-wife, Pamela Sue Martin (and later Emma Samms) was Blake and Alexis' daughter Fallon, Al Corley (and later Jack Coleman) was their son Steven, John James was Jeff Colby, Fallon's husband. Heather Locklear made her TV series debut as Krystle's niece, Sammy Jo.

- *Strike Force*, 1981–2, ABC: A cop show with Robert Stack and Dorian Harewood.

- *T.J. Hooker*, 1982–6, ABC: William Shatner starred as Sgt. T.J. Hooker, who patrolled the streets of L.A. with young cops, Officer Vince Romano (Adrian Zmed) and Officer Stacy Sheridan (Heather Locklear). Heather did double duty for me, working on both *Hooker* and *Dynasty* at the same time. How many actresses can boast they've done two series at the same time?

- *Matt Houston*, 1982–5, ABC: A show about a bored son of a multi-millionaire who ran a part-time private detective business. Lee Horsley played Matt. Beautiful Pamela Hensley was his partner, C.J. Parsons.

- *At Ease*, 1983, ABC: One of my few sitcoms, *At Ease* was a contemporary military comedy with Jimmie Walker and David Naughton.

- *Hotel*, 1983–8, ABC: An anthology set in a glamorous San Francisco hotel, where each week we saw the hotel staff intermingle with the guests. James Brolin, Connie Sellecca, Anne Baxter, and Shari Belafonte-Harper starred.

- *Glitter*, 1984–5, ABC: A series about a Hollywood celebrity magazine and the stars they covered, starring David Birney and Morgan Brittany.

- *Finder of Lost Loves*, 1984–5, ABC: Detective Cary Maxwell specialized in finding lost loved ones. Tony Franciosa starred in a show that was based on the real-life adventures of Los Angeles private eye Lloyd Schulman.

- *MacGruder & Loud*, 1985, ABC: John Getz and Kathryn Harrold were uniformed officers secretly married to one another.

- *Hollywood Beat*, 1985, ABC: Jack Scalia and Jay Acavone starred as undercover cops working the Hollywood club scene.

- *Dynasty II*: The Colbys, 1985–7, ABC: A spin-off of *Dynasty* that moved Fallon and Jeff into a story about Jeff's side of the family, headed by Constance Colby (Barbara Stanwyck) and Jason Colby (Charlton Heston). Also featured: Stephanie Beacham, Katherine Ross, Tracy Scoggins, and Ricardo Montalban.

- *Life with Lucy*, 1986, ABC: One of the great heartbreaks of my life. We signed the great Lucille Ball with great fanfare to return to prime-time with a sitcom, but times had changed. Viewers weren't interested in seeing a woman Lucy's age doing slapstick. It was my fault, not Lucy's. God, I loved her!

- *Heartbeat*, 1988–9, ABC: In the days before *ER*, we had a little medical show about a women's clinic. Kate Mulgrew starred as Dr. Joanne Springsteen. This also marked the thirty-second series we did for ABC. There were good times and bad times, but it sure was one hell of a run!

- *Nightingales*, 1989, NBC: A show I was crucified for about a group of student nurses. Yes, we did pour on the T&A a little too much in the beginning, but once we got the message and changed direction, it was too late. Suzanne Pleshette starred.

- *Beverly Hills 90210*, 1990–, Fox: My great comeback. The Fox network asked me to do a series about high school students, figuring that since I was the father of two Beverly Hills teens, I was uniquely qualified. We're still on the air, so we must be doing something right.

- *Hearts Are Wild*, 1992, CBS: A short-lived attempt to do for Las Vegas in the 1990s what we had done in the 1970s with *Vegas$*. This time around, our lead wasn't a private detective, but instead the owner of a Las Vegas hotel, played by David Becroft, who's since been on *Melrose Place*. The show was created by Eric Roth, who went on to bigger things with a little movie he wrote about a guy who sits on a park bench. What was it called? *Forrest something* . . . oh yeah, *Forrest Gump*. Eric's one of my closest friends, and that's no Gump.

- *Melrose Place*, 1992–, Fox: The only time in my career that I've been able to successfully spin off a show, this time from *Beverly Hills 90210*. Anyone remember the connection? Kelly (Jennie Garth) was dating Jake (Grant Show), a construction worker who lived in an apartment complex in the Melrose Avenue section of Los Angeles.

- *The Heights*, 1992–3, Fox: A short-lived series about a fictional rock band notable for the fact that the band scored a Top 10 hit during the show's run, but I'm sad to report that it wasn't enough to spike the ratings.

- *The Round Table*, 1992, NBC: The Peacock network was hoping for a little *90210*-style ratings boost with a show about first-year law students in Georgetown. Unfortunately, it didn't happen.

- *2000 Malibu Road*, 1992, CBS: A fun six-episode summer series set in Malibu with Drew Barrymore and Lisa Hartman Black. We would have been renewed, but we all couldn't come to terms on license fees. My dear friend Joel Schumacher (*Batman Forever* and *The Client*) directed every episode!

- *Winnetka Road*, 1994, NBC: A soap set in Illinois, starring Meg Tilly, Ed Begley, Jr., and Eddie Bracken.

- *Burke's Law*, 1994–5, CBS: The great Gene Barry returned as Amos Burke, 30 years later, on a network that was unfortunately in disarray upon arrival. We were scheduled in five different time slots in one season. Figure that one out!

- *Madman of the People*, 1994–5, NBC: Another one of our gallant attempts to have a successful sitcom. This one starred Dabney Coleman as an acerbic magazine columnist. It was canceled, despite being in the Top 10. Go figure.

- *Models, Inc.*, 1994–5, Fox: A *Melrose Place* spin-off that never found its legs. Linda Gray starred as the mother of Amanda from *MP*, who ran a modeling agency in Los Angeles. It's a smash in Europe. Funny business, huh?

- *Heaven Help Us*, 1994, syndication: Ricardo Montalban and I reunited in a short order series about an angel who worked with a newly deceased couple to help people. John Schneider also starred.

- *Robin's Hoods*, 1994–5, syndicated: Linda Purl starred as the owner of a bar who worked with recent parolees.

- *University Hospital*, 1995, syndication: Four young nurses again, but this time, no one complained. We learned our lesson on *Nightingales*.

- *Savannah*, 1996, WB: Our first show for the new WB network, a series set in the South about three women and the men who love them. Starring Robyn Lively, Jamie Lunar and Shannon Sturges.

- *Malibu Shores*, 1996, NBC: "West Side Story" meets "Romeo and Juliet" in a contemporary drama series about kids from the San Fernando Valley and Malibu. Starring Michelle Philips, Keri Russell, Tony Lucca, Greg Vaughn, Charisma Carpenter, Christian Campbell, Katie Wright, Susan Ward, Ian Ogilvy, and a young kid named Randy Spelling in his TV series debut.

- *Kindred: The Embraced*, 1996, Fox: A different direction for us in this unusual series about a detective (C. Thomas Howell) tracking down a clan of modern-day San Francisco vampires. Mark Frankel plays vampire leader, Julian Luna, and Kelly Rutherford is his lover. Stacy Haiduk is Lillie, who also loves Julian and is determined not to lose him.

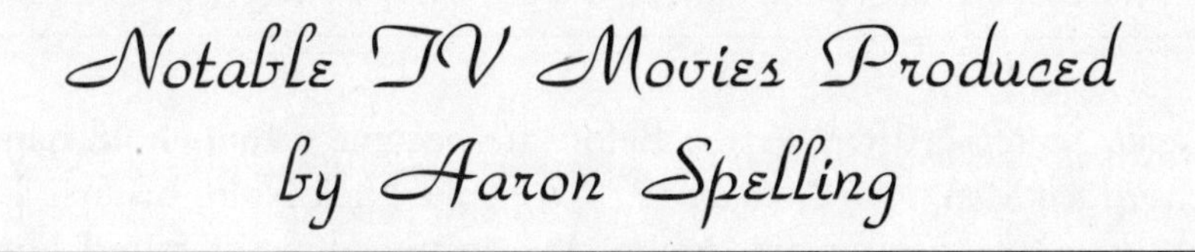

Notable TV Movies Produced by Aaron Spelling

WE'VE PRODUCED nearly 140 made-for-TV movies. Here are some of the highlights.

- *The Over-the-Hill Gang*, 1969, ABC: Our first made-for-TV movie, with a great cast of veterans, including Chill Wills, Edgar Buchanan, Andy Devine, Walter Brennan, and Jack Elam, about a town under the thumb of a crooked sheriff and a band of geezers that comes to save the day.

- *The Ballad of Andy Crocker*, 1969, ABC: Another one of our early MOWs, Lee Majors starred as a soldier who returns to his small hometown in Texas from the unpopular Vietnam war, only to discover that the town has turned against him.

- *Run, Simon, Run*, 1970, ABC: Burt Reynolds and Inger Stevens. Burt and Inger fell in love during the making of this film, about an Indian who gets out of jail vowing to avenge the death of his brother. We enjoyed Inger's work so much we hired her for our series *The Most Deadly Game*. A few days after she and Burt broke up, she committed suicide.

- *The House That Would Not Die*, 1970, ABC: Barbara Stanwyck. A great little horror piece about a haunted mansion.

- *The Affair*, 1973, ABC: Robert Wagner and Natalie Wood appeared together in only one film, and this was it. She played a songwriter with polio who experienced her first love affair with a lawyer, played by Wagner. From this movie, we became partners on *Charlie's Angels*, and worked with Wagner again on *Hart to Hart*.

- *Death Sentence*, 1974, ABC: Before he became a household name after *Rich Man, Poor Man* in 1976, we gave Nick Nolte his first TV break in this courtroom drama. My casting director found Nick acting in a small play in Los Angeles and thought he might be good for the TV movie we were doing. I think he turned out okay.

- *The Boy in the Plastic Bubble*, 1976, ABC: John Travolta showed his dramatic side for the first time during the *Welcome Back, Kotter* Sweathog era in a film about a boy who lives in an isolation bubble because he's been born without immunities.

- *Little Ladies of the Night*, 1977, ABC: Linda Purl starred as a teen runaway, with Carolyn Jones as her mom and David Soul as a social worker. The first of the "teenage hookers" movies, but ours really said something about teen runaways. The second highest-rated made-for-TV movie of all time, right below *The Day After*.

- *The Best Little Girl in the World*, 1981, ABC: Anorexia wasn't talked about when we made this film, but it sure was afterwards. Jennifer Jason Leigh portrayed a teenager who starves herself because she thinks she's too fat. Jodie Foster was originally set to star in the film, but dropped out at the last minute after she was accepted by Yale. Jennifer is now a big star.

- *Day One*, 1988, CBS: One of my all-time favorite projects, a three-hour film for CBS about why we shouldn't have ever dropped the atomic bomb. David Rintels wrote the script, and Brain Dennehy starred as Gen. Leslie Groves, who supervised the atomic bomb project.

- *And the Band Played On*, 1992, HBO: It took four years, but we finally got a forum on HBO to say one simple fact: The government wasn't doing enough to deal with the AIDS crisis. I'm so glad Randy Shilts lived to see the film finally air, after NBC dropped it and HBO picked it up. We attracted a stellar cast, including Richard Gere, Lily Tomlin, Alan Alda, Angelica Huston, and Matthew Modine. I'll never forget Robert Cooper at HBO. He was totally responsible for getting it done.

Theatrical Films Produced by Aaron Spelling

- *California Split*, 1974: George Segal and Elliott Gould played two compulsive gamblers; Robert Altman directed.

- *Baby Blue Marine*, 1976: Jan-Michael Vincent starred as a Marine dropout during World War II who was mistaken as a hero by residents of a small town. Richard Gere made his film appearance here.

- *Mr. Mom*, 1983: I couldn't find a film that was suitable to take my kids to, so we made one. Michael Keaton lost his job, so he stayed home and kept house while Teri Garr brought home the bacon, John Hughes' first hit screenplay.

- *'night Mother*, 1986: Adapted from Marsha Norman's Pulitzer Prize–winning play about a young woman (Sissy Spacek) who lives with her mother (Anne Bancroft) and decides to commit suicide. Mom spends the night trying to talk her out of it.

- *Surrender*, 1987: Romantic comedy with Sally Field and Michael Caine.

- *Three O'Clock High*, 1987: A high school drama about a big show-down between two students after school. We produced it with Steven Spielberg's Amblin Entertainment.

- *Cross My Heart*, 1987: Martin Short and Annette O'Toole starred in a story of a date where everything goes wrong.

- *Satisfaction*, 1988: A vehicle for Justine Bateman (then hot on NBC's

Family Ties) about a female rock band. Also featured the screen debuts of Julia Roberts and Liam Neeson. Whatever happened to them?

- *Loose Cannons*, 1990: Gene Hackman and Dan Aykroyd starred as two D.C. cops.

- *Soapdish*, 1991: Robert Harling came to visit the set of "Dynasty" and said more went on behind the scenes than went on the air. So we told him to write about it, and what we got was "Soapdish," a send-up of soaps, with Sally Field, Kevin Kline, Robert Downey, Jr., Elisabeth Shue, and Whoopi Goldberg.